GREAT NORTHERN RAILWAY
ENGINE SHEDS

FOR KENNETH LEECH

Published by
IRWELL PRESS
3 Durley Avenue, Pinner, Middlesex, HA5 1JQ
Printed and Bound by Netherwood Dalton & Co., Huddersfield

GREAT NORTHERN RAILWAY
ENGINE SHEDS

by
Roger Griffiths & John Hooper

Volume 1
Southern Area

IRWELL
PRESS

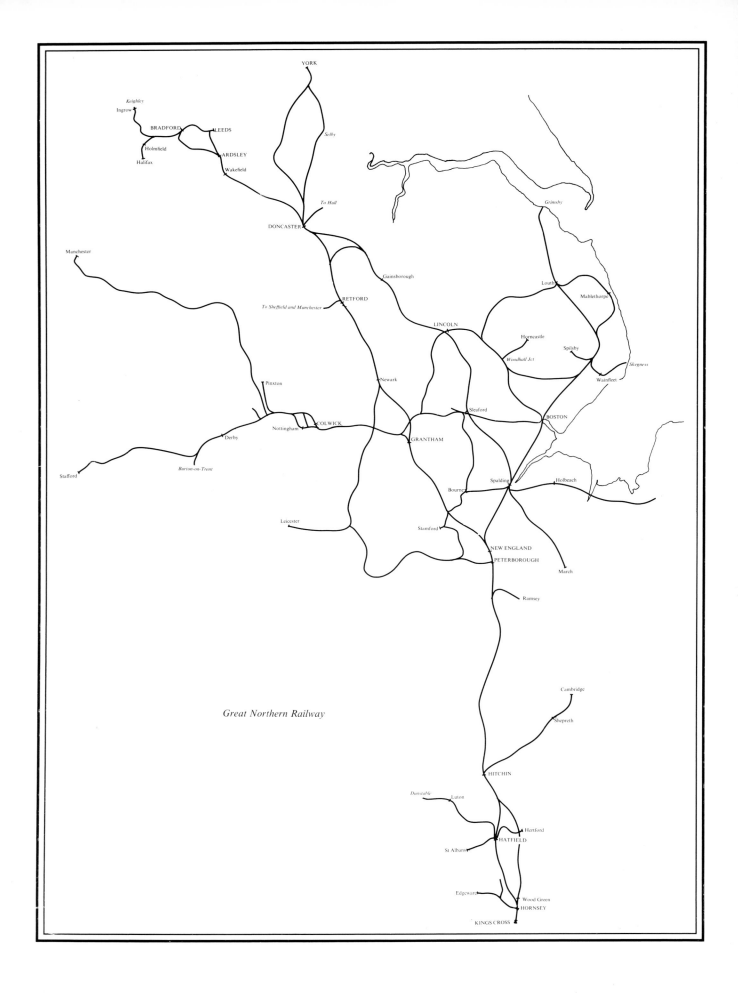

Great Northern Railway

CONTENTS

Cover: **Hatfield.** *J. E. Kite.*

Track plans are all based on official surveys and are reproduced to a uniform scale of approximately 2 chains to 1 inch. Structural drawings are again taken from official sources and are reproduced at 1mm to 1 foot unless otherwise stated.

283

Doncaster, heart of the GN Empire and later, the LNER. Many of the GN sheds acquired this nondescript look, through a general policy of neglect, remedied in some measure only in LNER days.

The Thompson Society

GREAT NORTHERN SHED DEVELOPMENT

The title 'Great Northern Railway' was first used in a scheme for a line from London (Whitechapel), through Cambridge, Sleaford and Lincoln, to York, but this Act was rejected by Parliament in 1836. There was a later scheme, for a Cambridge and York Railway, which itself gave birth to a London and York Railway. On 17th May 1844 a London and York Committee was formed to promote the line, but it was not until 26th June 1846 that the Act of Incorporation, for a company called the Great Northern Railway, received the Royal Assent. Support for the new railway was good, with paid up capital of £5,600,000 and further borrowing powers of £1,870,000 but opposition to it had been very strong too. Most of this emanated from the legendary 'Railway King', George Hudson. His many machinations and involvements in plans, and counter proposals, for various lines along the route from London to York, had badly delayed the GNR Act. Even after he had lost the fight, and the GWR came into being, Hudson did not give up trying to undermine the company's position and aspirations, until he fell from grace, the victim of his own questionable practices.

The first Meeting of the GNR Board took place on July 1st 1846, at 36 Great George Street, Westminster. Among officers elected that day was William Cubitt, who had surveyed the entire route on the line; he became Consulting Engineer, Cubitt's son Joseph was appointed Engineer for the Southern Section of the line (London to Peterborough, and on, via Boston, to Lincoln), while John Miller became Engineer for the Northern Section (Lincoln to Gainsborough and Doncaster to York). However, Miller only held his post for just over two years, resigning on 11th September 1848. His responsibilies passed to Joseph Cubitt who, by that time, also had the impending direct line, from Peterborough to Doncaster, to think about - all at no increase in salary it may be added!

Thus were the Cubitts largely responsible for development of the GNR route, with operations tackled on two fronts. The easier section, from Peterborough to Gainsborough, was contracted to Messrs. Peto and Betts, who made rapid progress and opened in 1848/9, what soon became known as the 'Loop' line, an appellation that remained in use for more than a century. The much heavier route from London to Peterborough was entrusted to that redoubtable contractor, Thomas Brassey. His operation was slowed down by the company, during the short financial crisis that followed the 'Railway Mania', so his section of the line did not open until 7th August 1850 - at first from a temporary terminus in London.

The direct line, from Peterborough, through Grantham, Newark and Retford, to Doncaster (less widely known as the 'Towns Line'), was contracted out later than the other sections. Several construction companies were involved, but some of them had financial problems, so progress was slow. Nevertheless, the major parts of the London and York Railway, as originally projected, were working by the Autumn of 1852. The exception was the section from Doncaster to York, which events had rendered unnecessary and which, in fact, never was built by the company. However, the very first length of line to be opened was precisely of Great Northern origin. This was part of the East Lincolnshire Railway, projected from Boston to Grimsby, and which the GN had leased on 2nd December 1846. The smaller company, nominally independent until the Grouping, opened the Louth to Grimsby section of its route on 1st March 1848, the first 14 miles of a system that would one day span 1051 miles. Thereby was a pattern set, with the GN embarking on a wide-ranging policy of leasings, absorbtions, running powers and Joint Agreements, in addition to the natural development of its own lines.

The earliest of the 'standard' GN sheds were the hipped roof buildings, Retford about 1900.

Dick Tarpey Coll.

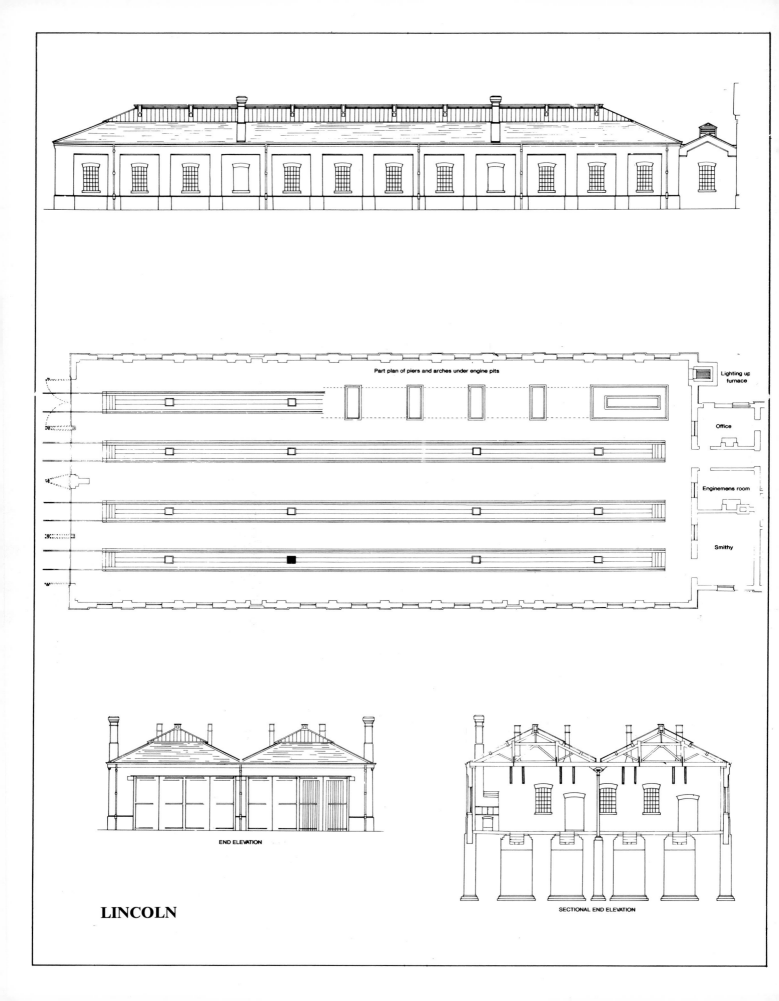

Part plan of piers and arches under engine pits

Lighting up furnace

Office

Enginemens room

Smithy

END ELEVATION

SECTIONAL END ELEVATION

LINCOLN

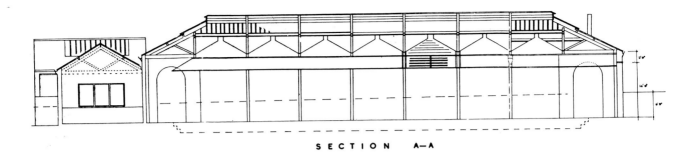

S E C T I O N   A—A

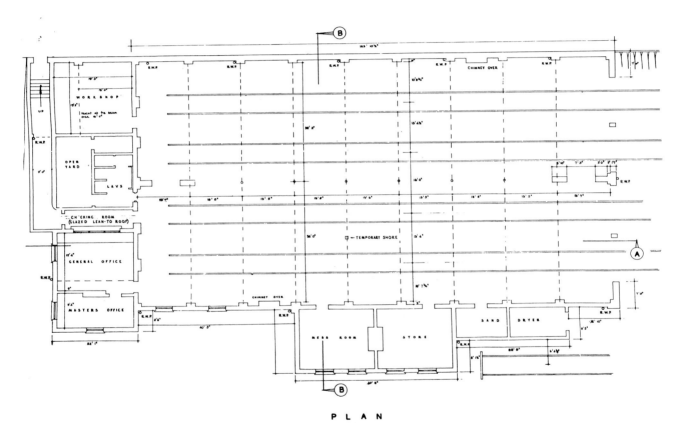

P L A N

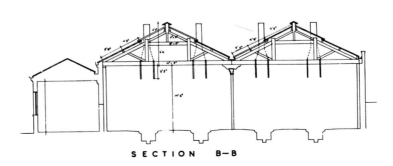

S E C T I O N   B—B

DERBY

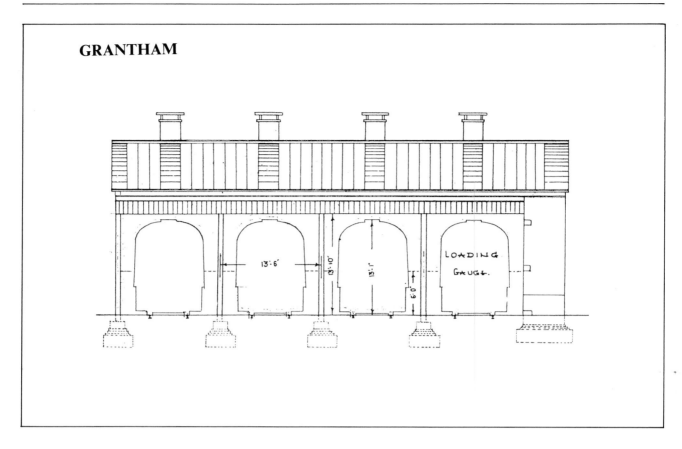

GRANTHAM

The later northlight style. Ingrow 1935.

W.A. Camwell

Deansgate, in Manchester, built by the GN, who were promptly prohibited from making use of it for locomotive purposes!

The Thompson Society

GREAT NORTHERN ENGINE SHEDS :
Evolution and Development

Responsibility for operations of the sheds lay ultimately with the Locomotive Superintendents but, from the beginning, this was devolved to the District Superintendents and ultimately the shed foreman. It seems that for many years at least loco superintendents had no hand in the design of engine sheds, resulting in a hotchpotch collection of styles and methods of construction, with no two buildings alike.*

The very first Great Northern shed was a temporary wooden building put up at Walton Junction, Peterborough, supposedly by the contractor, Peto & Betts, while the first permanent shed, in brick, was opened at Louth, by the East Lincolnshire Railway, a company leased by the GN. Further temporary wooden buildings were erected as line construction proceeded, for example, at Boston, while the early building at Lincoln was soon replaced by alternative arrangements at Gainsborough. The latter was short-lived, as will be seen from 'The Ledger of Boston Locomotive Department, 1848-1850,' : see volume two. It shows by March 1850 Gainsborough had disappeared from the list of active sheds (to appear for a further two months only, in another arcane document, the 'Cleaners and Firelighters Expenditure List'). The 'Boston Ledger' also shows Doncaster shed for the first time, in September 1849; this was a further wooden shed, single road and of a temporary nature, sited south of the station, which had two platforms and temporary buildings.

Larger, more substantial sheds soon followed, with gable-roofed brick structures at New England, Lincoln, Retford and Leeds, while at Peterborough Station, the shed formed an integral building with a carriage shed and the Great Northern Hotel! Other 'integral' buildings appeared in short order, at Hitchin, where the shed adjoined the up side station building, and at Doncaster, where the down side station building encompassed the engine shed. Elsewhere, small wooden sheds sufficed at Grantham Canal Basin, Shepreth, and the first branch line termini. Wood, was at first used for all roof construction, but as early as 1850, its incendiary tendencies were

This is an interesting point and one on which to make some coparisons. The influence of 'The Locomotive Engineer/Superintendent' (the 'CME' of later years) could be evident or negligible, according to his power and authority. On the Great Northern and Great Eastern, for instance it was not such all-powerful institution, as on say, the LNWR, the mightiest railway of its day. There Ramsbottom and Webb and Churchward on the GWR could impose their wills on every detail of construction, lending their names to distinctive standard buildings. Companies like the Midland were standardised to equal extent but buildings emerged more annonymously through a Civil Engineers Committee. All these features reflected in many senses the nature of the companies involved - it was no accident that variously inadequate cycles of 'standardisation' took place on the Great Eastern for instance.

Bradford Hammerton Street, where the northlight and earlier hipped style were married to considerable effect.

Coll. K. Leech

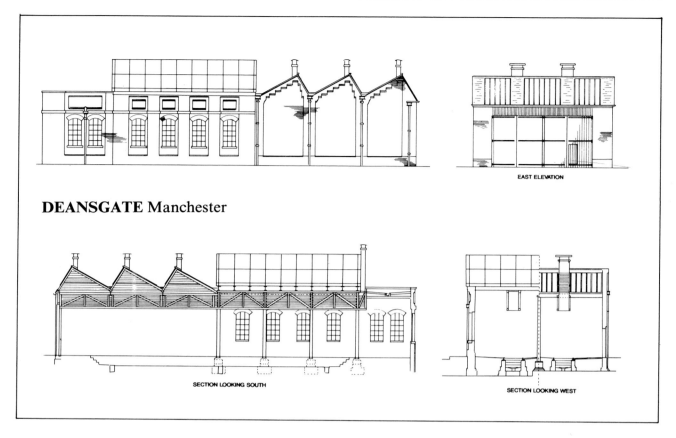

DEANSGATE Manchester

EAST ELEVATION

SECTION LOOKING SOUTH

SECTION LOOKING WEST

recognised and the use of iron mooted. The architect, Mr Goddard, was asked to incorporate iron in preference to wood 'when applicable'. The first iron roofed shed was, it seems, New England. Last in this early construction period was Kings Cross, where the unique twenty five road 'Crescent' in brick was opened in 1851, to remain intact for over 110 years.

New developments continued with further sheds to individual designs and employing a variety of construction materials, appearing at Hatfield, Luton, St.Albans, Kings Cross Station, Edgware, Wood Green, Spalding, Ardsley and Ramsey - to name but a few! To these must be added enlargements or replacements of earlier sheds, at places like Kings Cross ('Top Shed'), Bradford, Grantham Junction, Hitchin and Peterborough (New England). There was no common design to these enlargements / replacements either, with the exception of New England, where the original gable-roofed six road shed was extended on a number of occasions, to the same pattern. Perhaps the best example of diverse building styles was at Kings Cross Top Shed. There an eight road straight shed with a traverse-pitched roof, appeared in front of the crescent in 1862, to join a polygon shed which had been put up in 1859, for the Midland Railway. The MR traffic over the GN to London from Hitchin ceased when St.Pancras opened in 1868, at that time, the GN took possession of the roundhouse which, interestingly, was the only true shed of that type to have been built by the company.

It was the 1870s before any form of standard building came about. This was a brick construction, with two tiled hipped roofs, each covering two roads; offices were provided at the side or rear. Such buildings appeared from the middle of the decade, as replacements, at Lincoln and Retford, and from new at Colwick and Derby. Two road versions were provided at Pinxton and Newark, while a greatly enlarged variant, with four hipped roofs, each covering three roads, was erected at Doncaster (Carr). This 'standard' design did not last long for by the 1880s the GNR followed many other railways in constructing sheds with roofs of the 'Northlight' pattern. The new design appeared at numerous places - small versions at Ingrow, Leicester, Holmfield and Manchester Deansgate, and much larger ones at Bradford (Bowling Back, Bowling Junction, or Hammerton Street as it was variously known), Ardsley, Grantham and Colwick

Ardsley in GN days.

W.H. Whitworth

(two extensions to the original building). Having followed other companies in the northlight trend, the GN, like most others, came to regret their decision in later years, the lightly built northlights falling into disrepair with the rigours of use. All roofs were troublesome in some degree; for instance in July 1894, Stirling commented in his half-yearly expenditure report that one of the causes in an increase of £2,310, under 'General Charges', was that most of this had been expended in repairs to the roofs of engine sheds (and carriage shops). During the five years 1902-06, the GNR spent and average £5,000 per year on roof repairs. Following on from the northlight design, for one of the last sheds to be built by the GNR, Copley Hill, the company reverted to a roof with transverse pitches. Unfortunately this was another design that did not stand up well - the acid combination of soot and rain were a tough opponent, one which the GNR never properly got the better of !

On the branch lines there was little change; the earliest sheds were usually wooden (Ramsey was corrugated iron), while the later

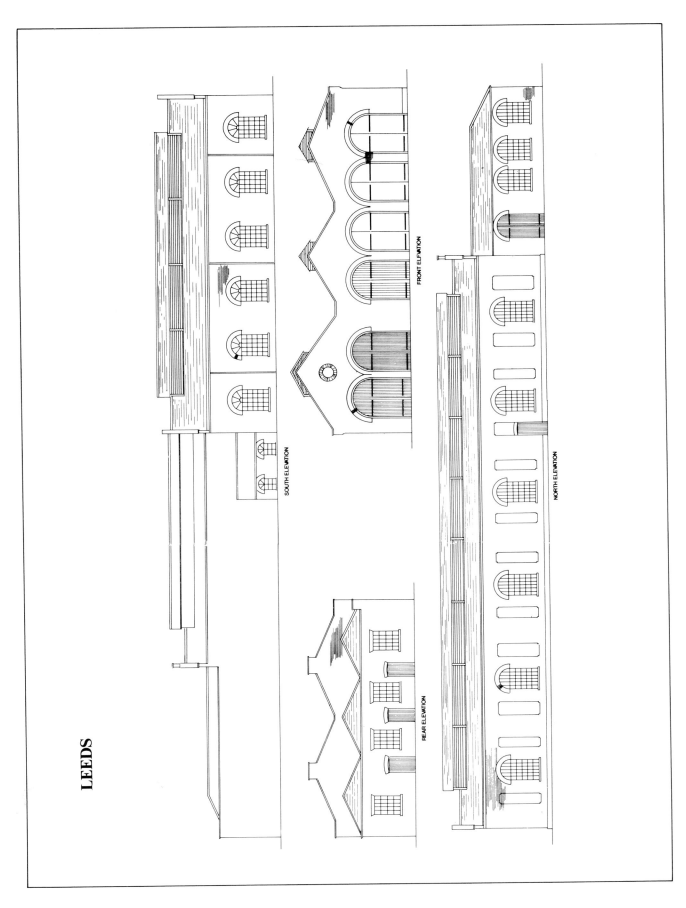

LEEDS

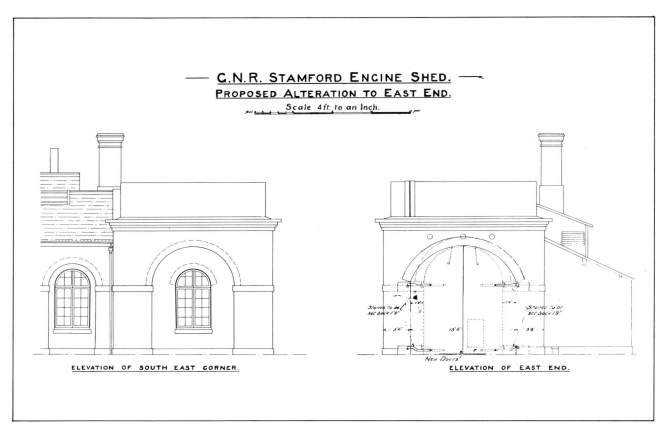

Mixed styles at Stamford.

J.H.Meredith

buildings were in brick. At Hertford yet another type of 'shed' was provided - the arch of a road overbridge, with a flimsy extension! Whatever their construction these small structures remained unaltered during their sometimes long lives - with another notable exception. This was at Stamford, where the original Stamford and Essendine wooden shed was extended by the addition of a brick building at the front. This unusual combination is difficult to justify, but it did produce a gem of a prototype for the modellers of branch lines! Finally, one other shed must be mentioned, the small building at Boston (Hall Hills) Sleeper Depot, housing the Departmental shunter that served the works.

The LNER did not build any new sheds for its Great Northern section, but of course carried out extensive maintenence and renewal work (the GN rivalled the Great Eastern in the general dilapidation suffered at its engine sheds) Yard layouts required special attention and aids to coal or ash disposal, mechanical or otherwise, were unknown. Such improvements are more fully described in a separate section, beginning on p129. A further shed, an oddity, did appear in LNER days, soon after World War Two and although strictly outside the scope of this book, it does deserve a brief mention. The LNER and BR(ER) used the small wooden shed at Ranskill Wagon Works - formerly a wartime Royal Ordnance Factory - for Departmental shunters, until 1959.

After Nationalisation the legacy of many years hard use, not to mention the battering handed out in the war, gave British Railways a major problem with shed roofs; replacements (though in essence 're-roofing' is an inappropriate term - the sheds were largely rebuilt) appeared at Ardsley, Boston, Bradford, Colwick, Grantham, Hatfield, Hornsey, Kings Cross, Copley Hill, Lincoln and Retford. In addition, BR reconstructed the sheds at Doncaster and New England, in projects costing many thousands of pounds. Eastern Region also had a constant programme of maintenance, a feature of which was reconstruction of the ashpits at a number of sheds. Later, the Region was to carry out modifications at a few of the sheds in preparation for dieselisation.

With the change to the New Order, nearly all the former GN steam locomotive sheds were closed, to be followed by demolition. Today (August 1987), the only GN sheds in existence are: Bradford (Hammerton Street), closed by BR in May 1984 and awaiting a decision about the future of the land on which it stands; Lincoln, albeit much rebuilt by BR, also stands empty and forlorn; Ingrow, where the small two road shed, in remarkably good condition, is in use as a warehouse; Derby, also in private use and sporting the only remaining GN-style hipped roofs; Retford, again in light industrial use and part of a factory estate, and St. Albans, where the only remaining branch line shed, long since disused, is in an advanced state of decay. Two more sheds survive, in use by British Rail: Doncaster, though much rebuilt, is the only one still to serve locomotives - plus the Civil Engineer, and with part of the site developed as a depot for the electrification of the East Coast Main Line. Which leaves Hornsey, somewhat altered and already serving as an electrification depot, thereby seeing the occasional visit from locomotives. These eight are all that is left of a long and complex history, which we now hope to unfold in greater detail, in the succeeding pages of this book.

Boston, site of the original works.

The Thompson Society

Kings Cross, quintessential *Norf London*

KINGS CROSS

TOP SHED

The story of what was to become the Great Northern Railway's most exalted engine shed started with purchase of land for the company's London goods station. This was an area of 40 acres off Maiden Lane, bought from St. Bartholomew's Hospital at a price of £1,000 per acre. Original plans for an 'engine repair shed', to be sited along the northern edge of the goods station, were drawn up in 1849 by the architect Lewis Cubitt, to the requirements of Edward Bury. Cubitt's design was for a crescent-fronted building containing eleven 50 ft. roads for locomotive repairs and two roads for tenders. Each of the loco roads was to be equipped with a 40 ft. pit, interconnected by traverser to the tender shop, the traverser being accessed through front and side entrances. However, as this design meant that all servicing and stabling of engines in running condition would have had to be carried out in the open air, the building was quickly recognised as inadequate and Bury himself re-designed it, on a larger scale.

This was no doubt why the GNR's London engine shed was not ready for use in time for commencement of services on 7th August 1850; even so, only 4 days later, Sturrock was able to report that the shed was 'nearly ready'. Initially, trains used a temporary station in Maiden Lane yard, pending completion of Kings Cross terminus, and for the period until the engine shed was brought into use, locomotives were dealt with in the goods yard area. Quite when Kings Cross locomotive depot was opened is not known, but it seems as if it was phased into use, being fully operational by mid-1851. This is supported by these three entries in the GN Minutes:

5th November 1850:.....That a tender from Messrs. Easton & Amos, of the Grove, Southwark, for the steam engine, pumps, blowing apparatus, etc, required for the Shops connected with the Locomotive Establishment in the London Station, amounting to £750, be accepted. Accepted.....

18th December 1850: Cubitt requested authority to order two 'Travellers' for the Locomotive Shops at London and Doncaster at £200 each. The Board resolved that these be ordered.

10th June 1851: Report from Sturrock, forwarding a petition from 37 of the Locomotive workmen employed at the London Station, complaining of the high cost of house rents they were obliged to pay. A letter from the men's Foreman suggested that the Company should build houses for the employees, on the spare ground behind the engine house. The Board resolved that the Company would not build houses, but if any party wanted to construct any such houses on the Company's property, then the offer would be favourably considered.

A similar plea by Kings Cross enginemen, two years later, met with an equally negative response. The redoubtable Locomotive Foreman, incidentally, was John Budge, recruited for the job on 23rd July 1850 at an annual salary of £170. At that time, Budge was only 35 years old; in 1858 he became London District Locomotive Superintendent, a post he held until retirement at an age of 65.

As re-designed by Bury, the shed was constructed in brick and stone, by the contractor John Jay & Co. The building consisted of the same 11 road repair shop of the original design - later designated the 'Back Erecting Shop'. It scaled about 195 ft. in width at the innermost ends of the tracks, by 55 ft. in depth. Inspection pits were provided on all 11 roads, either 36, 38 or 40 feet in length. With various workshops, a stores and a boiler house at its rear, the repair shop was itself centrally placed behind a 25 road crescent-shaped engine shed. Measuring 55 ft. in depth, with some 365 ft. 'around the curve', the crescent had a longitudinal slated gable roof with a raised smoke vent running along the ridge. Engine pits were on every road - 38 ft. long in the 7 roads at each of the north and south ends, and 36 ft. pits in the 11 roads fronting the repair shop. This was an altogether better design of building which, at first anyway, afforded plenty of covered accommodation for the stabling and servicing of engines. It was also like no other 'round' shed built in Britain, for the tracks fanned out from a single access road, rather than being led from a turntable. The 40 ft. turntable was sited away to the east while the coking stage was positioned nearer to the north end of the shed.

A first alteration was mooted on 28th July 1851, when the locomotive engineer asked for a carriage shed to be built in the area between the engine shed and coke stage, the work being authorised in the following November. It seems though that the GN did not actually

GREAT NORTHERN RAILWAY.

ORIGINAL LOCOMOTIVE SHED AT KING'S CROSS.

own the land and hardly had the building been completed, when it was subject to a change of ownership, and the railway company asked to vacate it! This led in 1853 to the construction of a carriage shed at Kings Cross station.

On 14th October 1852, Kings Cross station was opened for use and the temporary passenger station at Maiden Lane became a potato shed, which was expanded upon in 1855. To allow that expansion, and provision of more goods lines, the locomotive turntable was moved to the north side of the site; a new 40 ft. 'table was provided in fact, at a cost of £500. In 1856, expenditure of £1,063 was authorised for the laying down of additional coke sidings at the shed, while on 9th January 1857, the following tools were ordered for the repair shop:

Screw Machine	£83
Shearing and Punching Machine	£64
Hand Punch Press	£15
Grooving Drill	£65

The grooving drill was supplied by Messrs. Nasmyth, but all the other tools were made at the GN's Doncaster 'Plant'.

December 1857 saw the historic agreement between the GNR and Midland Railway, to allow the latter's trains to run over GN metals from Hitchin to Kings Cross, and provision for goods traffic and locomotive facilities for the MR at Kings Cross Goods Yard. In fact, the GN undertook a £30,000 scheme to accommodate the Midland. This included conversion of the potato shed into a goods shed for their use and construction of a new engine shed. That structure was to be in true 'Midland' style, a 'proper' roundhouse - the only one ever built by the GN - complete with its own coking and watering arrangements. To create space for the Midland engine shed the GN had to resite its turntable yet again - this time southwards - and carry out considerable earthworks. The builders moved fast though, as on 10th June 1858, the GN's Way & Works Committee heard that: .....*a large mound of earth has nearly been cleared away for the intended engine shed for the use of the Midland Company at Kings Cross. This earth has been deposited on either side of the main line for nearly a mile north of Holloway and has formed area for another line on each side. This space may presently be invaluable to the company*..... Then, on the following 2nd August, the Way & Works Committee was told: *Midland Shed: The area is cleared, the foundations, turntable pit and engine pits are built and the upperwork is begun*.....

The Midland Railway shed finally opened in February 1859, at a total capital cost of nearly £10,500, which the GNR charged to the MR at the rate of 6% per annum. Soon christened 'The Derby Shed', the roundhouse, actually polygonal in planform, was 167 ft. in diameter, centred on a 40 ft. turntable. At first, access was achieved from the western end only, through an ornamental archway, on to the turntable that served twenty-three internal roads of which initially only four had pits. The shed road immediately opposite the entrance was also taken through the eastern wall of the polygon and extended for some 20 ft.; in later years, at a date unknown, this track was connected to an access road, allowing locomotives to enter from two sides. Built in brick, the shed had a slated circular gable roof over the stabling roads, complete with a central raised smoke vent. Above the turntable a conical roof was surmounted by a circular structure, rather like the lamp room of a lighthouse, but unglazed, with above that, a tiled cone-shaped roof, topped off with a weather vane. At some time later, thought to be about the period of the First World War, this elaborate central covering was removed (or fell down), leaving the turntable open to the elements. The coke stage with canopy was sited in the yard to the west; parallel ash pits were provided in the coking road and in the track by-passing it and immediately on the north side of the roundhouse entrance, an office building was put up. Appointed as MR Locomotive Foreman at Kings Cross was William Kirtley, nephew of Matthew, the MR's Locomotive Superintendent. Some would have labelled such an arrangement as nepotism (literally, as a nephew was involved) - even more so, when William Kirtley left Kings Cross in January 1864 to take up a new job - as Superintendent of Derby Works. However, it must be commented that when Matthew Kirtley died, in 1873, William lost his sponsorship and did not get his uncle's job so left the MR in the following year, to become Locomotive Superintendent to the London Chatham & Dover Railway. in

No.1 before the 'Derby' on 30th June 1923. An obscure siding was afterwards laid more or less on the site of the MR roundhouse (the 'back pits') used for dead engines and known to the end as 'the Derby road', much to the puzzlement of contempary staff.

Collection K.Leech.

obtaining that post Kirtley beat, in the final interview, someone whose name crops up quite a lot in the early history of the GNR - the restless Mr. Charles Sacre.

Events at Kings Cross station in 1861 caused the GNR to look for a new site for a carriage repairing shed and it was decided to convert the seven northernmost roads of the crescent engine shed for just such a purpose. To make up for the lost locomotive accommodation and cater for increased demands brought about by expanding traffic, the GN also initiated construction of a brand new engine shed, with tenders being called in October 1861. Successful was the firm of Messrs. Kirk & Parry Ltd., with a bid of just over £22,000, the job completed in the Autumn of 1862. Apart from erecting a new locomotive shed and converting part of the crescent for carriage maintenance use, Kirk & Parry also undertook building works in the repair shop area and the final bill came to nearly £25,300.

An 1864 official plan shows that the new shed building contained 8 roads, stood about 60 ft. in front of the centre portion of the crescent and measured 152 ft. x 112 ft., with a 54 ft. x 14 ft. office block adjoining the rear wall at the south end. The 1864 plan has it marked as 'Running Shed', but other names were used later, the building being variously known as 'The Main Line Running Shed', 'The Square Shed', 'The Long Shed' and the 'Cleaning Shed'.

The new building was in brick, with a roof of a pattern new to the GNR - four slated transverse pitches, each with a smoke collecting trough running along the ridge for nearly the entire width of the building, and venting via a square chimney above each road. No internal inspection pits seem to have been provided initially for any of the eight roads, the fourth of which, when counting from the north end, passed through the rear wall to a traverser in front of the repair shop; this is shown to have been curved in layout to match the crescent, and scaled 25 ft. in length, in a pit of 120 ft. It served the ten northernmost roads of the repair shop, where the outside section, formerly used for running purposes, was now called the 'Front Erecting Shop'. Road number 11 in the repair shop was served directly by a track running along the south wall of the new straight shed, while the seven roads in the south end of the crescent were designated 'E.P.S.' which is assumed to have meant 'Engine Preparation Shed'. The yard outside the southern section of the crescent also received a name, being called 'The Continent' for a reason long lost in history.

Conversion of the crescent's seven northern roads for carriage repairs had comprised an extension to the rear, with seven tracks extended through the back wall. A new coking shed had also been provided, standing between the turntable and crescent; double-sided, it consisted of two 135 ft. x 10 ft. platforms with the wagon road passing between - this being equipped with a 110 ft. pit for some reason; later it was equipped with two hand-powered half-ton bucket cranes. The coke shed was complemented by a double-outlet water

column outside each coking road. Finally, facilities were completed by installation of a large hand-powered engine lift, spanning roads No.3 and 4, immediately outside the straight shed entrance. This very prominent structure was to become almost a 'trade mark' for Top Shed, when it appeared in numerous late 19th century photographs.

The above mentioned building alterations to the repair shop were made to accommodate additional tools. For example, a steam hammer ordered on 8th February 1862, at a cost of £190 and then on 28th January 1863, the following:

Shaping Machine	£140
15 inch Slide Lathe	£225
Drilling Machine	£95
Bar Cutter for Farrier	£80

In the next year, Sturrock asked for a new power source for Kings Cross repair shops and a second-hand beam engine was duly installed, to render sterling service until the shop machinery was converted to electric drive in the early 1930s.

The years 1862 and 1863 were busy ones for the GNR in London and apart from its own engine shed/workshops alterations the company also carried out some minor works at the Midland Railway shed. in December 1862, the MR asked for 7 additional pits to be provided inside the roundhouse, at an estimated cost of £91 each. The GN agreed and raised charges on the basis of 6% per annum on that amount.

April 1863, the MR asked for an alteration to the roof of its coke stage, at a cost of £50. Again the GN agreed to do with work, but as the price involved was so small the MR was asked to pay the full amount upon completion.

During all this, the Midland's own route into London was progressing and that company started making moves away from GNR territory as early as mid-1862. At this time the MR gave up its rented facilities in the GN yard, in favour of its own goods depot at nearby Agar Town. St. Pancras MR Goods Station started to receive trains in September 1867, but a further year was to elapse before Midland passenger services were switched from Kings Cross to St. Pancras. This took place on 1st October 1868 and the MR formally vacated its Kings Cross engine shed from that day. A year later, the Midland Company paid to the GNR the sum of £24,000, to clear its debt for construction and back rental of the roundhouse. The sum was about £700 in excess of the MR's actual dues, which probably explains why the GN settled an outstanding water account for the Midland, of over £800, from the Regents Canal Company. Although the bill was received by the GN in 1870, it took until 4th january 1874 before the

'The Derby', fully utilised by the GN.

Collection C. Brown

Stirling elegance at the coal stage, 1895.

National Railway Museum

Board decided to pay it!

So the Great Northern now had another engine house at its disposal at 'Top Shed', although locomotives did not at first use it (an 1870 Ordnance Survey map marks the roundhouse as a carriage shed); wagon repairs were later carried out inside, but before the end of the 19th century the building was in use again for stabling engines, which continued into LNER times. However, the coke stage provided for the MR's use was taken out and extra stabling sidings were provided in its place.

Complaints about smoke emission had, by 1868, caused the introduction of Welsh coal at Kings Cross and by the middle of 1876, average weekly consumption of all types of locomotive fuel in the London District had reached 794 tons. That figure included such important outstations as Hatfield, Hitchin and Cambridge, not to mention a handful of smaller sheds, but the great bulk of the fuel would have been loaded at Kings Cross. Exactly 28 years later, coal consumption at Top Shed alone had reached an average figure of 900 tons per week and by 1929 the amount had leapt to 1,530 tons per week.

April 1876 saw the doubling of the engine lines between Kings Cross locomotive depot and Pigeon House Signalbox. It cannot be denied that the new line, which cost £1,600 to lay down, certainly eased problems of access to, and egress from the shed, but the new arrangements could not disguise the fact that Top Shed was becoming ever more congested. So, by 1882 the Board decided to investigate a complete relocation of the locomotive depot to Harringay, enabling not only expanded engine facilities, but enlargement of Kings Cross Goods Yard, which was itself working at capacity. A site meeting enabled the GN's Directors to see the problems at first hand, but obviously the estimated cost, which has not been discovered, put those august gentlemen off the idea, as nothing came of the scheme. Five years later the matter was revived, only this time there were two projected sites for a new 'Top Shed', at either Holloway or Hornsey. On that occasion, a figure of £10,000 was estimated for the cost of moving the engine shed and improving the goods yard and surprisingly, the GN Board approved the plan. However, it is not surprising to learn that the project was then deferred! Yet again the subject was

raised, this time by Ivatt, on 28th July 1898, when he declared the shed room at Kings Cross to be 'inadequate'. For a third time, nothing was done about removing Top Shed, although a new engine shed did appear at Hornsey in the following year (see later). This of course did not alleviate the problem of congestion in the goods yard, which never was entirely solved.

Ivatt had asked, on 29th September 1896, for more engine pit accommodation, noting that: .....*the present pits are too short.....* and requested four 50 ft. pits .....*outside the old square shed, opposite the existing inside pits.....* The contracting firm of Messrs. Atherton & Dolman got the job for an undisclosed sum and by 2nd March 1897, Ivatt was able to report the new pits as being nearly ready. Ivatt's request reveals that at some time between 1862 and 1896, inspection pits had been provided inside the straight shed; the four outside pits built by Atherton and Dolman were excavated on roads 1-4; at an unknown future date, outside pits would also be provided for roads 5-7. As an aside, it is interesting to note that not until the 1950s was the space between the external pits concreted over!

Further improvements were soon forthcoming, with the award on 9th July 1898, of a contract worth £3,598 to Messrs. Kirk, Knight & Co., for the *'re-roofing of Kings Cross engine shed, to be completed in 18 weeks'*. The actual building involved was not stated, but almost certainly it was the 1862 eight road straight shed, as only a few years later much re-roofing work was carried out on the crescent shed (see below). Not long after Kirk, Knight & Co. had completed their job, another scheme was approved, on 14th April 1899, when £2,000 was sanctioned for new engine approach roads; once again, exact details of the work involved are lacking.

However, the next enhancement of Top Shed is well documented. It starts on 5th November 1900, with this section of a report presented by Ivatt on Kings Cross depot: .....*Coaling arrangements at this place are old and inadequate and the Company is paying sixpence per ton for taking the coal from the wagon and putting on the engines in London, as against two-and-a-quarter pence per ton at places where we now have new coal stages. Mr. Ross has drawn up an estimate and plan for a new coal stage and alterations to the sidings in the yard and moving the turntable, etc.; total cost of these alterations is estimated at £14,084. Of*

Saddle tank No.1212 with attendent cleaners. It featured in a 1919 visit 'by the courtesy of Mr H N Gresley, and in which the shed staff took the trouble to explain the mysteries of the break-down train and much else'

C. Brown.

this amount, some £6,148-10-0d is required for the renewal of the turntable and repairs to sidings, etc ...... Ivatt then goes on to say, somewhat confusingly: *.....whether the yard and coal stage are altered or not, I would be very glad to see the yard remodelled, because at present the place is a muddle of congestion. If the work is carried out, I can save the Company money by reducing the cost of moving the coal from 6d. to 3d. per ton, making a direct saving of £1,200 per year.....* That saving quoted by Ivatt doesn't quite add up: saving £1,200, at 3d per ton equates to a consumption of 96,000 tons of coal per year. That is over eighteen hundred tons a week on average, yet we know for a fact that coal usage 4 years later, in 1904, was just less than half that amount. It seems certain then that Ivatt was adding savings from elsewhere - manpower no doubt. Whatever, the work was not finally sanctioned until 3rd May 1901, at a newly estimated cost of £15,938.

At around the same time the above yard rearrangements were authorised, Kings Cross Locomotive Works, as the repair shop was known, ceased the heavy repair of locomotives, with completion of just such a job on Single No. 872. This was as a result of commissioning of the new Crimpsall Shop at Doncaster 'Plant', and transfer of all major repair work there; henceforth, Top Shed workshops carried out normal running repairs and inspections only - still a considerable workload, although a goodly number of men lost their jobs. Coincident with these various alterations taking place, and possibly a result of closure of Kings Cross Works, a second engine lift was installed in the depot yard, between the coaling shed and roundhouse; the hydraulically-powered hoist was of 28 tons capacity and would later be enclosed in its own building.

Various alterations from before the turn of the century took place at Kings Cross, to the coal stage, roof and doors, together with a number of minor changes, further pit accommodation for instance, approved in May 1909 at an estimated cost of £350. In the same year, a bell, which reputedly had 'hung over the entrance to Top Shed' was bequeathed to Hornsey, for use as a time-signalling device in the fitter's shop there. The bell had come to Kings Cross in 1884, off the American-built 4-2-2 'Lovatt Eames', which had the misfortune to be cut up in that year; for the subsequent history of this bell see the Chapter on Hornsey shed. In February 1911 Top Shed acquired an instructional locomotive for the Locomens' Mutual Improvement classes. This comprised the frames and running gear of an old Stirling saddle tank, converted in Doncaster Plant for hand-operated use, to demonstrate the finer points of valve gear functions, etc. Ivatt's last job for Top Shed came in 1911, when on 23rd February he made the following observation in a letter to the Locomotive Committee: *.....when we wash out locomotive boilers we use cold water, which is apt to do damage in the case of a hot boiler by reason of violent contractions, unless it is very carefully managed. Therefore is desirable to let the boilers cool down naturally, resulting in a loss of time and heat contained in a boiler full of hot water. It is recommended to purchase a plant from the Economical Boiler Washing Company, and put it down at Kings Cross.....* Provision of the hot water washout plant at a cost of £2,000 was sanctioned, but only for the straight shed it might be noted cold water washing-out continued in the roundhouse - and thus did Ivatt fade from the scene.

Ivatt's successor, Gresley, made an addition to Top Shed around 1917 when he asked for separate accommodation for the many female engine cleaners working at the depot due to wartime manpower shortages. On 1st October 1918, the locomotive engineer requested provision of a 22 ton hydraulic wheel drop for Top Shed, *.....as supplied by Cowans Sheldon and used by the Lancashire & Yorkshire Railway.....* Estimated costs were put at £1,166 for the drop pit and foundations, plus £780 for the drop mechanism itself. The job was sanctioned on 3rd October 1918, but work progressed slowly and a year later it was reported that the wheeldrop pit was 'under construction', while final completion did not occur until April 1921. It is probable that provision of this 'drop' resulted in removal of the hand-powered engine lift outside the straight shed.

28th December 1921 saw the last GN-authorised alteration work at Top Shed, the replacement of the sand furnace; Gresley described it as being in 'bad condition', recommending that it should be replaced 'at an estimated cost of £684'. The work was approved on 5th January 1922, to be completed just in time for the handing over of power to the LNER. The new company waited until about 1924 before making an 'adjustment' at Kings Cross, when the shed at last received an adequate breakdown crane, a Ransomes & Rapier 35 ton machine, ex-Great Eastern Railway, from Stratford engine shed. After that, five years were to elapse before the LNER announced an expensive and wide-ranging series of alterations and additions to Top Shed, to bring it into the 20th century.

The Plan was announced in mid-1929 and originally envisaged the complete rebuilding of the depot. This was not to come about, though the work took place during 1931 and continued throughout 1932, being completed in December that year. In these years the crescent building and 8 road shed were altered, while the roundhouse was taken down and replaced by 7 open stabling roads equipped with inspection pits, christened the 'Back Pits'. Apart from the 'Back Pits', new provisions included a 70 ft. turntable at the west end of the shed yard, in place of the existing model which had been enlarged from 52 ft. to 54 ft., at a date as yet undetermined. A new water tank of 25,000 gallons capacity replaced that of 18,000 gallons lost when the roundhouse was demolished; total storage capacity was therefore increased to 70,000 gallons. In the yard, a rotating drum-type sand dryer was installed, and track layouts changed. In addition, a 500 ton capacity mechanical coaling plant was erected at the south side of the yard with two 'dry' ash pits laid down and between the coaler and straight shed. The redundant coaling shed was demolished and replaced by office and staff amenity blocks and the adjacent hydraulic engine lift taken out.

Alterations to the crescent building meant the creation of the 'Met Shed' from the 7 road north portion previously noted 'in use as a carriage and wagon repair shop'. This would support the contention that although the then carriage repair shed was altered for locomotive accommodation in 1906 it had not in fact been put to such use. It has been suggested that the carriage shed was turned over to locomotive use *after* Bounds Green carriage depot opened in the 1920s. Whether this is correct or not, some work was definitely done to that part of Top Shed in 1933, and in its converted farm, the 'Met Shed' had room for only 17 engines, 5 fewer than the number of stabling places lost with the roundhouse. Further compensation was achieved by the alterations to the 8 road straight shed. It had its rear wall removed together with the office extension building, the traverser was taken out, as originally recommended by the General Manager in 1906, and Nos. 2-8 of the straight shed's roads were extended into the repair shop. Up till now, little mention has been made of the 7 southernmost roads of the 1850 crescent shed. By the time the LNER's scheme was promulgated, all but 1 of the tracks had been cut short outside the building (two were connected in 1920), allowing conversion of the inside into a stores for the repair shop, an oil store and an enginemens' noticeboard lobby. Use by engines of this portion of the crescent had probably dwindled after the roundhouse was taken over for such purposes. A water softening plant, erected at the extreme south west corner of the shed site, near the office building, was brought into use in 1934 and at last gave much-needed relief to the problems that had existed since the shed's inception, very unsuitable water from the Regents Canal. It should be added that for many years less troublesome water was taken from the New River Company, but never enough to replace the canal water. The final development came at the end of 1934, with vacuum tractor equipment from Cowans, Sheldon & Co. Ltd., for the 70 ft. turntable; vacuum accumulator tanks were also fitted, for engines not in steam, the first application of many such equipments by the LNER.

In 1940, after the outbreak of war, the 35 ton breakdown crane was superseded by a Cowans Sheldon 45 ton mode, this in its turn was shipped abroad in 1943 but was replaced at Kings Cross by another 45 ton machine, from Messrs. Ransomes & Rapier. Wartime depredations included a direct hit by a large bomb upon the sidings to the south of the straight shed - 'the Continent' - where a number of tracks were destroyed. In addition, severe damage was done to the 8 road shed's south wall and part of its roof, with a number of locomotives inside the shed affected, but none seriously so; engines, shed wall and roof were all quickly repaired.

In 1945 one of the repair shop pits was adapted for use with a portable set of weighing machines. These were intended to ensure correct weight distribution on all locomotive axles, with the aim of reducing the incidence of hot boxes but in practice this equipment, which must have been costly, was rarely utilised. In fact, a foreman fitter who spent two years at Top Shed, from May 1959 to May 1961, never saw the weighing apparatus used. A cleaning plant for locomotives, completed in 1947 was similarly ineffective. The chemicals employed by the plant did more than clean the engines - they stripped off the paint too and despite a series of tests which ensured that the correct 'mix' of solvents was eventually achieved and the plant worked well enough, its use dwindled, so that by the mid-1950s hand

The North London gloom permeated the district, coal dust, smoke and horse manure amidst a constant clamour of iron wheels on cobbles, enhanced by the occasional whiff of rotting veg, for Kings Cross was one of the principal London produce markets.

Collection W.A.Camwell

J6 0-6-0, numbered 624N in the early scheme of things.

Collection R.Tarpey.

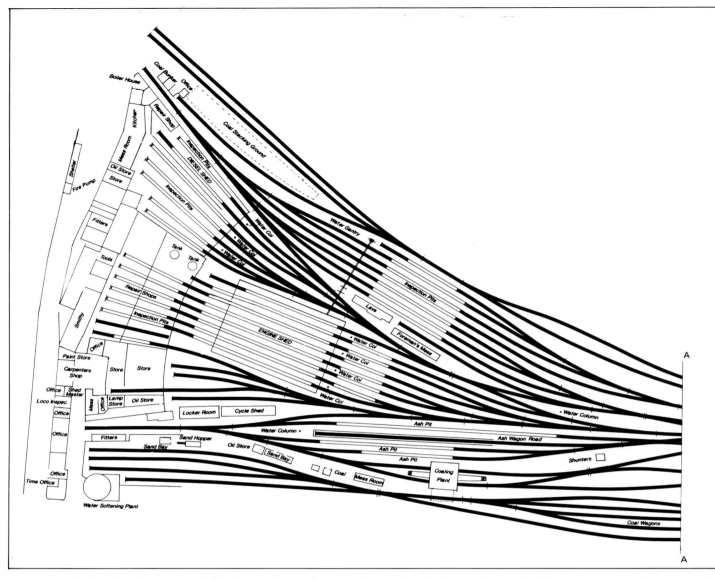

cleaning of engines, never wholly abandoned, was the rule at Top Shed.

In 1949, British Railways tacked the legacy of wartime damage, and re-roofed the straight shed. In doing so the distinctive transverse ridges were removed, to be replaced by a flat asbestos roof with longitudinal smoke troughs over each road. The Met Shed was also re-roofed, using corrugated materials.

In 1950, the busy months of July and August saw the mechanical coaler out of use, undergoing overhaul - a note uncommon event. During that period as many engines as possible were coaled at the station stabling point and Hornsey shed. The year also saw £70,000 spent in attempting to alleviate late departures of northbound trains from Kings Cross, due to engines being delayed by congestion at Top Shed. The remedy was simple - the laying of an additional incoming road to avoid the turntable. This allowed a more direct access to the 'table for tender engines, avoiding conflicting movements of tank types in passage to the coaling and ashpit area. That such a simple answer to the problem should cost £70,000 derives from the amount of existing plant that had to be repositioned to accommodate the new access road. Investing such a large sum paid off though, for within a few months, the late departure of engines was virtually eradicated.

In 1952 the water supplies were greatly enhanced by a new mains supply and erection of an overhead watering gantry at the Back Pits, with the hose over each road capable of at least 1,000 gallons per minutes. This facility was provided following the success of a smaller watering 'bridge' erected over three lines at York, Holgate Bridge Signalbox. The large gantry put in at Kings Cross was repeated very soon after at New England; these were to remain the only three examples in Britain. 1952 was also the time of the first arrivals of diesel

shunting locomotives at Kings Cross and the two northernmost roads of the Met Shed were partitioned off for their use, with a fuelling facility installed in the Oil Store.

By the Autumn of 1958, a quarter of a century of strenuous use had taken its toll of the Kings Cross turntable. Distortion of its framework had occurred, rendering manual assistance necessary. In October, the turntable was removed and sent to Barton works for overhaul, to be replaced by one of similar size, just removed from Melton Constable, in anticipation of the imminent closure of the M & GNR. This turntable itself had an interesting history, having been provided originally at Grantham shed in 1921. It served there for 30 years before being recovered, refurbished and laid down at Melton, where its great size at last enabled such types as B12 4-6-0s to be turned. However, it would be much more gainfully employed in its new position at Top Shed, even if it was to be only for 5 years.

With the exception of a 75 ton steam breakdown crane in 1960, all such works as those described in the last few paragraphs could only be considered as temporary, because the writing was on the wall for steam power. 1950 just about marked the beginning of the end, with a wind-down lasting until closure of Top Shed in June 1963. It would be true to say that in many ways, those final years of the steam locomotive and the men who worked with them were their finest. The period 1959-1962 saw hitherto unattained performances and levels of reliability that can only be described as incredible, much assisted when official blessing was given to the continued improvement of steam during the changeover to diesel power. So, Top Shed went out 'on a high', to use the modern idiom, and nothing could have been more appropriate, with Kings Cross spared the lingering end suffered by so many steam sheds over the succeeding five years. After closure, the

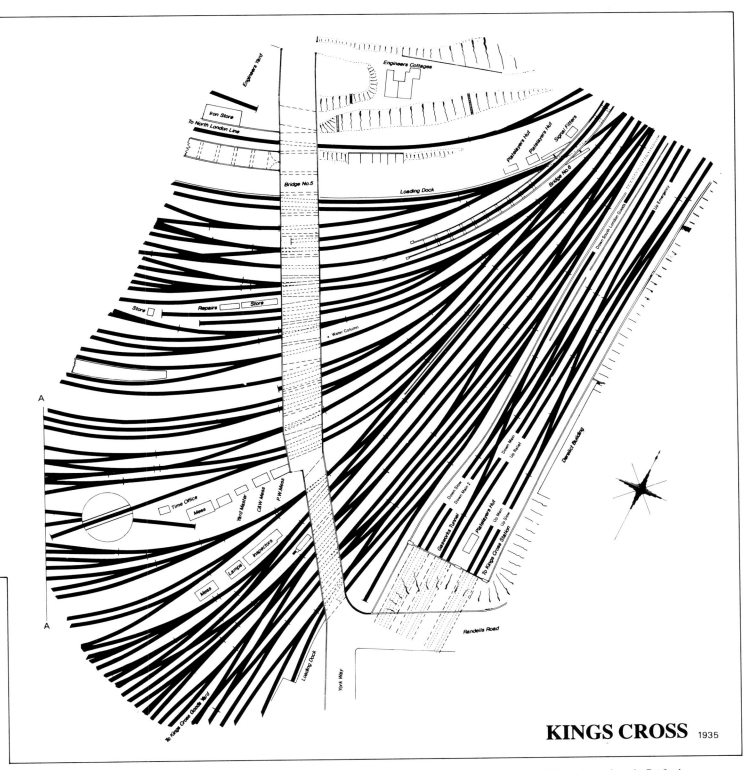

KINGS CROSS 1935

buildings and plant stood empty until demolition of all but the Locomotive Residence in 1964. The cleared site was subsequently used in part for a freightliner terminal which itself has since closed and a ready-mixed concrete plant still functions there today.

The locomotive history of Kings Cross is long and complex to say the least, clouded as always by the GN's practice of allocating engines to Districts rather than individual sheds. However, an allocation for Kings Cross shed in 1860 has been unearthed - there were 40 locomotives stationed at that time. These comprised 'Little Sharps' 2-2-2 and their 2-2-2T and 0-4-2T rebuilds, Wilson 0-6-0, Hawthorn 0-4-2 and 'Small' and 'Large Hawthorn' Singles, with Nos. 203-7 of the latter type allocated new to Kings Cross, for the most important express duties. A prime example of those were the 'Manchester

Specials', introduced on 1st August 1857 and running via Retford, Sheffield and Penistone in 5 hours and 20 minutes, a time reduced to 5 hours after only one month. The trains left Kings Cross at 1000 and 1730 and Manchester London Road at 0955 and 1720; from the September acceleration GN locomotives ran between London and Sheffield, 162 miles in 3 hours and 40 minutes, reputedly the fastest trains in Britain at that time. In 1858 the service was extended to Barston, for Liverpool and Chester, and from 1st September 1859, to Liverpool Lime Street. Going back even further, to 1855, the GN's Rule Book for that year shows the following duties being worked by Kings Cross shed, all in the Down direction, with corresponding return workings of course:

19

No 4492

No 4490

The Kings Cross coaler was something of a local landmark, like many of its contemparies and is one of the few to feature (albeit very distantly) in an Ealing Comedy - *The Lady Killers.*

Photo: National Railway Museum.

London to Hatfield	18 miles
London to Hitchin	32 miles
London to St. Neots	52 miles
London to Sandy	44 miles
London to Peterborough	76 miles

In addition of course, Midland Railway locomotives had been stationed at Kings Cross shed since 1859; records are scant, but it is known for certain that Kirtley 2-2-2 and 0-6-0 operated from the depot and later on, the same designer's 0-4-2.

In 1866 a pair of condenser-fitted 0-8-0Ts was delivered from the Avonside Engine Company, of Bristol. They were designed by Sturrock for the specific purpose of working goods over the Metropolitan lines, but were not looked upon with favour by the 'underground' company so they quickly passed from the scene. The same year saw twenty 0-4-2Ts delivered to the GN by Avonside and Neilson, for working over Metropolitan lines and out to the developing suburbs of the 'Northern Heights' and beyond. This was about the time that the renowned London suburban services began to bloom and soon became perhaps the most important task undertaken by Kings Cross shed, for nearly the next century. In 1872, Stirling 0-4-4WTs appeared and by 1881 there were 48 working in the London District. That year saw the next locomotive development with the first 0-4-4T of Class G2, eight being present by 1885, but virtually all had gone again by the early part of the 20th centruy, leaving one or two for empty coaching stock duties. Longer term residents were the G1 0-4-4Ts which first came in 1889 and increased until 1895, when 25 were stationed in the District. It was this class that first bore the official designation of 'Metropolitan' tank engines. but suburban services expanded so rapidly, demanding bigger and better engines that the G1's reign was relatively brief. Their replacement began in 1898 with the first C2 4-4-2T and was completed after 1907 when N1 0-6-2Ts came on the scene. The G1 survived on ecs work though, for example, in 1912, when Nos. 931 and 934 joined 767, all fitted with the Westinghouse brake for working foreign stock at Kings Cross. The

arrival of 931/4 allowed F4 0-4-2T No. 123A to be scrapped and G2 Nos. 247 and 531A to move to quieter pastures at Hatfield.

In 1903 came the trial of a Baldwin 2-6-0, working from Top Shed on commuter trains, mainly over the Enfield line it is believed. It was soon decided that the American engine was not suitable for the work and it went back to the West Riding. Between that same year and 1908 came the well known but brief interlude of the L1 0-8-2T. They were designed for the heaviest suburban trains, and the first eleven built came to London, but their weight and length, particularly on Metropolitan metals, and small wheel diameter were against them and all soon moved on to Colwick depot. Though unsuccessful on London suburban duties, the L1 did make a comeback to Top Shed. That was in 1919, when Nos. 116/8/9/32-4 were re-allocated for ecs work. They were painted in wartime grey and replaced in 1921 by Nos. 117, 125, 137, 151, 154 and 156 in green livery. This colour too did not last and all had been repainted black by the time the last was withdrawn in February 1934.

By 1902, the services required 107 engines and 47 coaching sets to carry 36 million passengers a year, a total still growing at an annual rate of one-and-a-half million passengers! Needless to say this resulted in serious overcrowding of a service that was limited by a capacity of 30 Up trains per hour at Finsbury Park. Even longer trains and more powerful locomotives were indicated, which meant that the 49 C2s working from London by 1907 would have a short tenure and only a decade later most had gone, and all had left by the Grouping. Two members of the class returned to Top Shed for 1948/49, when Nos. 67356/74 were push-pull fitted and participated in the Finsbury Park to Alexandra Palace workings. The C12 shared the duty with some ex-GCR F2 2-4-2T that had themselves arrived during the Second World War and worked until withdrawal late in 1950.

The C2s were replaced progressively on the suburban duties by Ivatts N1, with 35 working in London District by 1912. They formed the 'Metropolitan Link' at Top Shed, with regular double-shifted crews. The link included some turns that covered more than 200 miles a day, running from Moorgate to Alexandra Palace, High Barnet,

Suburban tanks and pilots on a Sunday, April 1939. Such engines characterised the interlacing lines around Kings Cross and were surprisingly far-travelled. There were over 100 tanks at 'The Cross' in this period, including more than thirty J52s, a dozen N1s, and no less than sixty two N2s.

W.Potter.

Hatfield and Cuffley and included some goods and ecs workings. The N1s also worked the Edgware branch and the Hatfield group of branches, but they were not very popular for the latter due to axle loadings. At the Grouping, there were 26 N1s at Kings Cross but from about 1931 the class started to lose its passenger workings to N2s and N7s and moved on to cross-London goods work, where they replaced Stirling and Ivatt 0-6-0STs. Southwards, the N1s operated coal trains to Herne Hill, Hither Green, Battersea Yard, Feltham and to the GN coal depots at Elephant & Castle and Brockley Lane. Van trains were worked to Victoria and Cannon Street and also summer excursions to the south coast, as far as Battersea. Mr. Hill's design of N7 0-6-2T also came to Top Shed in large numbers following the Grouping, 19 arriving during 1925-7, then another 17 in 1928. They worked on all the various suburban duties, including those to and from Moorgate and also took van trains over the Widened Lines to the Southern Railway. Almost as soon as they arrived at Kings Cross, the N7 started to move away again; 10 to Hatfield in 1930 and others to the GE section of the LNER, leaving only 10 at Top Shed by early 1931.

26 years. Of classes J15 to J17, ten, three and two respectively were allocated to Top Shed at the Grouping, but they dwindled away until the last - J55 No. 3908 - departed in 1943. Stirling's J14 and Ivatt's J15 (J53 and J52) came to Kings Cross between 1892 and 1909 and at first were mainly used on transfer traffic to the LCDR via Ludgate Hill. They moved to other duties in time, with 14 at the Grouping growing to 27 by mid-1934. Only one remained by 1959 - the last survivor in London District, No. 68846 which left in that year, ending an association of engine type and shed of over 60 years standing. Incidentally, after withdrawal, No. 68846 was the first BR locomotive to be privately preserved.

Sounding the death knell of GN saddle tanks in the London District was Gresley's J50 0-6-0T, the first three engines arriving in 1938, used on trips and shunting before leaving again 3 years later. However, in the early 1950s the 0-6-0T began to move from the West Riding to London in earnest, mainly to Hornsey shed, but some to Kings Cross, to eradicate finally the saddle tanks.

Kings Cross had many cross-London goods workings, but as far as

N2s under the water gantry in November 1954.

A.R.Goult

These too gradually dwindled until all had gone by 1942, but the class returned for the period 1951-1955, for use on the Alexandra Palace branch.

Thompson Class L1s completed the story of the Kings Cross suburban workings, the big 2-6-4Ts, of which the first arrived in 1949, were intended for ecs and commuter trains and the complement reached 23 within a decade. By that time they outnumbered the dwindling stud of N2, which however, remained more popular with the men. The L1s participated in outer suburban duties, taking over some turns from B15s, but the 4-6-0's larger wheels better suited them for such work, so after largely being relegated to ecs workings for a time, the L1 had gone from Top Shed by 1962, outlasted by N2s after all.

Shunting, tripping and banking work all concerned Top Shed until some duties were passed to Hornsey on its opening in 1899. Stirling J15 to J18 classes (J54 to J57) were present from the early 1880s, with all eight J18s at Kings Cross on trips to the East London docks until 2 moved away in 1905/6; the remaining 6 engines survived for a further

main line work was concerned, the shed was never very busy, even before Hornsey opened. Situated at the 'end of the line' as it were, much of the London long distance goods trains were worked into the Capital by engines from sheds to the north, on an out and home basis, returning whence they came with the empties. This is illustrated by the 1889 WTT which shows Top Shed to have had only 6 main line goods duties and the corresponding returns. Power for these trains would have been Stirling 0-6-0s and some 0-4-2s no doubt and there would be little change to that pattern for many years. For example, in 1905 there were only 15 0-4-2s of Classes F2 and F3 in the entire London District, together with 26 0-6-0s of Ivatt J5 (LNER J4) and Stirling J6 classes. By 1912 the 0-4-2 were down to 8 engines in the District, of which one or two may have been at Top Shed, while 0-6-0s had increased to 32 - 20 J5, 8 J6, 1 J7 (Stirling) and 3 J21 (first series - LNER J1); the actual allocation at Kings Cross from among this selection is impossible to divine.

The first accurate allocation available for Top Shed relates to the period just prior to Grouping. At that time 0-6-0 included 5 of Ivatt's

Much of the elegance and cleanliness of the 1930s was perpetuated under BR, for a minority of engines at least (contrast the A3 and the 9F). Official cleaning statistics of 1950 record the Eastern Region Pacifics as enjoying no less than *six full cleans a week at eight man hours each*. This was in essence balderdash contrived principally for the purposes of inter Regional minor politics. At Kings Cross full time cleaners, rather than lads on the footplate grade, were employed.

Camden Libraries.

For years the smoke and fume of 'Top Shed' was a feature of the Kings Cross/SomersTown/St Pancras district. It occupied a strange site, innaccessible and remote amidst its lines and yards. It was a strange area of high walls and guarded entrances, and a confusing bustle of road traffic.

Camden Libraries

J5, a single J21 and 3 J22 (LNER J6). These were used on night braked goods, goods workings across London and in the Northern Heights and on 'slow passengers' as far off as Cambridge. At the same time, Top Shed boasted an allocation of 17 of Gresley's Moguls-15 H12 and H3 (LNER K1/2) and a pair of H4 (K3). The H2/3 had arrived from 1913, been christened 'Ragtimers' in the idiom of the day, and been used on night braked goods and slow passenger turns. Three H3s converted to oil burning were stationed in London in mid-1921 to assist the very heavy and erratic services brought about by the miners' strike of that year. By the mid-1930s Top Shed's complement had dropped to 5 K2s and all had gone by early 1940. in January 1961 No. 61756 became a stationary boiler at the shed, a duty performed until the middle of the next year, when she was withdrawn, the last survivor of the class. The larger H4s made their appearance in 1920, the fashion of that era reflected in another nickname, the 'Jazzers'. By the end of 1930 there were 15 K3s working from Kings Cross with 10 of them assigned to regular cews in No.3 (Express Goods) Link, where they undertook eight express goods, one parcels and one slow passenger working. From the mid-1930s K3 started making way for V2 2-6-2s and all had left Kings Cross by the start of World War Two. A K3, No. 61912, replaced 61756 as stationary boiler, until closure in June 1963.

To continue with goods engines allocated to Top Shed, the years 1925-8 saw ex-GNR 'Long Tom' 0-8-0 No. 3447 on pick-up goods within the District, but the numbers of 0-6-0s and moguls changed little until V2 2-6-2s and afterwards B1 4-6-0s became available. Gresley's big 2-6-2 were to acquire something of a reputation No. 4771 *Green Arrow* arriving in July 1936 to spend almost its entire working life at Top Shed, Goods Link 3 with the K3, with special regard to one duty, the 3.40 a.m. Scotch Goods, as far as Peterborough, from where she returned on a fast fish train. V2s had reached 15 in number by the start of the war and replaced K3 on all express goods duties; by the early 1950s the type was rostered for York and Doncaster turns, on passenger as well as goods. Thompson B1 did not initially take part in much goods work, but in 1954 a lodging turn to Hull was introduced *.....which required hard running over the 192 miles via Selby (later, via Goole), returning on a fish train that stopped only at New England.* Nine of the class were allocated to Kings Cross initially,

taking over such duties as the 'Cambridge Buffet Expresses', semi-fasts to Peterborough and many summer extras like the workings to Skegness, for the large Butlins holiday camp there. The last new class entirely devoted to goods were the Standard 9F 2-10-0, which became particularly frequent sights after Hornsey closed to steam. Fitters recall the '9s' as being particularly light on maintenance, with faults usually restricted to such things as blocked injectors.

Top Shed was remembered above all for its passenger work, beginning as far back as 1857 with the fast Manchester trains. The singles operated the 'Flying Scotsman' on its introduction in 1876, with a time of nine hours to Edinburgh and the first non-stop runs of 100 miles or more - to Grantham - and the only run of that distance for another decade. by 1895 there were 14 at Kings Cross Top Shed, of both 7 ft. 6 ins. and 8 ft. varieties and they held down the fastest workings. Various types of 2-4-0 and some 0-4-2s handled the slower and heavier trains. Ivatt D2 (LNER D3) 4-4-0s appeared in 1898 and took over the most important main line turns, but the Singles were not quite finished, for between 1910 and 1912, four joined Ivatt 4-4-0s Nos. 49 and 50 in the 'Bradford Special Diner' trains. When the train was withdrawn, the Singles left Top Shed's allocation never to return-except No. 1 of course, which remained in store at the depot for many years.

Ivatt 4-4-0s had a short time in the forefront of passenger working, untilC1 Atlantics (small boilered version - LNER C2) appeared in 1900. The 4-4-0s were nevertheless to be present for many years, on secondary passenger trains and some fast goods, standing pilot at Kings Cross station and often double-heading larger engines on the heaviest trains. They also had a long span on the outer suburban workings to Dunstable and Baldock and even to Peterborough and Cambridge; the last left Top Shed just prior to World War Two.

The small-boilered Atlantics were not used in any great numbers, with three, four or five the normal complement. They were employed mainly on services to Peterborough and Cambridge and remained on the latter turns until the mid-1930s, but had all left for places like Hitchin, before the Grouping. Their large-boilered sisters of GN and LNER Class C1 came to Kings Cross in quantity from 1904 and by 1912 they had reached 22 in number.

B1s, K3s, and V2s were as much part of the scene at Kings Cross.

Camden Libraries

Pretty Polly, 'one of the LNER Pacific giants being cleaned after its run from the North during the night......the engines have to be just as spick and span for the next days run.' By this time the cleaning gangs were probably exclusively male but in wartime many women had been pressed into service: ' The Kings Cross depot of the Great Northern Railway was the first on that line to have women engine cleaners, and the majority of the workers are still with them. The women are middle aged, wives or widows of soldiers. Two working uniforms are supplied. Women are also employed in the lamp room, oil stores and messroom.

Clive Hardy Collection

The Second World War saw the stud increase again to help with the enormous traffic and at the end of the conflict many were worn out. The allocation in January 1947 still stood at the 22 engines: 2800, 2801, 2802, 2811, 2817, 2821, 2823, 2825, 2834, 2840, 2841, 2842, 2845, 2859, 2868, 2870, 2871, 2872, 2876, 2879, 2881, 2889. Most were in fact lying out of use at Hitchin and by Nationalisation only two remained on the Kings Cross roster, Nos. 2817 and 2821. The former soon moved on to Hitchin and 2821 went elsewhere.

Pacifics first came on the scene in 1922, with Gresley's A1. The first engine was only on loan from Doncaster and was used on a return passenger working to Peterborough. In the summer of 1924 4-6-2s started working to York on the 'Flying Scotsman' and by the end of 1925 six were allocated to Kings Cross with some duties extended Newcastle in mid-1927. Corridor tenders were introduced in 1928 for the first non-stop workings of the 'Flying Scotsman' and the allocation had increased to 11 by June 1929: 2546, 2547, 2552, 2561, 2744, 2746, 2750, 4472, 4474, 4475, 4476. It was in 1929 that the 4-6-2s first started working through to Aintree on Grand National Pullman specials, taking in Newmarket and Lincoln race meetings in succeeding years. October 1931 saw the provision of a 70 ft. turntable at Cambridge and Pacifics started working there, on the famous 'Beer Trains'. 1935 saw the debut of the A4s and the 'Silver Jubilee' express; further deliveries of the new streamliners enabled the replacement of A1/A3s on the 'Flying Scotsman' in 1936, succeeded in 1937 or 1938 by the 'Coronation' and 'West Riding Limited' trains, terminated, like the 'Silver Jubilee' by the outbreak of war.

To conclude, a few notes on locomotive allocations. We have seen earlier that there were 40 engines at the depot in 1860 and it is also known that the number for 1900 was 130. Figures for London District only are available for 1905 and 1912, but analysis of the District's various sheds' rosters at Grouping, in 1931 and 1934, show that Top Shed had about 55% of all locomotives. So, a reasonably accurate figure can be gleaned for Kings CRoss in 1905 and 1912 of 155 and 156 engines respectively. Grouping saw the allocation still standing at 156, with a climb to 180 by the first half of 1929, at which time there were 274 sets of footplatemen working from the depot, including 90 in the suburban links. By June 1930 the roster had decreased again, to these 162 engines and one railmotor (working on the Edgware branch):

A1 4-6-2
2543, 2546, 2547, 2552, 2561, 4474, 4475, 4476

A3 4-6-2
2744, 2746, 2747, 2750

A5 4-6-2T
5007, 5452

C1 4-4-2
3251, 3274, 3278, 3279, 3284, 3286, 3288, 3295, 3299, 3300, 3301, 4411, 4419, 4426, 4436, 4440, 4420, 4422, 4424, 4450, 4458, 4459, 4460, 4461

D2 4-4-0
4366, 4388, 4389, 4391

D3 4-4-0
4078, 4301, 4312, 4346

J1 0-6-0
3012

J3 0-6-0
3793, 4039

J6 0-6-0
3547, 3560, 3572, 3584, 3590, 3591, 3592

J52 0-6-0ST
3111, 3961, 3968, 3978, 4201, 4205, 4212, 4223, 4229, 4232, 4241, 4255, 4261, 4262, 4263, 4274, 4275, 4281, 4282

Kings Cross was closely bounded on all sides; the site was hemmed in so that expansion was next to impossible and problems were experienced in particular at the inlet/exit roads, compounded by light engine movements and the constant to and fro of up to *twelve* pilots. The ash pit area in the right foreground was the obscurely titled 'Continent', its origin long lost in time.

Kings Cross was amongst the most eccentrically arranged in the country, with its peculiar conjunction of straight shed and 'Crescent'. The place was much altered through the War (both 'the Loco and the potato market' had been hit by September 1940) and further renewals soon afterwards became necessary because of decay and neglect.

Sid Checkley

J53 0-6-0ST
4214

J54 0-6-0ST
3860

J55 0-6-0ST
3785, 3802, 3804, 3807, 3901

J57 0-6-0ST
3149A, 3684, 3685, 3687

K2 2-6-0
4644, 4645, 4649, 4668, 4679, 4689

K3 2-6-0
69, 91, 135, 140, 143, 156, 158, 163, 229, 231, 4008, 4009

N1 0-6-2T
4581, 4583, 4589, 4596, 4605

N2 0-6-2T
2662, 2663, 2664, 2665, 2666, 2667, 2668, 2669, 2670, 2671, 2672, 2673, 2674, 2675, 2676, 2677, 2678, 2679, 2680, 2681, 2682, 2683, 2684, 4606, 4607, 4608, 4609, 4610, 4611, 4612, 4613, 4614, 4615, 4741, 4742, 4743, 4744, 4745, 4746, 4747, 4748, 4749, 4750, 4756, 4757, 4758, 4759, 4760, 4761, 4762, 4763, 4764, 4765, 4766, 4767, 4769, 4770

N7 0-6-2T
913, 914, 915, 916, 917, 918, 919, 2653, 2656, 2657, 2658, 2660, 2661

Railmotor
51912 *Rising Sun*

At the end of October 1931 the allocation stood at 164 locomotives, increasing by 10 at 31st May 1934, to fall back again to around 165 in the Spring of 1937. A visit to the shed at that time - Sunday 25th April - found the following 'on shed':

A1
2560, 2561, 4475, 4479

A4
2509, 2510, 4482

C1
3251, 3273, 3274, 3284, 3288, 3300, 3301, 4444, 4458, 4459, 4461

D2
4370

J3
4039

J6
3539, 3560

J52
3111, 3961, 3968, 3970, 3978, 4201, 4205, 4212, 4213, 4215, 4223, 4229, 4230, 4232, 4239, 4255, 4262, 4263, 4265, 4274, 4275, 4279, 4282, 4289, 4290

J55
3908

K3
113, 116, 121, 140, 158, 229, 2425, 2427, 2428, 2455, 2761, 4009, 4649

Robert The Devil **on the Kings Cross turntable around 1959.**

Sid Checkley

N1
4575, 4583, 4587, 4596, 4601, 4602, 4604, 4605

N2
2663, 2664, 2665, 2666, 2668, 2669, 2671, 2674, 2675, 2679, 2681, 2682, 2682, 2683, 2685, 2686, 4606, 4607, 4608, 4610, 4611, 4612, 4615, 4725, 4727, 4733, 4738, 4741, 4742, 4743, 4744, 4747, 4748, 4749, 4753, 4756, 4757, 4760, 4761, 4762, 4763, 4766, 4767

N7
2646

O1
3456

O2
3481, 3498

V2
4771

Just the formation of British Railways the complement stood at 181, which fell to 160 by late summer 1950 and reduced again to 107, by the spring of 1959. That figure did not fall much further until just before the end, in June 1963. On closure all remaining engines were transferred to Grantham and New England.

Dante's Inferno!

Authors Collection

'Concrete mixers' at Kings Cross in June 1952. Resident 67797 alongside Stratford based 67727. They were useful engines, the half dozen regulars at 'Top Shed' working the outer suburban services (in conjunction with the Hitchin batch) and the drudge of empty carriage movements in and out of the terminus.

H.C.Casserley

Morning lineup in 1961. From left to right the engines are *Seagull, Royal Lancer, Sir Christopher Wren*(**the Britannias were a revelation on the Cleethorpes runs, replacing long underpowered B1 4-6-0s),** *Centenary, Sandwich,* **and lastly** *The White Knight.*
Photographer unknown.

'Bottom shed' evolved into a straightforward engine yard and was commonly known, at least in latter years, as 'the Passenger Loco.' Atlantics still dominated the main line work in the 1920s, when Gresley's Pacifics were yet to become the principal force.

Collection J.E.Kite.

'BOTTOM SHED'

Kings Cross terminus opened for traffic on 14th October 1852 and in the next year the GN had a land ownership problem affecting the carriage shed beside Kings Cross engine shed. That caused the company to erect a new building for coaching stock repairs, adjoining the departure platform (ie on the west side), and backing on to the station offices; cost of construction was £975.

There matters rested until the late summer of 1860 when came the first statement that operating problems were caused by having to send every tender engine over the single down line from the terminus, to the locomotive shed at Kings Cross goods yard for turning. Further congestion was caused by the need to reverse trains coming from the Metropolitan lines into Kings Cross and it was suggested the matter could be eased by installation of a turntable at the station, which was

On 10th March 1862 the General Manager asked for costs of £200 to be sanctioned for provision of a 6 inch water crane at *the new engine shed* at Kings Cross station. The price must have included a mains feed too, the expenditure was approved and the locomotive shed, converted from the carriage shed, opened later in the year. Tucked into a cramped triangular space formed by the west wall of the departure platform, the line coming up from the Metropolitan tunnels and Upper Edmund Street, the sheds facilities consisted of a 42 feet turntable, from which ran a dead-end spur used for parking coke wagons. The coking stage portion of the building measured about 110ft by 24ft, while the contiguous engine shed itself contained 2 roads and scaled 155ft by 20ft. Construction details are lacking, but walls were almost certainly of brick, with a slated gabled roof over the engine roads and possibly another gable, or lean-to type of roof over the coking stage. There was precious little room for anything else so the water crane was

'Bottom Shed', three roads at the west side of the station, with 8ft Single No.2.

W.J.Reynolds

agreed and expenditure sanctioned on 25th September. However, the GNs General Manager intervened and in a report of 30th October 1860, declared that the turntable would be 'useless' without an engine shed to complement it, and the engineer was asked to draw up the necessary plans. These were submitted to the Board on 19th March 1861 and envisaged conversion of the carriage shed into an engine shed for six locomotives, and construction of a new carriage repair shed in Kings Cross goods yard, all at an estimated cost of £6,710. The next minuted comment comes from 11th June 1861 when it was proposed that .....*improvements costing £400-£00 be carried out at Kings Cross carriage repairing shop*..... On 10th December that same year, the General Manager again intervened with what seems to have been an entirely new suggestion. He presented plans of a .....*proposed new engine shed at Kings Cross passenger station giving better access and more extended accommodation*.....Nothing further is stated about the shed.

positioned by the neck of the locomotive yard, where it could also serve engines standing on the station's short bay departure road.

The new depot was probably called 'Bottom Shed' soon after opening and must have certainly have alleviated some of the problems caused by light engine movements, but not all. Midland Railway engines had been using Kings Cross station since 1858, but as they were not allowed access to the new shed, still had to proceed to Top Shed for turning and servicing. In 1863, the Midland Company asked for its own coking stage and engine siding at Kings Cross terminus, which the GN agreed and had installed in the same year. The 240ft spur ran north from under Battle Bridge Road / Congreve Street bridge, where it made a junction with the line from the Metropolitan. The spur ran between the lines entering Gasworks Tunnel and the eastern retaining wall of the Gasworks itself, and about one third of the way along from the junction, a 38ft by 8ft wooden coking platform was built. Here a handful of MR engines could stand and take on fuel

No.94 at Kings Cross. These were the shed's 'peerless aristocrats' (in LTC Rolt's description of Stirling Locomotives), 'unsurpassed and unsurpassable'.

R.Tarpey Collection

Atlantic tank 1540, fitted for working the Widened Lines, awaiting a New Barnet working - 'the Northern Heights' so beloved of the early GN publicists. Enlargement of the station saw this cramped loco yard moved to a position adjacent to Gas Works Tunnel.

H.C.Casserley

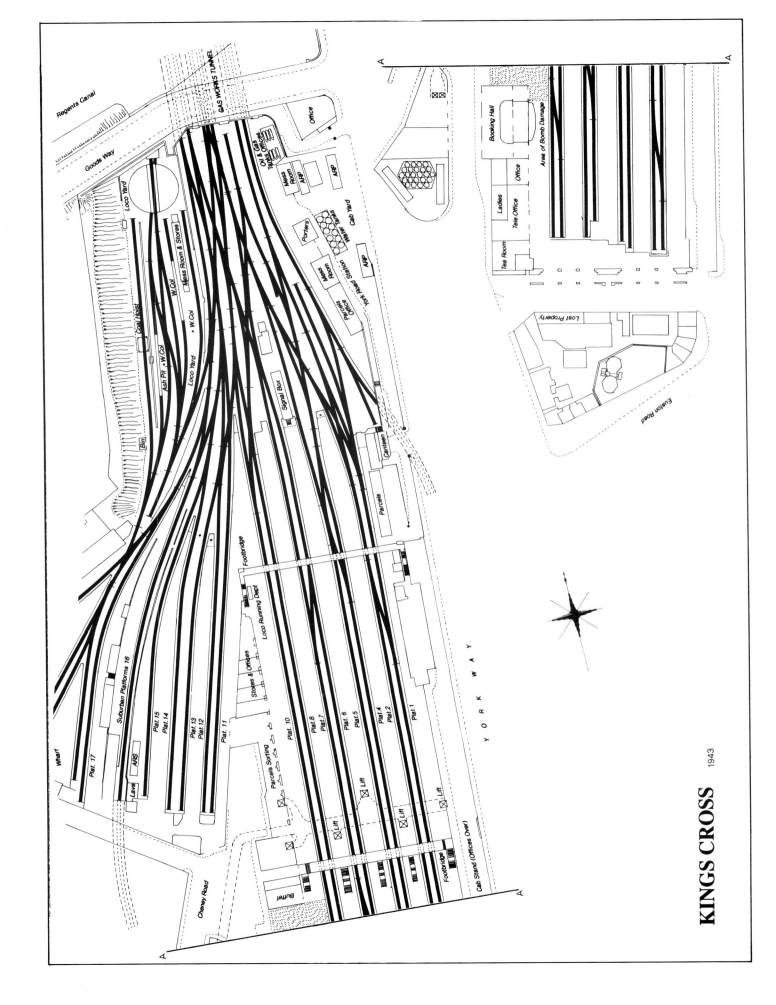

KINGS CROSS

1943

and so as not to make the whole affair a pointless exercise, it must be assumed the GN allowed the MR to use its turntable and water column.

Midland Railway trains stopped running into Kings Cross in 1868, but GN traffic was increasing to such an extent that the small shed at the terminus was becoming congested and more engines than was desirable had once again to travel to Top Shed. December 1871 saw the first recorded mention of a need for more stabling room at the terminus, but nothing was done about it until mid-1873, when statistics showed 200 trains were using Kings Cross station each weekday, including those over the Widened Lines. A scheme estimated at £50,000 was proposed for the creation of new local platforms, plans were produced and tenders invited for opening on 5th February 1874. The Way & Works Committee however recommended to the Board that a decision 'be deferred' until a committee of Directors had visited the site of the proposed work. At a subsequent meeting, on 21st March 1874, it was noted ..... *With reference to the meeting of 5th February, the Directors present at this meeting visited the site of the proposed Engine Shed and other works at the north end of Kings Cross passenger station, and also the proposed rearrangement and extension of the office accommodation on the accountants floor. They were accompanied by the manager and engineer, who explained the new works proposals. The tenders received were 10 in number and Messrs. Jackson, Shaw's tender £9,945 was accepted for the engine shed etc., provided that they would undertake the extension of the offices, estimated at about £3,000. on the same schedule of prices.....* Work was put in hand, with the shed closing about April 1874, to quickly be demolished. During the period of building it would appear that all engines once again made their way to Top Shed for servicing and turning.

The works involved were considerable: seven streets of housing and small commercial premises - Ashley, Essex, Norfolk, Northampton, Suffolk (East), Suffolk (West) and Upper Edmund Streets - disappeared, to clear a triangular area west of the station. New platforms were built over the site of the engine shed, while another platform was errected to serve the incline from the Widened Lines on its eastern face, with a further terminal road on its western edge; the remainder of the triangular space was taken up by new goods and milk docks and associated cartage areas. A new road, Cheney Street, ran along the south side, and on the north edge, the re-aligned Battle Bridge Road was accommodated on part of the gasworks site. The engine shed was built in the space between the high wall west of the new suburban platforms and the incline from the 'Metro' lines. Thus it was moved about 100 yards in a south westerly direction, to occupy an area formerly covered by Norfolk Street and the south ends of Northampton and Upper Edmunds Streets.

This second engine shed at the terminus was a three road dead-end building, in the south east corner of the new site, adjoining the wall of the suburban station; it measured some 43ft by 140ft with a large sand furnace on the west side. The new suburban platforms were brought into use during December 1874 and January 1875, with the new engine shed opening in the latter month. However, the overall job was not completed until some time later, and the final payment to Jackson and Shaw was not authorised until 6th April 1876. On that date, £3,158/8/9d was sanctioned, bringing the contractor's total renumeration to just over £17,658, for *formation of a new engine shed, workshops, offices, waiting rooms etc.*

The engine shed access road joined the line from the 'Met' tunnel under Battle Bridge Road bridge to skirt the gasworks before entering Gasworks Tunnel. The restrictions imposed by this were gradually eased by provision of new tunnels, on both up and down sides with the latter completed in 1892. Coincident with that work many other jobs were carried out at the terminus., with the first mention in a Minute of 8th January 1892. This records that the engineer *read a report about progress of the work of erecting artisan dwellings at Kings Cross.* This was Culross Buildings, loosely named after Lord Culross, and the basement was being fitted out for the use of gas and signalling fitters. The report concluded by mentioning that a site for a new engine shed would be cleared at the station.

By October 1892 the position had been reconsidered, as a minute of the 7th of that month noted: *.....Read engineer's report of the 6th, submitting a plan whereas lines can be laid at Kings Cross station to make the best use of the vacant land at the west side of the station. It is now found that an engine shed is not required and this will give space in the local station for three lines of way, with two good platforms and a booking office.....* This was suggested in an effort to avoid buying

additional property, but it was resolved to recommend to the Board that the premises of Messrs. Healey's and the German Gymnasium be purchased, although further consideration had to be given to this. Approval to go ahead with the revised plans was granted by 5th January 1893, the engineer was able to report on progress of work on the new shed etc., at Kings Cross passenger station. Of the £11,669 price accepted, £5,300 had been spent and the engineer asked for an additional £2,739 for extra works, not connected with the engine shed, which was agreed. Events are confused slightly by a tendency to mix the terms engine 'shed' and 'yard' but it was certainly the latter which was envisaged. Completion of the whole job took nearly another two years, with the engine facilities remaining in restricted use for most of that time. On 4th April 1895 it was announced that *the new locomotive yard and platform* had been brought into use, the latter numbered 11 - 13, while that serving the Met. incline became No.14 and its western edge, No.15.

Boring of the new down side tunnel meant that at last Battle bridge could be removed (the GN subsequently building a new road, 'Goods way', across the top of the tunnel portals as a substitute), with the result that both the gradient and curvature of the track from the Widened Lines were eased. A number of reports of this work mention that the alterations to the incline allowed the locomotive yard to be moved a few feet west, but comparison of 'before and after' plans does not readily show how this was achieved. What does seem to have occured though was that the 1875 engine shed's western wall was extended in length and height, to separate the suburban platforms from the engine yard; the associated sand furnace was moved further north along the extended wall. In addition, the turntable was enlarged to 52 ft. diameter, while in order to open up space for locomtive sidings, the coal stage was moved over 40 ft. closer to the turntable. This required removal of the tankhouse, with water thereafter supplied direct from the mains. The stage itself was larger than its predecessor, 50 ft. by 25 ft., with a tiled hipped roof. It retained the single bucket crane, wagon spur at the rear, and a 50 ft. ash pit in the track beside the coaling platform. Even so, stabling space was not great, a pair of through roads each of about 135 ft. and a spur ending between the turntable and station wall some 80 ft. in length.

Just prior to World War One it was again obvious that Kings Cross station required yet more expansion of its suburban platforms. Proposals were put forward for the locomotive yard to be moved, to create the necessary space and the company sought to purchase nearly 6 acres of the by then largely defunct gasworks site. This land had a chequered history, having previously been the property of the GN, acquired under the compulsory purchase powers of the Act of Incorporation. Later it was sold under the section of the GN Act dealing with disposal of surplus land, and purchased by the gasworks company under its own Act. When the GN wished to re-acquire the land for its new locomotive yard, the gasworks company questioned whether the railway, having once bought and disposed of the land to another concern under Parliamentary powers, a concern moreover that had made the purchase under its own Parliamentary powers, could again compulsorily buy it back!

2-4-0 No.257 at the first station loco yard

R. Griffiths Collection

The legal niceties of all this were eventually sorted out and the GN obtained the land, but the job got no further, due to onset of war, and it was 1922 before the matter was again taken up. On 3rd November that year the GN Board approved estimated expenditure of £39,000 for provision of two new platforms and a locomotive yard; on the 22nd, 23 companies were invited to tender by the 28th. A dozen replied and prices for the engine yard varied from £36,750-15-5d to the incredibly low figure of £13,775-1-4d from Messrs. Symington & Son Ltd., of Glasgow. Symington & Son offered completion in eight months to which the GN replied that the tender was accepted on the proviso that work would be completed in 7 months! The contractor's price was made up as follows:

Needless to say the target was an impossible one, as the LNER's quarterly report on New Works, for 31st December 1923, noted that: *.....spent to date, £17,231, work practically complete and signalling in hand.....* It looks at first glance as if Symington & Son had exceeded their tendered cost, but it must be remembered that the prices of such items as the turntable and signalling had to be added, not to mention the coal stage, construction of which was seemingly not part of the contractor's works.

Completion came early in 1924 and the facilities provided were a considerable improvement upon their predecessor. First came the 70 ft. turntable at the extreme north end of the site, which ended the necessity of having to send the new Pacific locomotives on an 8 mile

Enterprise, **the first A3, in the new, or third, loco yard.**

C.A.Appleton Collection

General condition	£35-00-0d.
Earthwork and fencing	£5,779-12-6d.
Drainage	£477-00-0d.
Retaining wall next to Goods Way	£3,371-01-0d.
Retaining wall next to Battle Bridge Road	£298-10-6d
Retaining wall between sidings in yard	£1,384-02-0d.
Foundation for locomotive turntable	£758-09-0d.
Engine pit and foundation for water crane	£316-13-0d.
Sundry items	£20-00-0d.

The earthwork cost did not belie the task involved, which started on 20th December 1922. It was necessary for Symington & Son to take down the retaining wall around the former gasworks, which amounted to about 2,500 cubic yards of brickwork and concrete. This was followed by excavation of the land behind the wall - an area of about one-and-a-half acres - to a depth varying between 15 and 27 ft. giving some 23,000 cubic yards of clay and gasworks foundations to be removed. And all this to precede construction of the new locomotive yard - in the total time of only seven months!

round trip to Ferme Park to turn. On the eastern spur would be parked the terminus stand-by engine; a pipe was brought to the spot so that steam from the stand-by locomotive could be used for heating coaching stock. The mains-fed water column completed the locomotive facilities sited between the yard's two easternmost tracks.

Improvements were not long in coming. In about 1928 a half-ton skip hoist coaling plant was installed at the southern end of the site and the original coaling platform removed.

Came April 1949, and it was necessary to take the turntable out of use for overhaul; during the period of the work, engines went to Top Shed and some to Hornsey for turning. before long the turntable was again giving trouble, such were the demands that had been placed upon it. This time the 'table was removed and sent to Gorton works for overhaul. It returned and was re-installed on 14th December 1952, requiring the use of two breakdown cranes - those from New England and Neasden officiated, as Top Shed's own crane was itself not available, undergoing overhaul. In 1958, for a third time, the turntable began to show its legacy of years of hard work and it was again sent to Gorton for attention. This time though it was replaced by another 70 ft.

Coranach **on the new yard turntable, winter 1931. Kings Cross was amongst the last of the great London termini to be thoroughly rearranged, about 1923/24 and the new engine yard was a principal consideration.** *To turn the Pacific engines a turntable 70ft in diameter is requisite; those in Kings Cross locomotive yard and depot are 50ft. It is therefore at present necessary for the 4-6-2 engines to run light between Kings Cross and Hornsey, where there is a 70ft turntable, in order to turn. This means light running for 8 miles between the up and down journeys on each London train worked by these big engines. This necessity might not be so serious in itself, but other factors are also involved, such as the occupation and wear and tear of the lines between Kings Cross and Hornsey, the increased time that must be allowed between the arrival of the up train and the departure of the down one for which the engines are diagrammed etc.*

Collection Brian Hilton

'table that had recently been removed from the sleepy little backwater of Witham, on the former Great Eastern Railway. Quite why so large a diameter turntable had been provided at such an out of the way spot was merely in line with a policy of standardising on that size, so it must have come to 'Bottom Shed' in almost new condition and there were no further problems with turntables at Kings Cross locomotive yard.

The same year saw the first influx of diesels and in the early 1960s BR erected a diesel inspection shed over the standby engine spur and added a fuelling facility, with 2 tanks being installed. not long after that came erection of a large office and staff amenity block above the diesel fuel tanks, on the sloping ground at the west side of the yard; here was housed the locomotive foreman and his various depot personnel. Two more fuel tanks were added before steam finally bowed out in 1965, at which time the turntable, water columns and coaler were quickly removed. Then, for the next 15 years, new generations of railway enthusiasts watched 'Deltics', Class 47s, the one-off DP2 and numerous others of their ilk behaving exactly like their steam forebears had done for the preceding 103 years. The end finally came with the large scale introduction of High Speed Train sets, when the need for locomotive facilities ended. 'Bottom Shed' closed in 1980, after its four separate installations had amassed a 118-year history, thereby exceeding even 'Top Shed's' life span by some 5 years.

Today the site of Kings Cross station's last locomotive yard lies derelict soon to be redeveloped in connection with the Channel Tunnel Link.

Kings Cross on 24th March 1933. The alterations had been contemplated for some years; 5½ acres were acquired from the Gas Light and Coke Company and the 'Congreve Street' bridge removed ('so called by the railway but for at least 40 years past this sole entrance to the gas works has been un-named'). The new road formed above the Gas Works Tunnels, linking York Road and Pancras Road, and still so familiar, was named with scant inspiration, 'Goods Way'.

Great Northern Society

Sir Frederick Banbury in the last years of steam at Kings Cross. It was always a marked contrast to the remote and inaccessible Top Shed; everything was visible and even in diesel days there was a constant fascinating movement, engines straining and shrieking round the sharp Milk Yard curve before reversing into the yard.

Sid Checkley.

The Hornsey coaling plant. The official description reads thus: *Locomotive coaling plant supplied to the London & North Eastern Railway Co. at Hornsey. Inclined hoist capable of handling 6 wagons of up to 20 tons each per hour. Reinforced concrete bunker providing storage for 200 tons of two qualities of coal.* **Further pencil notes add:***Note hinged arms on cradle and canopy. Red tiles on roof. Residential district; dust important! Homes in background - Mondays washing...*

HORNSEY

The need for more engine shed accommodation pressed ever harder in London and soon became apparent, even in the early years, to the GN Board. Little enough was done apart from expanding Top and Bottom sheds at Kings Cross, as far as the sites would allow, and opening a small shunting engine shed at Wood Green; proposals for a new shed did not come until 1882. The idea then was to entirely relocate Top Shed but despite Directors site meetings and much discussion, nothing came of it. In 1887 the matter re-surfaced and this time Hornsey is mentioned for the first time, the Board approving a 100,000 scheme to move Top Shed to either there, or Holloway. This scheme was also deferred, never to materialise.

The first developments of note came at the start of the 1890s, when engine servicing/stabling points were created at Clarence Yard and Ferme Park. They were an attempt to provide servicing for shunters from the neighbouring yards and reduce delays to engines running to and from Kings Cross shed. They were more 'stopgaps' than real answers to what was progressively becoming a serious problem and proposals soon followed from Stirling, in 1892, for a shed at Hornsey - or Ferme Park, as it was equally and confusingly known in the early days - for 50 engines, with attendant shops, turntable and sidings. Approval was subsequently given and during 1894/5 the contracting company of Messrs. Bowdry & Yarburgh carried out a large-scale site preparation project - landfilling, consolidation and grading. The firm had won the contract with a price of £12,196 and on 26th March 1895 Stirling was able to report its completion, at a final cost of £11,793. The engineer continued by asking that: .....*plans for the new shed now be prepared, for tendering to builders.....*

On 1st May 1895, Stirling presented plans for a shed for ninety-six engines - nearly double that originally proposed. The archive continues to record that the engineer also presented plans for enlarging the existing shed .....*in Kings Cross goods yard, capable of accommodating 43 engines.....*, upon which the Board approved the issue of tenders for the construction of Hornsey shed. In the absence of more documentation it is assumed that Stirling was saying he needed shed room 'at London' for 96 engines, but as Kings Cross held only 43, was justifying

to the Board the need to house fifty further engines at Hornsey. Whatever, and despite the already complete foundation work, the new shed was not embarked upon for another *three years* or more. From the General Manager's report of 28th July 1898: .....*At the present time the engine shed in Kings Cross goods yard is altogether inadequate for the number of engines requiring to make use of it. The approach to it and the departure from it cause serious delays to goods traffic, and light engines running between Kings Cross and Ferme Park help to congest the lines between those two points. The provision of further engine shed accommodation at Kings Cross is impracticable and undesirable and it is suggested that a new shed be provided at Ferme Park, at an estimated cost of say, £49,000.....*

This report led to tenders being issued and eventually, on 29th September 1898, a contact was let for the construction of Hornsey engine shed. The successful firm was Kirk, Knight & Co., which had some very swingeing terms and conditions to meet, in obtaining their £32,499 job! Able to start work only at the end of September 1898, Kirk, Knight & Co. were expected to have Hornsey coal stage ready for use by 1st May 1899 - or earlier - and the entire engine shed in operation by the following 1st July! Clearly, with most of the work having to be done during winter months, these were impossible targets. Therefore it is not surprising that Ivatt's progress report, of 24th June 1899, one week before the final completion deadline, went like this: .....*£17,884 has been expended already. The main walls are up, ready for the girders and these are being fixed. The engine and ash pits are nearly completed. The north wall is completed and the walls of the shops and offices are about 8ft above ground. The coal stage is being slated-in and about half the tank plates are fixed. A third of the brickwork of the turntable pit is done.....* In other words, the job was nowhere near completion and the GNR would have been lucky to see its depot finished much before the latter part of 1899, but the coal stage was almost certainly in use earlier. In fact the whole shed was most likely brought into use in phases, which may explain why an 'official' opening date has not been traced Kirk, Knight & Co. received their final payment in 1900, when it was stated that the shed and its accoutrements had actually cost more than the tendered price, due to 'other works' that were not specified - neither were their costs. There was no mention of any 'penalty clause' deductions from the contrac-

Perhaps the most enduring of the varied Hornsey complement were its 0-6-0 saddle tanks, noted for their far ranging activities across London. R.C.Riley in his youth, as a confirmed South Londoner, encountered them almost as emissaries of a foreign land: *These were completely unlike the familiar Southern engines....Most of the SR tanks were green, while these strangers from North London were black; some were even dirty, a sight less usual than it is today. The 1930 allocation shows 46 of these engines at Hornsey, the shed largely responsible for the SR transfer trips, while 16 were at Kings Cross.*

Brian Hilton Collection

PORTABLE BATH FOR ENGINES BATH NIGHT. The LNER have installed at one of their principal engine sheds a portable plant for washing locomotives. The 'bath' consists of a high pressure injector which supplies a mixture of steam and hot water at a pressure of 400lbs per square inch thus enabling one man to thoroughly clean an engine in a couple of hours. Hornsey, February 28th 1936

Collection Clive Hardy

tor's emoluments either, but it is doubtful if the GN failed to enforce any such clauses that might have been written into the contract!

With the doubtful distinction of being the last GN engine shed to be opened, Hornsey comprised an eight road dead-end building for 40 (!) engines. It was constructed in brick, with a northlight roof and measured 240 ft. x 116 ft. The ramped coal stage stood at the east side; this was built in brick, with a wooden face at the front and at one end supported a 50,000 gallon water tank. At the east side of the shed there was also a 52 ft. turntable, purchased from Cowans Sheldon in a separate contract, at a price of £402. Various offices, stores and workshops were ranged round the walls, but a purpose-built repair shop was not provided. This deficiency was mostly made up very soon after opening, in a number of improvements/additions requested on 19th February 1900 and approved on the succeeding 6th April. These comprised the creation of a coal stacking ground, with £2,200 allowed for site preparation and £235 for the necessary siding. Repair facilities were considerably enhanced by the purchase of shearlegs, which with foundation would cost £350, plus £240 for the hydraulic pump and lift for the hoist.

After but a short time of operation, a problem emerged at Hornsey that was to persist throughout its steam days, and although largely contained in later years, this was done only at considerable cost. The problem was smoke emission, the shed sited squarely in a residential area, having houses to the north, east and south. With the prevailing wind from the west, smoke was usually going in the direction of the houses and on 4th July 1901, the General Manager reported to the Board the first complaints received from the public. He concluded that two courses of action were open to the company - use expensive (Welsh) coal for lighting-up, or try to successfully defend a law suit in the courts. It seems the latter course was adopted and perhaps successfully at first, as the subject does not re-appear in the Minutes until a Way & Works Committee entry of 2nd April 1908. This concerned the reading of the Solicitor's report of 30th March, about the Borough of Hornsey taking the GN to court over four complaints about the smoke nuisance. Two cases had been dismissed, while in the others, fines had been imposed upon the company, but the amounts were not stated. This is the last mention of smoke problems at Hornsey to be gleaned from GN papers, so it is assumed the company were

constrained to employ Welsh coal - as at Kings Cross.

While all this was going on, the subject of locomen's accommodation came up twice. On 5th November 1903, tenders were called for erection of a mess room at Hornsey, the lowest being accepted, at a price of £132-12-0d. On 1st October 1906, Ivatt wrote the following letter to the Locomotive Committee: .....*A good many of our drivers, especially those working trains from Peterborough, have to be booked off duty and lodged at Hornsey prior to their return trip. The men complain that it is very difficult to get beds and ask the directors to put up a Company Lodging House at Hornsey. At present the average number of men lodging at Hornsey in the 24 hours is 15 sets (30 men). The greater part of them go to bed between six o'clock in the morning and twelve midnight and this would mean that 30 beds are required. But if we do build a lodging house, I think we should start with not less than 50 beds, as the number of men having to lodge there are increasing, owing to Board of Trade interference. Probably Mr. Ross could design the building in such a way as to allow expansion without too much difficulty when required.....* It is illuminating to note that even the humanitarian Ivatt considered the Board of Trade's action in reducing the men's hours of duty as an 'interference'. Not surprisingly perhaps, further word about a hostel does not appear in the Minutes and the GN never did provide such a facility, anywhere on its system.

Still with regard to working hours, these were rigidly enforced in British industry, often by some form of audible signal, and the shed staff at Hornsey were no exception. However, from about 1909, the fitting staff did at least have a unique device to indicate their duty hours, although it is doubtful if they would really have appreciated the fact! The device was a handsome bell, taken from the American 4-2-2 *Lovatt Eames*, when she was scrapped in 1884, and bequeathed to Hornsey by its first owner, Kings Cross Top Shed. (For the earlier story of the Baldwin Single and its bell, see the sections on Wood Green and Kings Cross sheds). That bell rang the Hornsey fitters' working hours until 1938 when, suitably engraved and mounted, it was presented by Sir Ralph Wedgwood to a Mr. R. Pennoyer, of the United States Embassy in London. What became of the bell after that is not known, but perhaps the 106 year old instrument, with strong GN engine shed connections, still adorns somebody's trophy cabinet today.

Because of the policy of simply allocating engines to the various Locomotive Districts, it was not until the Grouping that it becomes possible to say exactly what engines were working from Hornsey. On the last day of the GN, the following were stationed at the shed: 2 J4; 4 J5; 17 J13; 24 J14; 24 N1; 6 N2; Total 76. One can safely assume that such a locomotive 'mix' had been more or less standard up to the Grouping, as Hornsey's prime functions never really changed. First, it was sited so as to provide servicing for locomotives working in from the north, on goods and coal trains, before they returned to their home sheds. 0-6-0s were seen from the outset, joined by 'Long Tom' 0-8-0s from 1901 and Gresley's 2-8-0s from 1914 (01) and 1921 (02); after Grouping, ex-GC 04/5 became regular visitors. During the Second World War a new type of eight-coupled engine became a common sight at Hornsey - the Riddles' WD 2-8-0 and the LNER was quick to purchase some at the war's end. Before entering LNER service the 'Austerities' were given a shopping and some at least came to Hornsey during 1946 for painting. Nos. 77230 and 77395 are two examples known to have been dealt with, before going on to their designated sheds; it does not seem as if any of the 2-8-0s were ever allocated to Hornsey though. Regarding the 'Long Toms', Hornsey actually had two on the complement from 1925 to 1929, Nos. 343/5, which undertook local goods work. No. 3435 went to the breakers from Hornsey.

Hornsey also provided pilots - Ivatt 0-6-0ST - for the many shunting duties in such goods places as Ferme Park, Clarence Yard and East Yard. The shed also provided the pilots on duties like the Holloway Carriage Sidings job and New Southgate shunters, while a solitary C12 4-4-2T, No. 4503, was retained for many years as Highgate Park carriage pilot. A sister C12, officially allocated to Hornsey, performed stationary boiler duties at the carriage sidings until 1951. In addition, from the early BR period, Hornsey condenser-fitted N1s took over banking duties from Farringdon Street to Ludgate Hill, formerly the shared preserve of Kings Cross and Kentish Town MR/LMS depots. From 1951 a steady influx of J50 0-6-0Ts replaced N1s over a five year period, with Hornsey's last, No. 69470 withdrawn in August 1956. J52s were another victim of the J50 transfers and Ivatt's saddle tanks disappeared from London around 1959.

Having received and sorted all that goods traffic, its distribution was a principal Hornsey concern. Goods trains were run all over the north of London and to some extent, south of the Thames too. Favourites for this work were the 0-6-0 and 0-6-0T classes, their duties taking them to such destinations as New Southgate, Hertford, Enfield, Mill Hill, Edgware and Alexandra Palace. North London Railway and Great Eastern tracks were taken to Temple Mills, Poplar, Victoria Docks and Royal Mint Street. For those East London workings, it was a long-standing tradition at Hornsey to keep one engine in pristine condition. For many years up to the Second World War, which put a stop to such smartness, the 'Pride of Hornsey' was J52 No. 4252. After the war, it took a while to regain certain practices, but in January 1950, N2 No. 69547, freshly out-shopped in new BR black livery and emblem, became in turn 'Pride of Hornsey'.

Further incursions on to other railway companies' lines were made to Acton (GWR) and Feltham (LSWR), both via the Tottenham & Hampstead Joint line. Condenser-fitted engines worked over the 'Widened Lines' to Snow Hill and Blackfriars (LCDR), Bricklayers Arms (SER) and Hither Green (SECR). In LNER days, particularly during the emergency years of the 1939-1945 War, ex-GER engines operated from Hornsey, on the shed's heavy Acton and Feltham interchange duties. Of significance were J17 Nos. 8164/84, 8204/8/35/6, which all appeared for varying times during the middle period of the war. In BR days, in 1951-3, four ex-GE J20s were given the same duties.

Last of Hornsey's main functions was to take some of the suburban load off Kings Cross, with C2s initially, then N1s from 1907. By 1912, fifteen of the 0-6-2Ts were at Hornsey, forming a separate 'Metropolitan' link. Six N2s joined them in 1921 and by 1925 four of Gresley's 0-6-2Ts were working in the Metro link, with triple-shifted, regular crewing. By the next year, N2s had six of the link's turns, taking over all ten by 1929. N2s also took their turn on goods duties, especially on the branches to Mill Hill and Edgware. Surprisingly, the post-Grouping ubiquity of the ex-GC N5 0-6-2T hardly applied to Hornsey; only one is known to have been working from there, in the summer of 1935.

Crowded and bustling through night and day, the shed and yard

The Ferme Park turntable in its new position at Hornsey shed. Over the years the turntable saw quite a number of accidents with engines sometimes ending up in the shed foremans office.

J.E.Kite

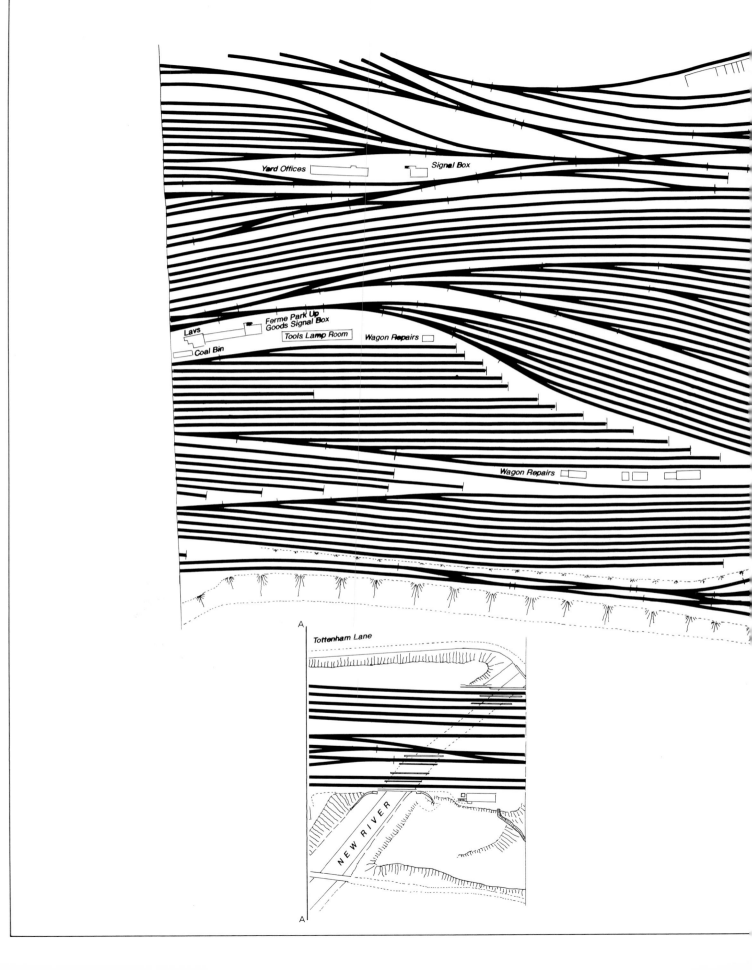

Yard Offices Signal Box

Lavs
Ferme Park Up
Goods Signal Box
Tools Lamp Room Wagon Repairs
Coal Bin

Wagon Repairs

A

Tottenham Lane

NEW RIVER

A

Coal Merchants
Coal Merchants
ARS
Old Stables
Platelayers Hut
Water Tower
ARS
Railway Hotel
Hornsey No1 Signal Box
Wharf
No.24
Cafe
Hornsey No.2 Signal Box
Footbridge
Site for Oil Fueling Plant
Canteen
Huts
Sand
ARS
Coal Hopper
Offices
Cafe
Ash Pits
Building
Contractors
Compound
Water Cranes
ENGINE SHED
Offices & Shops
Lavs
Bin
Hoist
Water Tank
Ash pit
Coal Stage
Tank Over
Cycles
Water Softening Plant

HORNSEY 1950

The original coal stage with adjacent sand-house.

Hornsey from the north in March 1947. Excavations for the planned fuel-oil installation are proceeding. The footbridge, opened in November 1900 and damaged by enemy action during the War, has still to be replaced.

The Thompson Society

was ever more severely taxed - the old northlight pattern roof had to be largely replaced as early as 1921 and from 1928/29 proposals were got out for a new turntable and mechanical coaling plant. An oil fuelling depot was made ready by 1948 but the programme collapsed in ignominy before, it seems, it could be put to use for steam locomotives. It was, like many such abandoned plants, to prove later very useful for diesels. The re-roofing work of 1921 had not been particularly comprehensive and BR gave Hornsey a wholly new roof around 1955. The usual materials of asbestos, steel and concrete were used, but BR changed the pattern from the northlight to one employing transverse pitches - a rare change of style. This was followed by the last notable steam locomotive development, when five Class J94 0-6-0STs came to the shed in the late 1950s. The big 'Austerity' tanks had a short future though, as Hornsey's 1948 oil tanks provided a ready made fuelling facility for the New Order that was to sweep the steam engine away, in a flood of dieselisation.

The revolution in motive power had been forecast in an HMSO report of about August 1957, from which the following pertinent paragraph is taken: .....*The maintenance of steam locomotives is to cease at Hornsey and the use of Kings Cross MPD by steam locomotives by the end of 1961 will be much diminished. A new Diesel Electric Depot will be built near Finsbury Park (on the down side in Clarence Yard), and will have an allocation of 136 Main Line and Shunting Locomotives. The Diesel Depot (Stage 1) will be completed by March 1959, by which time the 40 Main Line Diesels will have been delivered and temporarily accommodated at Hornsey. Stage 2 will involve the construction of an Electric Depot.....*

Of course, with the benefit of hindsight, we all know that the above plans did not quite work out as intended! But, in preparation, fitters from Kings Cross were moved to Hornsey in order of seniority to acquire the necessary diesel experience to man the depot at Clarence Yard. This only partly worked as some of the staff would not adapt to the new conditions. But nothing could stop the advance of the diesel and accordingly, English Electric Type 4 No. D201 arrived at Hornsey, early in 1958, soon to be followed by sisters D206-9 and BRC&W Type 2 Nos. D5300/1. By November 1958, the Type 4s were rostered for 4,500 miles per week, on London-Newcastle passenger workings, plus some goods work on the GN and GC sections of Eastern Region. In January 1959 the 'Deltic' prototype came to

Hornsey to commence trials, the outcome of which is well known. Meanwhile, other diesel classes proliferated remorselessly, with the more mundane jobs increasingly undertaken by further Type 2s of BRCW origin, soon joined by the Sulzer and North British versions. In time all of these Bo-Bo classes would be transferred away, to be replaced, by the seemingly everlasting Brush Type 2 (today's Class 31) and the short-lived 'Baby Deltics'.

It is not suprising then that Hornsey would officially close to steam at a relatively early date, an event which actually occurred in June 1961, when the remaining steam locos went to Kings Cross, New England and Doncaster, for a brief stay of execution. For some time before this though steam had become a bit of a pariah, as is well remembered by a Kings Cross fitter who on 13th May 1960, had to take a badly ailing V2, No. 60853, off the main line and into Hornsey shed for attention; the steam loco was not well received and what happened next is unknown as the fitter was told to report back to Top Shed immediately! Steam continued to run into London though and for a while after Kings Cross depot closed in 1963, engines had to visit Hornsey for turning and watering; for coaling they had to proceed to Kings Cross station stabling point. Then, there was an eyewitness to what was probably the last steam engine to visit Hornsey in normal traffic, when in 1965 a very sorry-looking B1 (unfortunately, record of its number has been lost) took water there. The very last steam engine to use the shed was somewhat inappropriately not an East Coast Main Line denizen, but GWR No. 7029 *Clun Castle*, which visited Kings Cross on enthusiasts' specials during 1967.

Diesel locomotives continued to operate from Hornsey until about 1971, after which the shed lay disused for some years, until it was taken over as a Permanent Way Depot. In recent years it has additionally been used as a base for the electrification of the ECML and as such, saw its first visit from an electric locomotive, when the unique 87 101 *Stephenson* was billeted there for a while, for test purposes. The former Hornsey engine shed is being used at present as stores annexe to the electric multiple unit depot, with the rear end cut away for a new roadway and only two of the eight shed roads in use. Such duties seem set to continue for some time, so there is a faint chance perhaps that Hornsey steam shed - albeit in altered form will survive to celebrate its centenary.

J52 3927, the shed pilot, pushes N1 4595 to the coaling plant in 1935. The modifications to the coaler's jigger feeders were obviously successful as no further trouble was reported. In BR days a procession of Pacifics would sometimes arrive on shed for coaling during periods when the Top Shed facilities were hard pressed.

J.E.Kite

The 1948 Locomotive Exchanges saw Hornsey play host to the ex Great Western 2-8-0 No.3803 which was working goods trains along the GN Main Line.

Authors collection

N7 69618 of Southend Victoria has its bunker replenished by the coaling crane in 1959. N7s had been employed by Hornsey duringa number of periods from 1955.

W.Potter

The diesels have arrived. Brand new BRCW Type 2s and ancient J50s.

WOOD GREEN

Goods and coal traffic into London escalated rapidly after the GN main line opened and the company was forced to build a number of yards to handle it. By about 1865, these required the frequent movement of shunting engines, running light, to and from Kings Cross shed and in an effort to reduce this activity - and thereby, costs - it was decided to erect a small shed for their use, somewhere in the northern suburbs. The site chosen was on the down side of the main line, between Hornsey and Wood Green stations. This was a sort of no-man's-land, which caused the shed to be referred to by several names : Wood Green, Hornsey (Wood Green) and even Hornsey (Waterworks),after the adjacent New River Works. However, from (admittedly few) references found, it is evident that simple 'Wood Green' was the official GNR designation.

Opened in 1866, the two road dead-end shed was built in brick with arched entrances and a slated gabled roof. It measured 113ft by 35ft, just large enough for six tank engines, which seems to have been precisely the number outstationed from Kings Cross. No turntable was necessary, only a small wooden coal platform and water tank outside. Access to the shed was via Wood Green South signal Box; the 1881 WTT Appendix shows a Whistle Code of '4 whistles' for locomotives wanting to take the 'engine road'. This they did, running south on a long spur, passing the shed and then branching off onto another spur whence reversal took the engines into the south-facing building; altogether an inconvenient and laborious set of manoeuvres. Ten years after opening, on 21st February 1868, the GN Board agreed works at Wood Green station, to cost an estimated £3,650. This was in connection with race traffic to the newly built Alexandra Park racecourse and comprised : .....*new lines of railway and stabling room for carriages*..... It was entirely possible therefore, that some locomotives off race specials may have sought refuge at Wood Green engine shed - after having been turned elsewhere of course. One locomotive definitely given refuge was *Lovatt Eames*, an American engine imported to Britain in 1881 by the man whose name it carried. This 4-4-2 - the 5,000th locomotive to be built by the Baldwin Works at Schenectady - was fitted with Eames' patent vacuum brake and he used it to demonstrate his invention to British railway companies. First exhibition runs were for the Lancashire and Yorkshire Railway and on 16th March 1882 *Lovatt Eames* ran a demonstration for the GNR. Seemingly unimpressed, Stirling immediately banned the engine from further use over company metals! With no further demonstrations in prospect, the undoubtedly dispirited Mr. Eames returned to the USA, after which his engine was put into store at Wood Green, during July 1882. The unfortunate inventor was assassinated in May of the following year, and after some legal haggling, the Baldwin 4-4-2 was auctioned by the GN on 24th April 1884. Successful bidder, with the ridiculously low offer of £165, was

one J.T.Williams, a scrap merchant, who shortly afterwards broke the engine up, within the confines of Wood Green shed. The GN claimed arrears of rent from proceeds of the sale and retained the locomotive's handsome bell; a distant reminder of the ill-fated inventor which stood for years, first at Kings Cross, than at Hornsey sheds.

Regular residents of Wood Green would almost certainly have been Sturrock and Stirling 0-6-0STs, with perhaps one or two 0-4-2T and 0-4-4Ts at times. By 1889 the WTT shows weekday pilot duties from Wood Green, to East Goods Yard. Their timings were :

Wood Green Engine Shed Dep. & East Yard Arr.

Dep: 3.30am 6.45am 10.45am 5.54pm 11.45pm
Arr: 3.40am 6.55am 10.57am 6.00pm 11.57pm

It would seem all five pilots ran a trip, or trips, from East Goods to Clarence Yard, before returning to their home shed and the WTT gives these workings, to get the engines back to Wood Green :

Clarence Yard, Light Engine Dep. & Wood Green Arr.

Dep: 5.42am 6.50am 3.26pm 7.18pm 7.52pm
Arr: 5.51am 7.01am 3.36pm 7.25pm 7.59pm

Eight years later, the 1897 WTT reveals six weekday duties operated from the shed, of which one was a passenger turn, commencing with the 6.18am Wood Green - Kings Cross. What the engine's remaining duties were, and how it returned to Wood Green, are not clear. The other five duties featured exactly the same times from Clarence Yard to Wood Green, but outward times were different, as shown below - each pilot then took an average of twelve minutes to reach East Goods Yard :

Wood Green Engine Shed Dep :

Dep: 3.35am 4.37am 7.30am 11.15am 5.57am

Undoubtedly this had been the pattern of services throughout and it is interesting to note that Wood Green engines, although operating at Clarence Yard, did not stay at the 'stabling point', opened there about 1890. By 1897 nonetheless the shed had little future left, and the opening of Hornsey, two years later, brought about the end of Wood Green; it was closed and all traces of the building removed.

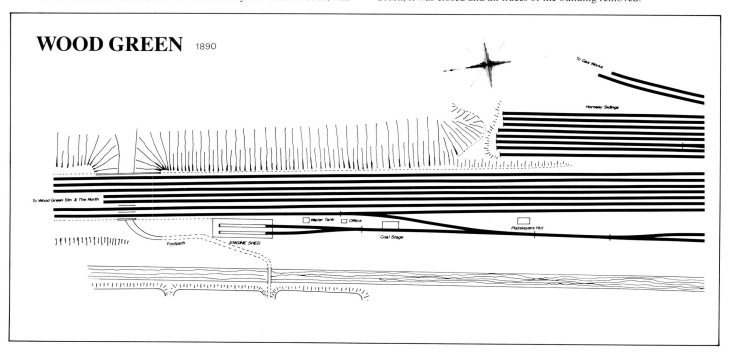

WOOD GREEN 1890

To Gas Works

Hornsey Sidings

To Wood Green Stn. & The North

Footpath   ENGINE SHED   Water Tank   Office   Coal Stage   Platelayers Hut

Ex-Great Eastern N7 0-6-2Ts at Hatfield in the 1950s. There were few Great Northern sheds where space was generously provided for; Hatfield was no exception and the shed building was almost a hindrance, to what was little more than a crowded engine siding.

B.M.Wykes

HATFIELD

The Great Northern opened the London - Peterborough section of line on 7th August 1850; an engine shed was not provided at Hatfield straight away and indeed it is not until late 1851 that Sturrock first mentions Hatfield, when he requests the placing there of a 16ft turntable, 'for carriages'. On 15th November the next year Sturrock followed this up with a request for a carriage shed to cost an estimated £130 which the Board approved. This may mean an engine shed was provided as well (why stable coaches and not locomotives?) but it is not until 1854 that the archive definitely indicates an engine shed in use; presumably the place stood on a site of some importance, the sort of place that would provide sufficient traffic to justify its own service to and from London. Whatever reason might lie behind its provision the shed would soon have been necessary for the working of the various branches out of Hatfield; the Hertford and Welwyn Junction and Luton Dunstable and Welwyn Junction Railways whose Acts of Incorporation were passed on 3rd July 1854 and 16th July 1855 respectively. These two lines, worked by the GN, were completed through to Hatfield on 1st March (from Hertford) and 1st September 1860 from Luton : by the latter date both companies had been amalgamated into the Hertford, Luton & Dunstable Railway.

The shed then, opened in the early part of the 1850s, a two road dead-end building in brick measuring 215ft by 35ft. The roof was a single gable with slate on wood all supported by iron beams. Water came from a nearby spring to be stored in a 10,000 gallon tank and a coking platform, probably built of wood stood north of the shed. At first no turntable was provided but as a requirement by the Board of Trade Inspectorate a 40ft unit was duly installed at the north end of the yard during August 1860.

By March 1862 Sturrock reported that the Hatfield water tank was 'too small' and requested approval for £150 to deepen it by 4ft and thereby double the capacity to 20,000. Sturrock regarded the shortfall as .....*particularly noticeable during periods of heavy demand - or on stormy days..........* This last comment is made the more mysterious by the locomotive engineer's report on 7th March 1864, that Hatfield's water supply was .....*good at present due to heavy rains.....*

The original water supply at Hatfield was certainly problematic, a state of affairs confirmed on 1st February 1864 when the loco engineer announced that the spring could not be further developed. He gained approval for an estimated expenditure of £1,085 to dig a well that would yield 40,000 gallons a day and install the necessary engine pumps and pump house. In fact two wells were eventually sunk, annually producing 30 million gallons of water of excellent quality. Just a year later on 3rd February 1865 Sturrock indicated that as Hatfield was now 'so important a centre' a breakdown train ought to be stationed there. His request was turned down by the Board and it was not until 1876 that Hatfield got its breakdown train based on a Doncaster built 8 ton hand crane. The 'importance' alluded to by Sturrock was enhanced further during 1865 when on 16th October the six mile GN - operated branch of the Hatfield & St.Albans Railway opened - the Act authorising construction having been passed on 30th June 1862.

Summer 1866 saw considerable congestion in the London District of the GN leading to many complaints about late running - especially from commuters, seemingly as vocal in the mid-19th century as they are today and John Budge the London Locomotive Superintendent visited the outer suburban centres (see also Hichin) and his report detailed the locomotive allocation at Hatfield which at the time seemed to be under some pressure.

Engines stationed there were:

Sharp 2-2-2T
1,2,15,31

Sharp 0-4-2
3,25,44

Hawthorn 0-4-2
101,102,104,107,108,112,115

Wilson 0-6-0
154,156

Hatfield over many years saw a continous to and fro of the various 0-6-2 tank types. The previous generation of London commuter tank had been the 4-4-2s, Stirling engines which came to predominate from around the turn of the century.

Collection Allan Sommerfield

The shed was no stranger to tender engines, particulary in earlier years and 0-4-2s were long used on London trains

Collection Kenneth Leech

No.11 on the cramped Hatfield turntable. Most views of the shed and its environs show how closely bounded it was by housing and not, unforunately for the railway, particularly of the 'labouring classes' sort. Their complaints could be brushed aside (more often they were servants of the company in any event and maintained the silence of self-preservation) but owners could cause problems. Welsh coal for lighting up seems to have been the favourite GN recourse

Great Northern Society

Nos. 31 and 154 were noted as 'spare engines' and two - unknown - were reported to be 'in shops'. Of the remainder each loco was averaging 104 miles a day in traffic with a 'shed day' being managed only every nine days. The Sharp Single tanks were used on branch services - Hertford and St.Albans mostly but appearances were made on the Dunstable line. Backbone of Hatfield's fleet, the Hawthorn and Sharp 0-4-2s were employed on services to London and over the Luton line but infrequent journeys were made on the other branches too. As usual the 0-6-0s were employed on goods traffic which was considerable - particularly on the Dunstable branch. A surprise omission from John Budge's record were the four Sharp 0-4-2s, ex-Kings Cross 'Metro' engines reportedly working Hatfield branch services from January 1866. Anyway things must have improved as the matter of timekeeping does not re-emerge in the archive even when from April 1867 further duties befell the shed. London Chatham and Dover Railway locomotives and trains commenced through running via Ludgate Hill; reciprocal services were worked by the GN but it is not clear if Hatfield locomotives participated.

The next 20 years were seemingly a quiet time at Hatfield but 1886 was a fairly eventful year with a plan produced on 31st August for 'new works' and resignalling of the station area. Part of the work included extension of the south sidings and demolition of the carriage shed beside the engine shed making the latter a through building. Notes accompanying the plan indicate the GN's original intention had been to move the entire depot to a point north of the station but .....*this will cost too much at present so the engine shed will remain for the time being*..... Extension of the roads through was apparently not proceeded with either but the water tank was enlarged again to 29,000 gallons and the turntable was replaced by one of 44ft 7inches diameter. It was during this time (probably) the GN started the practice of keeping an engine and coach on more or less permanent standby to transport Prime Minister Lord Salibury to London - with speed of the essence 2-2-2s and 4-2-2s were employed. His four terms of premiership spanned 1885-1902 but how long the GN maintained the facility is not known. Only six years later resiting of the engine shed was again considered. This followed a complaint on 7th January 1892 from residents of adjacent houses, objecting to the more or less continual nuisance of smoke. A new site for the shed 60 chains north of the station, was put forward as suitable. Its use would have entailed doubling the St.Albans branch for 53 chains which with necessary station platform alterations, put the total estimated cost up to £13,000. The General Manager was to report further but record of his findings has not been traced. Suffice it to say Hatfield's engine shed never was moved and the 1892 problem must have been alleviated in some way, as it does not re-occur: through the use of Welsh coal, more than likely, as elsewhere. (see Hornsey for instance).

Smoke made itself a nuisance in another way, after 47 years combined with the buildings permanent dampness, mild sulphuric acid had considerably corroded the iron beams supporting the roof. In his July 1901 report to the Locomotive Committee Ivatt highlighted the problem - also present at Hitchin (though to lesser extent) and announced that complete replacement of the roofs of both sheds should be considered, at an estimated cost of £1,500 each. The Committee asked Ivatt to investigate further with the upshot that the existing roofs remained with the iron beams being supported by wooden trusses. Total costs for both sheds are quoted as only £370, the bulk of it spent at Hatfield. There must have been some hidden costs in the Hatfield job or other work was carried out soon after for which authorisation has so far not been traced. Photographs from the very early 1900s shows the westernmost road to have been extended 'through' to the rear, allowing southerly ingress/egress and an increase in outside stabling room. Possibly the opening had been an accidental occurrence - 'shunting' mishaps vis-a-vis engines and shed walls were a not uncommon experience! Whether accident or design the new opening was secured by a rolled steel joist in the wall, bearing on new pad stones. New brickwork was formed above this lintel but the roof retained its original profile and central raised vent. However, this was changed by a further job that does not seem to have warranted official mention; in late (or more likely very early LNER) days the Hatfield roof was raised by about two feet, smoke vents were fitted over each road and at the same time a new chimney was built for the hearth in the foremans office. The reason for the roof heightening may only be speculated upon - a fire perhaps or a fresh attempt to eradicate Hatfield's 'hanging smoke' nuisance.

The next mention of Hatfield in the Minutes comes from those of

the Locomotive Committee on 21st July 1902, when a letter from Ivatt broaches the subject of staff housing .....*several of my men at Hatfield have enclosed a memorial asking for cottages to be built. Some of these living in houses belonging to Lord Salisbury have received notices to quit and others expect similar notices very shortly. There are no other houses available and I recommend the memorial be considered by directors*..... The memorial had been signed by 12 drivers 10 firemen and 3 labourers, but no further mention of the problem has been found in the archive so we can only wonder what fate held for those unfortunate men.

At the turn of the century engine power in the London District was considerably enhanced by arrival of Ivatt's C2 4-4-2Ts. They became daily sights at Hatfield from 1899 on the London services some of which ran through onto the Dunstable branch.Their arrival displaced the Sturrock and Stirling Metro tanks from workings into the capital with the last Hatfield - Moorgate duty by a Sturrock 0-4-2T taking place in 1903. However, the Metros stayed on at Hatfield on branch services mainly to St.Albans and Hertford although 0-4-4Ts were frequently on the Dunstable line.

Dominance of the 4-4-2Ts was threatened in 1907 by the arrival of No.190, Ivatt's prototype N1 0-6-2T but its axle load made it far from ideal for the branches and it was restricted to Luton and Dunstable workings. At the time of the N1s appearance passenger services over Hatfield's three branch lines were probably at their peak, viz;

Hatfield in 1922

K.A.Ladbury

HATFIELD - HERTFORD

Twelve up and thirteen down trains ran on weekdays with two up and three down on Sundays. Between 1904 and 1909 these services were as often as possible in the care of Kerr Stuart Petrol Railbuses Nos.3 and 4, in a test project overseen by one O.V.S.Bulleid. If the railcars proved a success it was the intention to order more and build a special shed for them at Hatfield. Nos.3 and 4 consistently proved unable to meet the demands placed upon them and they faded from view - here it is worth noting that their steam counterparts, the railmotors, were also seen at Hatfield but it seems they were never based there. Sightings were confined to weekdays-only visits from Hitchin during a few years immediately prior to World War One. A major part of railmotor lore is the present day dispute over whether they ever worked over the Hatfield-Hertford branch.

HATFIELD - ST. ALBANS

Operated by a 'shuttle' service controlled by staff only, no tickets being necessary. It comprised ten return trains on weekdays and three on Sundays.

HATFIELD- LUTON - DUNSTABLE

By far the busiest branch at any time, it was in the early 1900s supporting nine up and ten down trains Hatfield-Dunstable of which five up and four down were through services to and from Kings Cross.

The Hatfield coaler in March 1935. A lightweight type introduced to Britain by the LNER, this and some similar units were provided by Stothert & Pitt, of Bath. The type was subsequently usurped by the LMS as the 'Stranraer' or 'Lynn' type of 'tub elevator'. Together with the plant at Hitchin, the Hatfield example was put up in 1929; at both sheds space was at a premium: *The structure is of the minimum width, enabling the coal and locomotive roads to be as close together as practicable. Ample stability is provided by a wide base, and the structure is entirely clear of the railway construction gauge. Ladders give access to the winch and to the chute for its adjustments (The Railway Gazette, April 26th 1929)*

National Railway Museum

HATFIELD 1947

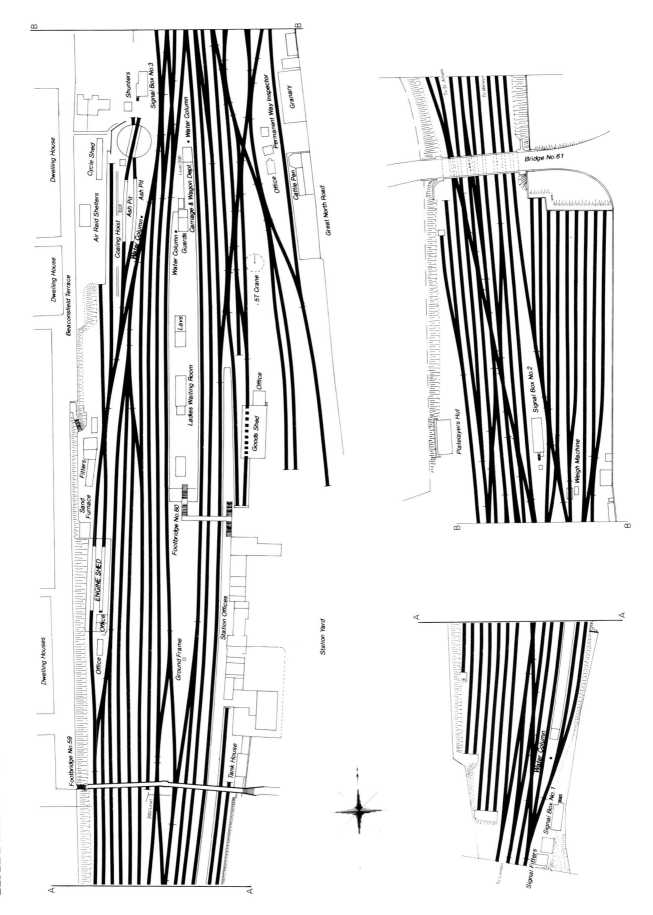

Hatfield on 4th March 1961. This was very close to closure; DMU sets eliminated the 0-6-2Ts with a sweeping suddenness and though it provided a retreat for diminishing numbers of steam engines on goods, it spent most of the final months in a semi-deserted state. Diesel shunters had arrived late in 1957. Unlike the 0-6-2Ts, they were required to pay very few visits to the shed. This was a revelation which took some months to make itself felt, at a shed where the daily streams of engines 'off' and 'on' in tune with the daily commuter tides, was ingrained

A.R.Goult

Hatfield on 24th April 1960, rebuilt in the 'blockhouse' form beloved of the Eastern Region. The style made for a particularly unlovely if highly functional building. No doubt the staff, used to tumble-down dereliction, paid little heed to this sort of nicety, an indulgence reserved for the enthusiast.

Ken Fairey

In addition the GN ran fourteen up and fifteen down trains between Luton and Dunstable only (to which must be added three return workings by the LNWR - extension of that company's Leighton Buzzard-Dunstable service).

All three branches saw considerable goods traffic, especially straw hats (!) and Vauxhall cars from Luton, parcels of Salvation Army literature and orchids from St. Albans and any manner of GER exchange traffic from Hertford. All this was marshalled at Hatfield before proceeding onwards and there was a Stirling 0-6-0ST or two engaged in fairly continuous shunting.

So Hatfield's men and machines were kept pretty busy and following the 1919 reduction in locomens daily working hours from ten to eight engine turn-rounds generally became more frequent with consequently heavier demands placed upon the engine shed. At Hatfield this resulted in an additional 75 ft. ashpit being dug late in 1920, its estimated cost of £165 approved by the Locomotive Committee on 15th April that year. Seven years later Hatfield's wells began to peter out after more than 60 years of exploitation, a new borehole was put down, completed in 1928 and another LNER improvement followed in 1929, a half ton skip-type mechanical coaling plant identical to that provided at Hitchin in the same year.

Gresley N2 0-6-2Ts arrived in 1921 and brought much change to Hatfield, five C2 and three 0-4-4Ts were allocated from Kings Cross to take up duties on the branches whilst four of the big new tanks came onto Hatfield's roster to allow withdrawal of the venerable Stirling 0-4-2s and 2-4-0s that had been pottering about on the branch lines. By the Grouping the allocation consisted of 5 C2, 1 D1, 1 D3, 2 G1, 4 J4, 1 J5, 1 J15, 4 J21, 1 N1, 8 N2. In January 1929 it had increased by one engine to 29 worked by 55 sets of men, four of which formed a 'Suburban Link'. Late in 1931 Hatfield's roster peaked at 30 engines to drop slightly soon after with the following complement on 30th June 1934: D2 3041/2, 4372; J1 3003/11; J3 3384, 4169; J69 7389; N1 4567/82; N2 2686, 4734; N5 5533, 5930; N7 2642-52/4-6/8. From then on the allocation stayed at about 26-28 engines, until the late 1950s.

The N2s apparently had a predilection for derailments when working on the Dunstable line so N7s came around 1924 to replace them on some duties. Thus commenced a triangular situation involving N2, N7 and the Dunstable branch that was to last until the

The shed yard in 1956, when DMUs were still a distant threat. Hatfield, along with Hitchin, was regarded by the 'cockneys' at Kings Cross and Hornsey as parochial places, which in a sense they were. They were deemed to 'keep themselves to themselves', though most London men would spend time there on relief, or between some turn or other. In the 50s it was still a 'country' area though spares and various items were still delivered by road, using the Kings Cross 'little blue (LNER) Bedford van, Reg. WB 4302' (!)
B.M.Wykes

end of steam, N2s periodically falling out of favour and N7 work increasing for a time. Even a pair of N5s was allocated between 1934 and 1941 (see above) on Hertford and Dunstable workings. Prior to that GN 0-4-4T had done but for a short time in 1929 ex-GE 0-4-4T 8100 and 8124 were working from Hatfield - presumably without success.

Perhaps the 'grandest' locomotives to work from Hatfield, Ivatt 4-4-0s were present for some while, their main duty being the Kings Cross-Dunstable through trains. An eye witness describes their progress along the Luton branch as 'always stately'. D1 Nos. 41 and 42 (LNER D2 3041 and 3042) are remembered as Hatfield's 'star' engines, kept in pristine condition for handling the exacting through commuter workings; on Summer Sundays the same engines would be seen at places like Southend, on excursion trains. By 1936 J6 0-6-0s started arriving at Hatfield to replace the 4-4-0s but the 0-6-0s were moved away again during World War Two. During the latter period of the war and for a time after, a number of Sentinels were allocated for varying periods, to shunt the Luton works of Laporte Chemicals Limited. Y3 Nos. 61, 62, 63, 65 and 66 all took their turn on that job.

By 1947 N2s were 'favourites' again as evidenced by the allocation in January of that year: two J67, nine N1, thirteen N2, and eight N7. This trend continued under British Railways; the August 1950 complement saw the addition of two N2s and two N7s but in 1952 N2s were formally barred from workings on the Dunstable line and N7s took over all duties. As before N2s gradually crept back again, seemingly this time for goods work only.

Also during 1952 - August to be precise - BR put forward a proposal to close Hatfield engine shed 'in the near future' and in preparation for this Hornsey footplatemen began route-learning over the St. Albans and Dunstable lines.

Hertford branch services and another Hatfield duty, the Welwyn Garden City shunt would become the responsibility of Hertford ex-GER depot and all this would make redundant a considerable number of the Hatfield staff. The scheme quickly foundered in a storm of trades union protest never to resurface; BR retained Hatfield shed and promptly spent a lot of money giving it a new roof. The materials used were the BR favourties of lightweight steel and asbestos sheeting; profiling of the brickwork gable ends was also changed to a decorative 'stepped' pattern and the foreman's office chimney was rebuilt yet again. Around the same time owing to the all-tank engine allocation the turntable was removed. For some years previously the operating diameter had been increased by the use of extension rails to 46 feet but it was unlikely that tender engines would ever again be allocated and it was surplus to requirement. The pit was not immediately filled in and as may be expected it had a magnetic influence - so much so that on 24th May 1954 N7 No. 69638 found the attraction too great and fell into it. Fortunately the only damage was to some locoman's pride, the 0-6-2T being quickly extricated and the pit filled in soon afterwards.

Even so the end was not far off, presaged in December 1957 by the appearance of no fewer than six new diesel shunting engines: D2000-2 and D3476-8 with D3476 almost immediately becoming Luton Bute Street pilot. The inexorable wind-down of Hatfield shed had begun earlier than this; the St. Albans branch passenger service stopped running on 1st October 1951 and the Hertford passenger trains had preceded that, ending on 18th June 1951; Hertford (Cowfield) station had closed on 2nd June 1924 but passenger trains continued to run using a connection to Hertford (North) station on the 'Loop' line. Then came the introduction of Cravens DMUs on the Kings Cross suburban services which wrote finis to the 0-6-2Ts and accordingly Hatfield shed. It closed in June 1961 around its 107th anniversary with the last seven N7 0-6-2Ts going to Kings Cross; eight diesel shunters were transferred to the new diesel depot at Hitchin.

Luton kept its passenger service, latterly diesel powered of course, until 26th April 1965 with goods traffic continuing from Hatfield until 3rd January 1966 when the line was cut back to Blackbridge Siding between Ayot and Wheathamstead and closed completely between there and Vauxhall Sidings, Luton. Access to the severed portion of the branch was then by means of a new connection from the former MR route opened on the same day. The Luton-Dunstable section is still in use today but the Welwyn Garden City-Blackbridge Siding length closed on 2nd November 1970. Meanwhile St. Albans goods services had ceased on 5th October 1964 and Hertford goods followed on 18th April 1966. It was not long therefore before Hatfield's yards ceased operation and the diesel shunting engines went away, their reign the merest fraction of the time that steam held sway.

Hitchin in ancient days. The shed (to the left, close enough to be more or less integral to the station buildings) was another of those 'retreats' which owed as much to early limitations of the steam engine as to any perceived system of working. In this regard Hitchin was akin to Hatfield, Watford on the LNWR, Basingstoke on the LSWR and others ringed about 'The Great Wen' of London.

Hertfordshire Libraries

HITCHIN

Two important factors determined very early on that the North Hertfordshire town of Hitchin, on the River Hiz, would be the site of a GN locomotive shed. The Act of Incorporation for the Royston & Hitchin Railway, on 16th July 1846, three weeks after the Act incorporating the GNR ensured Hitchin would be a junction on the proposed main line. Whilst the somewhat limited capacities of early locomotives more or less demanded servicing arrangements at regular intervals, at nearly the halfway point, between London and Peterborough, Hitchin was a natural spot for coke and water supplies and standby locomotives.

Thus, on the same day when the Kings Cross-Peterborough main line opened to the public, 7th August 1850, Hitchin was also brought into use. Adjoining the south end of the up platform station buildings, the engine shed was of two roads, measuring some 120 ft. x 25 ft. The brick structure had a single gable roof, the construction of which had been the subject of some discussion, when the whole matter of roofing materials for 'Engine Houses' was being decided, in terms of a general GN policy. On 9th January 1850 the architect, Mr. Goddard, asked whether various shed roofs should be .....*of (corrugated) iron or wood and slate*..... In the event, both types were employed at different sheds, the decision for Hitchin favouring a wood/slate variety - fortunately, as iron sheeting very quickly proved to be markedly less durable. (Hitchin's roof was supported by iron beams though, which eventually gave trouble - see below). A substantial coke stage was put up, so positioned that it could fuel an engine standing in the shed yard, or at the head of a train stopped at the up platform. No turntable was provided at first but a 40 ft. model was authorised on 1st July 1851, to be sited east of the shed entrance. A water crane stood near the coke stage: on 8th May 1855, Sturrock got approval for expenditure of £85, to site an additional water crane on the up platform, on the other side of the stage.

On 23rd October 1850 the Royston & Hitchin Railway opened, to be leased by the Eastern Counties Railway from 1st April 1852 and bring that company's engines into Hitchin on a daily basis. The ECR paid £300 a year for use of GN 'station facilities' at Hitchin and it may fairly be assumed this included access to the engine shed - if only for turning and watering. In May 1857, the Midland Railway line from

Bedford arrived at Hitchin and that company began its well-known ten year stint of operation over the GN to Kings Cross, from 1st February 1858. The MR built its own shed (the first of three in fact, on the down side, in that company's goods yard), so although the MR did tap the GN water supply, it did not burden its host with the need to accommodate engines. However, the added traffic caused Sturrock to comment, on 4th February 1858, on the need to station a breakdown train at Hitchin. The Board concurred and an 8 ton hand crane was duly purchased; the date of its arrival is not known, but there is a reference to it in 1866, when the archive noted that a breakdown train was .....*based at Hitchin*..... Traffic increased over the GN and R & H/ECR, to such an extent that on 3rd March 1861, Sturrock requested provision of a new ashpit, two sidings and a water crane, which was passed to the Executive Committee for approval. By Christmas 1861, accommodation problems caused Sturrock to propose 'alteration' to the shed, at an estimated cost of £430. The precise nature of these works is not clear but one or two clues may be gleaned from maps and plans.

On 7th March 1865 Sturrock commented that Hitchin engine shed again required extending, for which he had obtained an estimate for £440. The Board approved the expenditure and it seems to have been at this time that the (original) shed was lengthened to 160 ft. The new section of roof followed the original in outline, but was supported by wooden beams, as opposed to iron; a brick screen formed the south end gable. At the same time, moves were underway to enhance the water supply at Hitchin, where yearly consumption was around 80 million gallons. All this passed through the 12,000 gallon tank and on 1st October 1862 Sturrock asked for approval to raise it by 8 ins., increasing the 'head'. The tank filled only slowly, impeding the prompt departure of trains. On 8th may 1866 the loco engineer not surprisingly mentioned that the present 10 year old water pump/engine was having to work continuously, which made it very awkward during breakdowns or routine maintenance. Sturrock recommended spending £670 on an additional pumping engine, pumps, pump house and water crane - this was approved. Before the latest improvements could be put in hand, the London Locomotive Superintendent, John Budge, came to Hitchin to investigate complaints of poor timekeeping. His findings give accurate information as to what locomotives were stationed at Hitchin, as he detailed them in his report, and the duties they were then undertaking. The locomotives were: Sharp 2-2-2T

The shed around the turn of the century. In later years, such was the dereliction, stop gap repair work and the general crowding-in of the site, that it was difficult to appreciate what a substantial, (grand, even) affair it had been

Hitchin Museum

No.746 at Hitchin.

Collection Kenneth Leech

Nos. 6, 9, 21 (21 stopped for repairs); Sharp 0-4-2T No. 12; Sharp 0-4-2 No. 47; Hawthorn 2-2-2 Nos. 53, 62, 65, 66, 70 (65 spare engine); Wilson 2-4-0 No. 76; Wilson 0-6-0 Nos. 171, 347. Operational engines were averaging 105 miles a day each, with most enjoying a rest on Sundays. Of the seemingly over-extended locomotives, the Sharp 2-2-2T were used on services to Cambridge, which had become a GN responsibility on 1st April 1866, with termination of the Eastern Counties - by then GER - lease of the R & H. The Hawthorn Singles, Sharp 0-4-2s and Wilson 2-4-0s would have been used on stopping passenger and some goods trains, in both directions, while the 0-6-0s of course were assigned to goods work. Nine years after Budge's investigation - which seems to have resulted in an improved performance - Stirling's first 8 ft. Singles arrived in the London District and by November 1875 one of them would be seen daily at Hitchin, on main line pilot duties. The engine worked down on the 7.00 a.m. slow train from Kings Cross - the 'Old Parly' as it was known to locomen - then stood pilot during the morning, before returning to London on an afternoon all-stations 'stopper'.

Some years before the '8 footers' arrived, on 27th September 1871, the Hitchin turntable, after 21 years service was, as Stirling informed the Way & Works Committee: 'worn out'. He said that work was in hand on foundations for a replacement which would be fabricated at Doncaster Works and installed by company servants. it is believed to have been 45 ft. in diameter, positioned on the same site as its predecessor, and thereby encroaching further upon the shed entrance. This was probably the cause of the coaling shed being moved from the platform end, across the shed yard, to a position next to the cutting side. No mention of this move has been found in the records, but certainly it had been moved by the mid-1880s. The new turntable operated for the next 34 years, until July 1905, when Ivatt asked that it be replaced by a 60 ft. version, as 'Small' Atlantics had by then appeared, rendering such a diameter a necessity. Costs were estimated at £850 for foundations and siding, plus £540 for the 'table, from Ransomes & Rapier. It was situated further east of the shed, opening up the narrow neck there, and its placement required more of the chalk hill to be removed. This last factor was responsible for a £282 cost overrun, which was 'admitted' to the Way & Works Committee on 6th February 1906 and approved - not that the Committee had much choice! In later years, the site of the original turntable was covered by office buildings.

Following the fairly steady activity through the 1850s, '60s and '70s, Hitchin seems to have settled down, as it did not disturb the archive again until July 1901. At that time, Ivatt reported the iron roof beams (and those at Hatfield) were corroded and estimated replacement costs were £1,500 each shed. In the event re-roofing was not resorted to - instead the iron beams were supported by timber trusses, at a total cost for both sheds of £370! As the Hatfield roof was reported to be in the worst condition, a larger percentage of the repair cost must presumably have been incurred there. On 29th July 1903, Hitchin's water 'bugbear' reappeared, when Ivatt asked for a water crane to be moved. He also requested that the 12,000 gallon tank, by then with 100 million gallons through it annually, be replaced by a 100,000 gallon specimen, at a cost of £1,700. Having seen the existing tank cope with its marathon task for over 50 years (100M gallons a year meant that the tank's 12,000 gallons were consumed almost 23 times a day, on each of the 365 days!), the Way & Works Committee deferred its replacement. It never was superseded!

Steam railmotors appeared at Hitchin in April 1907, working until 1914 on the Baldock service. The steam cars' arrival was closely followed by mass movement of Kings Cross' surviving 8ft Singles to Hitchin: Nos. 34, 221, 666, 1007, 1008 were among those which came there, but some soon moved on to Cambridge and further afield, and all had gone by the start of World War One. In 1916 the pumps supplying the tank from the two wells were replaced by an electrically-driven centrifugal pump. Not surprisingly, the 60 years old 3-throw steam driven devices were then in a bad condition, but what a stirling service they had rendered!

Post-war improvements in railway workers' conditions of service caused Gresley to comment, on 31st March 1919, about ashpits, as follows: *.....the enginemen at Hitchin have complained from time to time about the lack of simple pit accommodation for the preparation, examination and inspection of locomotives. At the moment there are 29 engines stationed at Hitchin and only covered pit accommodation for 5. Now that the enginemens' hours have been reduced from 10 to 8, it is necessary to turn more engines round at Hitchin than was formerly the case, with the result that the shortage of pit accommodation will become more acute .....*Gresley went on to estimate the cost of extending the existing pit by 49 ft. and provision of an additional pit outside the shed, at £350. The expenditure was approved on 4th April 1919. At about the same time further 'thoroughbreds' were sent to Hitchin for

HITCHIN

1947

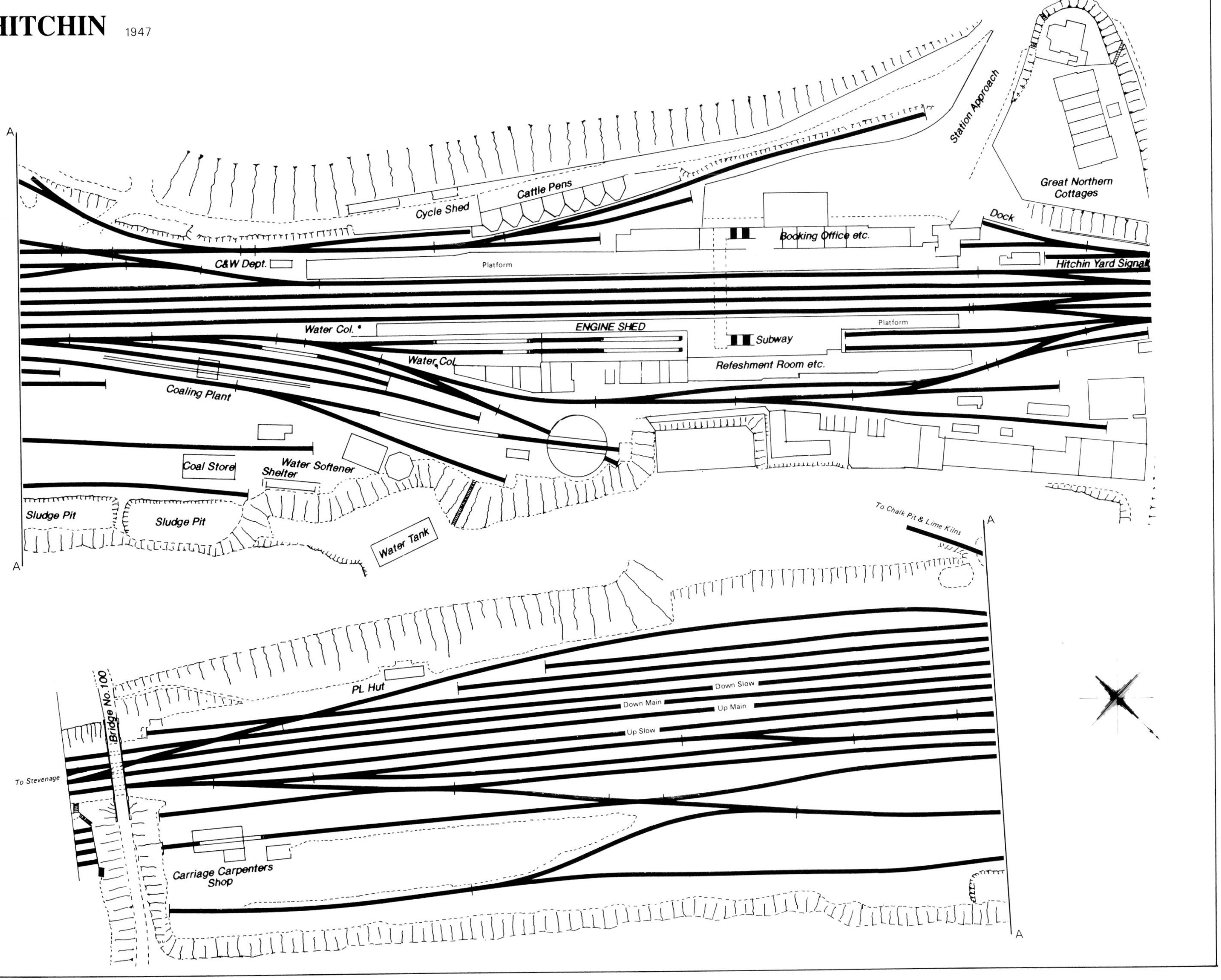

Great Northern Cottages

Station Approach

Hitchin Yard Signal

Dock

Booking Office etc.

Subway

Platform

Refreshment Room etc.

Cattle Pens

Cycle Shed

C&W Dept.

Platform

ENGINE SHED

Water Col.

Water Col.

Coaling Plant

Coal Store

Water Softener Shelter

Water Tank

Sludge Pit

Sludge Pit

To Chalk Pit & Lime Kilns

A

Down Slow

Up Main

Down Main

Up Slow

PL Hut

Carriage Carpenters Shop

Bridge No. 100

To Stevenage

A

A

A

the first time, with 'Large' Atlantic No. 299 from Kings Cross. This was to begin an association between the class and Hitchin engine shed that would last until 26th August 1949, when the last C1, No.(6)2828, was towed away for scrapping. During this thirty or so years the big 4-4-2s were to render stalwart service on the London - Cambridge workings and perform countless acts of rescue, substituting for ailing locomotives. Gradually their usefulness dwindled until the final days, when mournful lines could be observed, standing south from the shed yard, cold, dirty and uncared for.

Within a few days of Grouping, and the LNER but eleven days old Gresley asked for a second electric centrifugal pump, at a cost of £500, which was agreed. Six years later, with the allocation standing at thirty-four locomotives, operated by sixty-six sets of enginemen, considerable further improvements were made. These were first mooted on 16th November 1927, by Alex Wilson of the Locomotive Department, in a memo to the Loco and Works Committee. Wilson said .....*The facilities are inadequate for present day requirements and are not conducive to economical and efficient working. There is only one road into and out of the depot, the ashpit accommodation is insufficient and the coaling facilities stand in need of improvement. The number of engines located at the depot is 34, the number being coaled daily being 31, while the quantity of coal used amounts to 20,000 tons per annum. A scheme is therefore submitted:*
(1) Separate inlet and outlet roads
(2) Additional ashpit accommodation, viz: lengthening the existing ashpit from 45' to 115' and providing an additional ashpit 120' long
(3) A mechanical coaling plant and twelve 10 cwt. tubs, with coal shelter and coalmen's cabin
(4) Crossover road between out and inlet sidings
(5) Additional coal stack sidings
Estimated cost of the scheme was £2,982 and it was calculated that annual savings would amount to £398. The scheme was approved and on 5th January 1928 the LNER accepted a tender of £840 for the coaler, from the Bath-based firm of Stothert & Pitt. Of girder construction, the coaling plant was installed at the extreme south end

of the loco yard, which had its layout improved, much as suggested by Alex Wilson. In a further improvement, not specifically mentioned by Wilson, a small, electrically-powered machine shop was built, equipped with a lathe, drilling machine and shaping machine.

Locomotive allocations fluctuated, with strangers being C14 No. 6126 between 1927 and 1930, used on Hitchin-Baldock trains. No less than two Q1 0-8-0s arrived in 1928; what they were used for is not known and both had gone again by 1930. In September of that year Y3 Sentinel No. 55 came to Hitchin for a stay of over two years, on shunting duties at the Engineer's Yard. By late 1931 the allocation was down to twenty-five, which included a couple of railmotors for working the Hertford North shuttle and Letchworth service. These

No.711 at the coal stage. For most of the earlier period at Hitchin, as at Hatfield, tender engines predominated.

Collection Kenneth Leech

Atlantic No.279, on the 21st May 1923, on the Ransomes & Rapier turntable of 1905/06. The first 'table (see page 59) though itself enlarged, proved inconvenient for the working of the shed and its site was afterwards given over to offices and other buildings.

Collection Kenneth Leech

Hitchin in the 1930s. Despite its awkward elongate site a road running the length of the chalk cutting, to the rear of the shed, remained in use, an advantage in such a cramped layout. At the time of Sturrock's alterations of the 1860s the road led through to a site at the rear of the shed, where a two road building stood, measuring about 60ft by 25ft. It was built in wood, with a tiled gable roof. How long it stood, or what its precise purpose was remains unclear. There are suggestions that it was the mysterious Shepreth Shed, translocated and dating originally from 1851. Any clarification of this must, likely enough, remain impossible.

W.A.Camwell

Hitchin on 12th July 1936. At this byway, astonishingly, over twenty locomotives were present.

W.A.Camwell

The coaler in December 1934: *The firm of Stothert & Pitt, Engineers, Bath, has recently developed and installed at several British railway depots an electrically-operated plant designed for readily depositing coal in the tenders and bunkers of locomotives, and a typical installation is shown in the photograph reproduced herewith.*

National Railway Museum

devices had been re-introduced in the first year of the LNER and lingered for a while, before spending most of their time out of use. Two railcars, *Rising Sun* and *Expedition* are especially remembered as fairly long term Hitchin residents during that era. For the rest of the 1930s during which time the shed was re-roofed and a water softening plant installed, allocations hovered around twenty-eight with, for example, on 30th June 1934: C1 3272, 4427, 4437; C2 3949; C12 4511; D2 3049,3050, 4326, 4333, 4336, 4374, 4375; D3 4073; J1 3001, 3002, 3007, 3010; J3 3302, 4081, 4100,4137, 4154; J6 3539,3585, 3602; J69 7395; Railcar 51908 *Expedition* - 26 locomotives, of nine.classes, and one railcar. Two years later C1s had increased to five: 3272, 3286, 4427, 4437, 4451. The presence, in 1934, of Ivatt C12 4-4-2T No. 4511 was significant. It arrived that year and stayed for some 10 years, more or less replacing railmotors on the Hertford North service. Next, in November 1935, ex-GC Class A5 Pacific tanks, Nos. 5007 and 5412 moved to Hitchin, to spend 18 months on outer suburban work.

The Second World War saw much activity, including the very busy service to the large RAF camp at Henlow, on the Midland line from Bedford. The war also brought further strange classes of locomotive, not least of which was an armoured one, numbered WD 'A'. This apparition was, in reality, ex-GER Class F4 2-4-2T 7172, and she stayed at Hitchin, threatening but never needed, from June 1940 to May 1943, before returning to 'civvy street'. A year after the war's end, a visit to Hitchin on Sunday 15th September 1946, found four C1s, a J15, a J20, a J39, a K3 and six N2s. This was only one month before the invasion by Thompson B1 4-6-0s, Nos. 1089-99, which came to Hitchin to replace the Ivatt Atlantics. They took over the former suburban duties of the 4-4-2s, Cambridge workings and main line standby - the latter being a very heavily-used feature in the immediate post-war years of run-down Pacifics. Thompson 4-6-0s markedly dominated events for the rest of Hitchin shed's existence. Their onslaught can best be appreciated when one compares the 1946 'on shed' list, with the allocation on the last day of the LNER when thirty-four engines comprised fourteen B1 4-6-0s, four C1s, a couple of D2 and a D3 4-4-0, seven J3 and one J6 0-6-0, and three J67/9 0-6-0Ts. Ivatt 4-4-0s had been a constant factor for over 40 years, being favourites for summer extras, to places like Southend-on-Sea. Common factors also, were Ivatt's 0-6-0 types. In fact, J1 No.65013 was the last of its class, employed on Henlow camp trains until withdrawal in November 1954. 65013s finest hour came in 1951, when she replaced a failed 4-6-2 on a 490 ton, 14 coach train, and steamed triumphantly

Hitchin in the late 1950s. DMU sets had started to eliminate the tanks on London trains and plans were being made to build a diesel depot nearby. The steady operating patterns of years were to be severely put out. Main line failures still turned up though on a regular basis (as they had done for years). The solitary 4-6-4 No.60700 was no stranger to Hitchin and receives once again, remedial attention.

into Kings Cross with it! Her replacement on the RAF camp trains was initially ex-GE E4 62785, then J15 65479. N2s had first arrived in 1921, with No.1764, but there were never many of the type at Hitchin - only sufficient numbers for the services to Sandy and Royston. Ex-GE J67/9s which would be replaced by J68s in 1956, had themselves superseded older GN-design saddle tanks. In the first year of British Railways came a second Thompson locomotive invasion, six Class L1 2-6-4Ts. By 1950 there were nine of the 'Concrete Mixers' at Hitchin, where they seem to have been well received by the crews and the big tanks were utilised on various duties, some of which incurred mileages of around 1,500 per week. August 1949 brings a mystery, when it was reported that the Hichin turntable had been 'destroyed'. This resulted in multiples of light engines proceeding to Cambridge to turn and work up trains. New England B1s also assumed some Hitchin duties during the emergency, but exactly what they did is not known. As to the turntable, it was restored to service on 3rd December 1949, by the installation of a completely new unit, but the cause of the original's destruction has not been discovered.

The sheds complement stayed at around the thirty mark until the late 1950s, when loss of traffic and new rostering etc. saw the allocation inexorably dwindle. The arrival of D2003 on 22nd December 1957 boded ill and in April 1960, work started in the former MR goods yard on construction of a diesel depot, for the servicing of thirteen main line and six shunting locomotives. Choice of the site (where incidentally, the MR shed still stood, until 1989), was determined by considerations of space for expansion of the station and the handover of part of its yard to the Civil Engineer. In 1960, the entire steam allocation was transferred away, but the shed continued to function with engines loaned by New England, until finally closed in June 1961, two months short of its 111th anniversary. The building was soon demolished and most of the tracks taken up, although the turntable survived until the late 1970s, when it was recovered for a new lease of life at Quainton Road, now known as The Buckinghamshire Railway Centre. In time came the end even of the diesel depot and today Hitchin is merely a station on the electrified and very modern, ECML.

Hitchins lonely J15, in 1959, stationed there for working RAF leave trains.

B.M.Wykes

7ft single No. 63 at the Peterborough station coal stage, probably around 1892-3. It carries front vacuum hose and side chains together with (a combination of some import, apparently, to initiates) lined out splasher slots. The 'classic simplicity of outline' with, in LTC Rolt's phrase, 'a certain unsteadiness' is readily apparent. Such engines haunt the ancient days at Peterborough.

: K Leech Collection

PETERBOROUGH

Lying by the Nene some 70 miles from London, Peterborough in the late 1840s was by no measure a large town; it nevertheless proved important enough to attract the Eastern Counties (later Great Eastern), Midland and LNWR, all of them sharing a station on the south bank of the river. The Great Northern began in earnest upon the construction of its first section of line, from Peterborough to Lincoln ('the Loop') in 1847 and it was almost certainly in the early part of the next year that a temporary engine shed was put up, north of the town at Walton Junction. This, the first Great Northern shed of all, is accordingly shrouded in obscurity. It was probably erected by the contractor, Messrs Peto and Betts, but no plan of any sort has been discovered and the precise date of its opening is not clear. Even the exact location is in doubt. Great Northern trains ran into the existing (ECR/LNWR/MR) station from opening of the Peterborough - Lincoln section in October 1848 until a separate GN station could be brought into use, in August 1850. Access to the joint station in this period had been gained over MR tracks, from a junction with the GN Loop line; study of a plan of 1876 shows two levelligs of the land where the shed might conceivably have stood but any suggestions must remain speculative. It is known at least that the shed was built in wood but what sort of coke platform might have been provided is not clear and there was surely no turntable installed.

Some word of the engine complement is recorded; on 3rd May 1848 Bury was able to inform the Directors that ......*The Locomotive Department has to report for the information of the Board that seven engines and tenders are now in the Companys shed at Peterborough.....* A month later, on 1st June, nine locomotives were housed there, made up of five passenger and four luggage engines. The former would have been 'Little Sharps' and possibly the odd 'Small Hawthorn' single while the luggage engines were Hawthorn 0-4-2s and the obscure Bury-type 0-4-0s. The next three months saw another seven engines arrive at Peterborough and on 29th August the locomotive engineer was able to report that these were made up of .....*10 passenger and 5 goods engines, with one other goods engine on loan to Peto and Betts.....*

On commencement of the first public services on 17th October 1848 Bury advised that a former colleague from London and Birmingham days, Thomas Owen, was acting as Locomotive Foreman at Peterborough at a weekly wage of two guineas (£2/10). Within five weeks his responsibilities were deemed to be 'much increased' and Bury asked for a raise for Owen of 50%, to be paid monthly, 'or £150 per annum'. This figure actually equates to rather less than three guineas a week which no doubt assisted the board in its deliberations. 'Walton Junction' fades from the record, until 11th August 1850, four days after London-Peterborough services commenced, when Sturrock was able to report that the (permanent) engine shed at Peterborough was 'nearly ready'. Very soon after that, Thomas Owen took his men and locomotives to the new premises and Sturrock wasted no time in seeking permission to remove 'Walton Junction' shed to Boston, to be used for the repair of engines. However this request seems not to have been granted, for in January 1851 the locomotive engineer again asked for the 'temporary' engine shed to be moved to 'my yard' at Boston, for temporary accommodation for carriage repairs. This time Sturrock got his way and by 8th March 1851 he was able to note that the shed had been 'removed to Boston'. Thus passed the first GNR engine shed, cheaply built no doubt, after a brief but 'interesting' existence.

PETERBOROUGH STATION

Sturrock's report of 11th August 1850, that Peterborough engine shed was 'nearly ready', referred to the structure adjoining the north end of the up side station buildings. Designed by the Lincoln architect Henry Goddard, as part of the GN station/hotel development, all the buildings were put up by the contracting firm Messrs F W Costar. First mention in the GN Minutes comes on 9th January 1850, when Goddard asked the company if it wanted an iron or wood/slate roof for its engine shed, with the latter style being adopted. Opening may safely be assumed to have occurred in the latter half of August 1850, indicated by Sturrock's request of 1st September to resite Walton

Junction temporary engine shed. The new Peterborough engine shed comprised eight roads, a structure 120ft wide by 95ft long, in brick, with an internal wall subdividing it into two four road sections. Each was covered by a slated gable roof with raised smoke vent running almost the full length of the ridge. There were separate arched entrances for each road, which occupied 89ft inside (with 80ft inspection pits), accommodating about sixteen engines of the period. Along the east side a 62ft by 22ft office and workshop connected the shed with a repair shop, at the rear of which stood the Great Northern Hotel. A 40ft turntable stood in the yard, some twenty five yards to the north of the offices, with the coal stage nearby. This simple structure measured 90ft by 20ft with a 23,000 gallon tank (water was pumped from the Nene) astride its north end.

The engine shed dealt with all Peterborough traffic for about two years, until New England opened in 1852. Thereafter the 'station' shed was concerned only with passenger duties and was officially referred to as 'Peterborough Passenger Engine Station'. Expansion plans commenced in 1854 with, on 14th July, Sturrock requesting a smithy and a carriage and wagon repair shop, at an estimated cost of £560. The matter was postponed and only a few years later, with New England repair shops already in being, it seems the locomotive shops at the station shed were turned over to carriage and wagon work. Sturrock's 'smithy', in his request of 1854 was resurrected six years later when on 26th June 1860 the locomotive engineer asked for alterations .....*to the Passenger Engine Station at Peterborough*. Additional office room was proposed for the clerk of stores and together with 'space for the smiths' costs were estimated at £283, which was approved. What materialised seems to have been a large structure for such a small price - a building 70ft by 25ft, extending from the front of the engine shed/carriage shed and reaching almost to the edge of the turntable pit. In 1853 the first Peterborough breakdown crane, an 8 ton hand powered model, had been authorised and delivered from the Kirkstall Forge Company and in December 1857, Sturrock asked for *a small siding at the north end of the coke stage for the accident crane and van, to cost an estimated £65*. This was sanctioned.

For the first eleven or so years of running trains to and from London, it was the practice to change engines at Peterborough, in both the up and down directions. However in 1862 ashpits and water cranes were completed at the station, which allowed through running of engines between London and Grantham. In this way Peterborough lost a lot of its importance, but it was still necessary to maintain locomotives at the shed; some engine changing still went on and there was always a need for standby locomotives. To this end the shed was equipped with an engine hoist, ordered after Sturrock's request of 20th May 1862. It was duly installed over road number 5 (reading from the west) about 30ft from the front of the shed. It is also worth commenting that the turntable was enlarged to 45ft at some time - certainly it was of that dimension by the early 1880s.

From 1865 comes a tragic report concerning the station shed. That was on 14th January, when the boiler of engine No. 98 exploded. She was a Single, delivered by the obscure firm of Longridge & Co. in 1851, as a Crampton type, only to be rebuilt as a 'normal' engine not long after. The report of the explosion merely states that it occurred in the repair shop and that some damage had been caused to the roof of the engine shed. Only then did the account mention that three people had died, including one poor apprentice lad whose body was literally propelled through a wall by the force of the blast, with what was left of him landing in the tender of an engine, standing 'many yards away'. There must have been an inquiry into the incident but the Minute books are henceforth mute on the subject. However, what can be further said is that the report of No. 98 standing in the repair shop is not correct, as photographs of the wrecked locomotive clearly show her to have been occupying No. 5 road. Also, the comment that 'some damage' had been done to the shed roof was a gross understatement as those same photographs reveal a massive hole in the roof and damage to rear and internal walls, all of which was doubtless swiftly repaired.

There is little mention of the shed for the remaining years of the century, apart from entries regarding water, a subject which engaged the Great Northern greatly. It had proved a problem as early as 1862 and on 1st October that year Sturrock commented that the tank atop the coke stage was too low for sufficient pressure to be generated; he asked that expenditure be sanctioned to raise the tank by 8ins.

Two months after asking for the tank to be elevated, Sturrock noted, on 4th December 1862, that water consumption at Peterborough and New England engine sheds then totalled 300,000 to

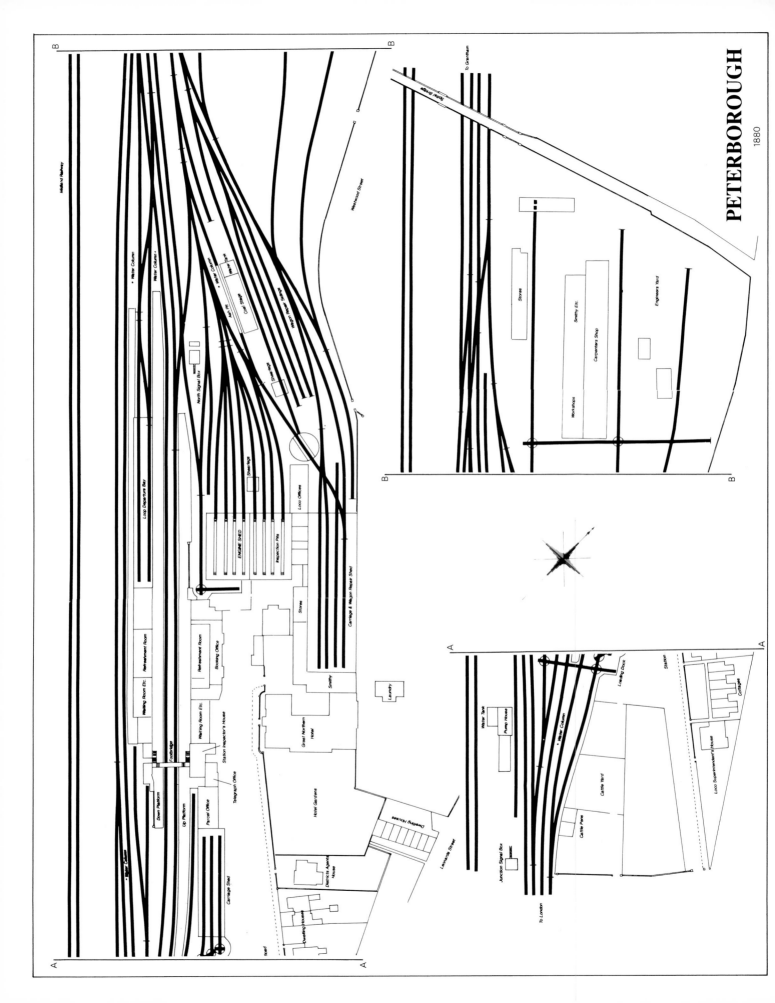

PETERBOROUGH

1880

350,000 gallons *a day* and that an 8ins main should be laid alongside the existing 6ins between Peterborough station and New England. In addition, Sturrock suggested that the spare pumping engine at the station be moved to the banks of the River Nene, to increase capacity there; estimated costs were £1,400 - £1,500 for the main and £500 for the removal of the pump and were approved on 9th December 1862. On 14th February 1866 Sturrock advised that he needed an additional pumping engine for Peterborough and recommended purchase from the firm of Messrs Easton & Ames, who had supplied the original appliances. A quote of £537 had already been received for a 12 horsepower engine, to which would have to be added costs of the necessary carriage pipes, estimated by the Locomotive Engineer at £54. The Board accepted Sturrock's view that additional pumping capacity was needed, but did not agree to Messrs Easton & Ames. Instead it was resolved that supply of a new pumping engine should be by tender. The precise outcome is not known but presumably Sturrock got his pump and water thereafter proved sufficient. In 1870 came a court case against the GNR, at which it was accused of illegally taking water from the Nene. Little else is known and while it seems that the complaint was justified, the GN continued to use river water over the next 20-odd years, though the company did seek alternative supplies. For example, from 10th October 1893 comes an Engineer's report on 'the borehole at Peterborough', read out to the Way and Works Committee; there was no previous reference in the Minutes to a boring at Peterborough, but there had been an unsuccessful drilling at New England in 1885. By October 1893, good quality water had been struck at Peterborough at a depth of only 15ft. Drilling had continued to 26ft when pumps had been installed, coming into use on 30th August, providing 100,000 gallons of water per day to Peterborough and New England engine sheds. That would have satisfied only part of the daily requirement of course, but it reduced what had previously been total reliance upon the River Nene. However, the new Peterborough borehole fed New England for only a few years for in 1898 the massive subterranean water body at Warrington Junction was tapped; soon it supplied New England and afterwards the Peterborough bore supplied only the station shed.

The shed at Peterborough station fell increasingly under the shadow of its larger contemporary at New England and complete removal was contemplated as early as January 1896, when the Engineer brought to the Way & Works Committee a proposal to 'rearrange' the station.

The whle scheme, which was estimated to cost £96,000 envisaged replacement of the Thorpe Road level crossing south of the station by an overbridge, re-alignment of the tracks and building of a new station, to allow faster through running. This in turn would require removal of the engine shed and wagon works, to a suggested new site at Westwood Bridge, some distance to the north. The cost of moving the shed and wagon repair shop was put at £29,000, but Mr. Webster of the Locomotive Department intervened to urge construction of a yet larger shed to hold forty engines, at an additional cost of £2,000; the new building however would have to have been put up at New England, where there was little space available. As usual, the matter dragged on somewhat, with further discussions at Board level in 1898/9 but the costs of moving the station, shed and wagon works still proved too much for the GN budget and the final outcome was an extension of New England shed in 1904/5. Eventually Thorpe Road crossing was superseded by a bridge, in 1913, but it was a further 60 years before Peterborough station was moved and the notorious speed restrictions eased.

The alteration at New England in 1904/5 brought about the end of Peterborough station shed, at least in the usual operating sense, and on completion of work at the former 'Goods Engine Station', passenger locomotives were housed there too. The station shed did not entirely go out of use; the breakdown crane - a 15 ton model from 1899 - continued to be stationed there as did standby pilot engines, for which the turntable, coal stage and water tank remained in service. In fact on 1st June 1905 Ivatt remarked that *.....the turntable is too small to turn the largest passenger engines which have to go to New England to turn, incurring extra mileage and loss of time. Messrs Ransomes & Rapier can supply a 60ft turntable for £540.....* The Board resolved to make plans and issue tenders, and by 27th July 1905 the Locomotive Engineer was reporting again, with an estimated cost of £675 for enlarging the turntable pit. Expenditure was sanctioned by the Board which directed that GN employees would carry out all the work of excavation and installation. The job moved so swiftly that by 25th November 1905 Ivatt was able to advise *.....work will be completed next week.....*

As stated above standby engines continued to be kept at Peterborough station, and after closure of the former Great Eastern Peterborough East shed, in 1939, engines off the former GER lines came to turn, water, clean fires etc. Whether any of the engines using

No 61 by the Peterborough tank, which like so much of the torturous Peterborough water arrangements, tried Sturrock and his successors unduly.

K Leech Collection

the shed after 1905 actually stabled inside it is not completely clear. Certainly by 1911 an official plan shows the building entirely in use by the Carriage & Wagon Department, but another from 1913 shows all eight roads in use as 'a locomotive shed', with only the repair shop earmarked for carriages, as hitherto! A 1920 Midland Railway drawing furthermore still shows the shed in use to its full extent for engines, while an undated LNER version has only the four western-most roads for engine use, a situation confirmed in a 1940 wartime fire precautions plan. All very confusing and the weight of evidence indicates that the shed building continued in use for engines after 1905, with eight roads reduced to four sometime after the 1913 enlargement of the Great Northern Hotel. At this time the eastern section of the shed became the hotel garage, its four entrances bricked-up in the process. It is interesting to note that these entrances - and the four in the western section of the building - were not the original arched variety but square steel-framed types, so at some previous time the old entrances had been replaced. When was Peterborough station shed finally closed? Possibly not until early British Railways days but even after that standby locomotives continued to stable in the yard, as did the breakdown crane - a 35 ton Cravens machine, delivered in 1913.

During its lifetime Peterborough station shed housed all the earlier types of GN passenger engines, starting with 'Little Sharps', 'Small' and 'Large Hawthorns', Sturrock 0-4-2s, 2-4-0s and singles. By 1855 the GNR Rule Book showed the following duties operated by Peterborough shed - separately identified from New England:

Up Peterboro' to Hitchin - 44 miles
London - 76 miles
Dn Peterboro' to Doncaster - 80 miles
Grantham - 29 miles
Leeds - 110 miles
Retford - 62 miles
York - 115 miles

In 1865 it is recorded that there were twenty two passenger engines based in the town, with a further five on order. In making this known, Sturrock was seeking additional locomotive accommodation for Peterborough and he added the perplexing comment that only eight engines could be housed at the station shed. Whether half the building was in use for other purposes at the time, or Sturrock was 'trying it on'

is not known, but almost certainly it was a case of understatement on the part of the Locomotive Engineer! After Sturrock came Stirling and his famous singles were prominent inhabitants of Peterborough. Initial allocations of his three types were:

7ft-0ins
Nos. 4, 21, 39, 41, 63, 222

7ft-6ins
Nos. 92, 233, 234, 237, 874, 875

8ft-0ins
Nos. 7, 8, 22, 48, 69, 98, 221, 545/9, 663/668, 772/776,1001, 1003, 1004, 1005

They roamed as far as London, Leeds and York with one of the prime duties for the 8 footers being the Leeds Luncheon Car Express, leaving Peterorough at 12.29 p.m. to arive in Kings Cross at 1.55. That meant 86 minutes for the 76 or so miles, 53.2 mph average with usually 250 tons load; early arrivals were frequent. Return to Peterborough was by means of the 3.25 p.m. from Kings Cross, which went on to York - another smartly timed run. Dispersion began in the late 1890s and even though Nos. 1003/4 stayed at Peterborough all their days most of their sisters were sent to sheds such as Boston and even Louth - or were broken up. Cause of the singles' demise was the introduction of such types as Ivatt's 4-4-0 and his first Atlantics, both of which saw out the shed's fully operational days. Large boilered 4-4-2s were resident on standby duties, as were the various types of 2-6-0, but Pacifics were not used, being too long for the turntable. Most common engines for standby pilot duties in latter LNER days - and favourites in BR times - were the V2 2-6-2s and many are the tales of their performance after substitution for ailing locomotives. This was particularly so during the transition period from steam to diesel although A3 Pacifics (despite the 60ft turntable), B1 4-6-0s and even a 9F on one occasion , were also used. Subsequent to the end of steam traction on the East Coast main line, diesels were parked in the yard, but after a while even that ceased. As to the shed buildings themselves, they were finaly demolished about 1963 (the turntable was removed in January 1965) but the rear wall of the carriage shop survives today, as an integral part of the Great Northern Hotel.

Peterborough station shed, reduced to an engine yard, a guise indeed in which it apparently served more or less until the end of steam. It enjoyed a history as tangled as any on the Great Northern; plans for its removal surfaced as least as early as the 1890s and precisely how each portion was eventually divided up has never really become clear.

Brian Hilton Collection

PETERBOROUGH (NEW ENGLAND)

Previous reports and articles on New England engine shed over the years all indicate its opening to have been in 1851; this would seem to be incorrect, with the shed actually brought into use the following year. In support of this come seven entries from the Minute books, as follows:

23rd July 1850: In answer to the Minute of 11th June 1850, read report of 15th July from the General Manager, Locomotive Engineer and Engineer, recommending Peterborough as the most appropriate centre for the permanent locomotive works.
Resolved that it be recommended to the Board to adopt Peterborough as the site for the permanent locomotive works and to give instructions to obtain the necessary land and for the preparation of plans and of obtaining tenders for the works.
27th July 1850: The Board approve that the locomotive works will be at Peterborough and 20 acres of land required by Mr. Cubitt's plans be purchased. (A contemporary report in a local newspaper reveals that this land purchase was completed in October 1850.)
23rd April 1851: Report from Locomotive Engineer of 22nd intimating that to admit of the large quantity of Coals being brought into London through Peterborough, early next winter - as is proposed - it will be requisite to provide at once additional stables and coke sheds as well as coal sidings at Peterborough.
Resolved that the General Manager, Locomotive Engineer and Engineer confer without delay with a sketch and estimate upon this subject, preparatory to the site they recommend for the sheds and sidings, being inspected by the (Way & Works) Committee.
6th May 1851: Report of the 28th April, from the General Manager, Mr. Sturrock and Mr. Cubitt, recommending with the view to the economical working of the Coal Traffic by having full trains, viz: That a line be laid from the present station at Peterborough to the field lately purchased by the Company and on the field to make a series of long sidings, some to be used for the purpose of standing coals, and some for the purpose of placing full trains. That an Engine House be built, connected with the sidings by a turntable on the south side and by points on the north side, with room for 24 engines and a coke stage and water tank for the supply of engines, and intimating that in order to get in the proper length of siding a small piece of additional land be purchased at each end of the field in question.
Resolved that this report be considered after the decision as to the locality of the General Workshops.
10th June 1851: The Peterborough Coal Sidings etc. job adopted and the extra pieces of land to be purchased.
17th June 1851: Joseph Cubitt advised that at present the works, ordered for the working of the Coal Traffic at Peterborough, be limited to the Engine Stable, the building which supports the tank and contains the smithy, workshops, offices etc. and to one of the coke stages, about four of the sidings, the large turntable and the requisite water cranes and water supply. Mr. Cubitt stated that it will be necessary to purchase a piece of land and to make arrangements for diverting the road which crossed just to the north side thereof, for which compensation must be made.
Resolved that Mr. Cubitt's plan be adopted and that the works be carried out as the traffic becomes developed, such accommodation as is absolutely necessary only being provided in the first instance.
30th December 1851: Works at Peterborough: Mr. Cubitt requested to proceed.

It would appear from the above that London went short of coal in the winter of 1850/1 (and during most previous winters no doubt) so the GNR dcided to 'climb on the bandwagon' and supply as much as it could by the use apparently, of the first 'block' trains. However, the Board does not seem to have been too keen to spend money on setting up the necessary facilities - presumably waiting to see if they were justified; by the end of 1851 they seem to have been sufficiently convinced to give the go-ahead for construction of sidings, engine shed etc., and it is therefore patently clear that New England could not have been operational before 1852. No doubt it was not far into that year before the job was completed - builders moved very fast in those days! The only indication about progress comes from 21st February 1852, when Sturrock requested a small engine, boiler and fan for the shed. He suggested purchasing from Nasmyth & Co. who had quoted £164

for the boiler and engine and £18 for the fan; expenditure was approved.

This first New England engine shed was a six road through building with brick walls and two iron-clad gable roofs, each covering three roads. Standing roughly on a NNW-SSE axis, and measuring 180ft in length by 78ft in width, the building would have held twenty four locomotives of the day, as intended. An 1853 official plan shows, on the west side of the shed, and separated from it by one track, a 291ft × 26ft structure comprising from the north; 88ft coke stage, 115ft smithy etc (which supported a 128,000 gallon water tank) and another 88ft coke stage. As noted above, Cubitt recommended the use of only one stage, so the latter space was in fact utilised for a sand furnace. Water was pumped from the River Nene, nearly two miles to the south and a 40ft turntable was sited east of the shed, accessed by a single track from both north and south ends - this device would be somewhat shortlived. Less than a year after opening, Sturrock was having problems at New England. He wrote to the Board on 7th February 1853; *.....I have the honour to inform you that the men employed at the new locomotive shed at Peterborough New England, are leaving me in consequence of there not being any cottages near the works for their accommodation and from enquiries I have made it does not appear to be any intention on the part of the public as yet to erect such dwellings near the new station for the men. There should be about 80 cottages to accommodate the staff of the station and Mr. Cubitt informs me there is a suitable piece of land belonging to the Company on which such houses could be erected.....* However, Cubitt then added his own suggestion that the land should be *sold to certain individuals who would erect houses at their own expense.....* It would seem no such individuals came forward, so it was left to the GN to put up the 80 cottages. It should be said that the Minute of 7th February 1853 contains the first official reference to 'New England' found so far.

Six months later, on 2nd August 1853, Sturrock sought more accommodation - this time for locomotives. He applied for *..... Mr. Cubitt to enlarge the engine stables at the Coal Station, Peterborough, to expand the room for an additional 12 engines, the cost of which is estimated at £3,400.....* The Board resolved that *.....the Executive & Traffic Committee be authorised to order these works if they see proper.....* They did and the job went ahead, involving extension of the shed walls and roof by one engine length (about 45ft at each end, with completion some time in 1854, the length of the shed was then some 270ft).

Despite the new houses for New England staff, Sturrock had to report on 10th January 1954, a letter from the shed foreman, Thomas Owen, that he was 'still losing men' because of lack of accommodation. The Board reacted quickly and on 1st February authorised the building of 50 more houses - those of seven rooms to cost no more than £200 each and the 'smaller' type £120 each; just how many of each size was built is not recorded, but the larger properties would have been very few in number for the Yardmaster, Shed Foreman etc. As an aside, Thomas Owen'a sponsorship of the men's housing need was his last recorded act as foreman, Owen, who had served at Walton Junction and Peterborough station sheds before moving to New England on its opening, was replaced 'early in 1854' by Charles Sacre, who moved from a similar post at Boston.

Subsequent expenditure in this period was minor; Sturrock requested on 22nd June 1854 *..... a new engine pit by the Coal Station, for raking out and blowing off .....* An estimated cost of £68 was approved and the pit duly appeared between the shed and turntable. This was followed in March 1855 by Sturrock making a plea for yet more staff housing, plus additional engine accommodation and repair facilities. The result was a deputation of Directors and on 17th April 1855 the Board heard a report on that visit which resulted in a number of recommendations. These were that 50 more cottages (third class) be built for enginemen and space measuring 40ft x 25ft be provided 'for use as a school room'. In addition the deputation declared that covered engine space should be increased by again extending the building one engine length at each end and absorbing the smith's shop. To compensate a new smithy would have to be built to accommodate twelve fires. The Board resolved that the engine shed extension and new smithy should proceed, but erection of 50 cottages and the school room be postponed. That postponement was short, however, and on 25th May 1855 the cottages were given the go-ahead; nothing was mentioned of the classroom but it may safely be assumed to have been approved also. 1855 closed with Sturrock faced with yet another 'domestic' affair. He reported to the Board about meeting a deputation of New

That 'certain unsteadiness' again, on the Petrborough station 'table. The jacked up wagon is evidence of the wagon repair depot(see plan).

K.Leech Collection

England staff .....*asking if they can buy coal from the Company, because they have to go into Peterborough to purchase supplies, and spend an extra 3/- (15p per ton transporting it to New England. The men agreed between themselves they would pool their requirements into wagon loads and I think that if the Company does not agree to sell coal, then a demand for more wages will be made .....* The GN Board obviously preferred to make money selling coal than lay out money in extra wages, so the mens' request was acceded to. The distance that had to be travelled to and from New England, by any personnel residing in Peterborough itself occasioned the GN to provide a staff-only station (a simple wooden platform) adjacent to the depot and yards. Mentioning the platform here may be out of chronological sequence; its opening and closing dates, even its precise location are unknown, but exist it did. It was March 1856 before New England again appeared in the Minute books. On the 4th of that month it was noted .....*Mr. Brydone presented a request that the blow-off pit, taken up in the extension to the engine shed, be rebuilt, at an estimated cost of £137.....* This was sanctioned. The same month also saw a punch/shearing machine ordered for New England at a price of £64, while two months later on 20th May, came approval for yet another 50 staff houses, as .....*35 drivers still do not have suitable accommodation.....*

A year later came the start of a big change at New England. The first reference is on 3rd April 1857, when the Locomotive Engineer gave the estimated cost of intended additions to the GN works:

Building, according to bills of quantities, will cost £4,968/4/7d
Traveller; £250
Hoist: £200 from Kirkstall Forge Company, Leeds; 25 tons capacity
Removing of vice benches, machines and shafting etc. £75

It was noted that 2,637 cubic yards of soil and materials would have to excavated for the new workshops and on 21st April came a brief note that with regard to the new repairing shops, the estimated cost of new Permanent Way alone would be £1,258. On 2nd May Sturrock commented again on .....*the lack of space and tools at New England and*

I refer the Board back to my comments of March 1855, when I said that more room was necessary for stabling and repairing engines at New England. It is now more than two years since and the problem has worsened. I feel that something should be done and I have prepared plans and estimates for a workshop to free stabling room in the sheds ..... Sturrock went on to say that: .....*repairs to engines are being carried out in the open and a small shunting engine is employed solely to move locomotives about the yard where they are kept in all manner of places. The new workshops will cost £5,793/4/7d., and if they are built the small shunting engine could be dispensed with and a saving made from this source alone. The workshops are necessary for the safe and economical working of the railway and I hope the Board will do something.....* Two days later it was resolved that the Board meet at New England on 18th May, at 1 p.m., to look at the problem.

The visit took place as scheduled and the Board .....*inspected the cottages, both those built and those in course of construction, the workshops for engines and the sites of the new repairing shop as proposed by Mr. Sturrock.....* On the next day, the Directors' report was referred to the Engineer and by 18th August, tenders had been issued for opening on that day. Seven were received for the job, which included the construction of an engine shop, turning shop, stores and other offices. Lowest tender was £4,343 from Messrs George Holme & Co. which was accepted. By 31st October, Sturrock was able to report: .....*Mr. Brydone is so advanced with the building at New England that we will have to order a hoist and an engine for the traveller, which are included in the estimate that accompanied my report.....* Sturrock then went on to say he had applied to the Kirkstall Forge Company for the hoist, and E.B. Wilson & Co., for the transverse frame (traveller, or traverser), ...*as they supplied us with similar articles before.....* On 3rd November next the Minutes record that hoist and traveller engine had been ordered as indicated by Sturrock, at costs of £200 and £220 respectively. After that all went quiet until 29th March 1858 when a Way & Works report noted: .....*The erecting shops for the use of the Locomotive Engineer have been well built by the contractor and are nearly advanced to completion.....* Even so, it was not until 3rd August that there came the comment .....*the new locomotive erecting shops at Peterborough have not been completed by the contractor.....*

Now some confusion comes out of all this activity between 1855 and 1858, with regard to changed building plans and additional workshop space. First, Sturrock's comment on 3rd May seems to suggest that the engine shed extension authorised in 1855 was not in fact carried out, yet Mr. Brydone's request in March 1856 for a new 'blow-off' pit was specifically occasioned by the old pit having been obliterated by an extension of the engine shed! There have been many (and many more suspected) instances of Locomotive Engineers either embroidering or understating their case to get some job or another approved by an eternally parsimonious Board. Sturrock was typically prolific in such manoeuvres and, maybe, he was telling only part of the story on 3rd May 1857, even though some sort of an extension *was* carried out in 1856. It will be recalled that the recommendation in 1855 was to extend the engine shed by lengthening the building at both ends. This was not done it seems - rather, a new three road shed was added to the eastern side, for use as a tender and paint shop, thereby freeing space in the locomotive depot. The new shop had a roof indentical in style to the

produced in 1865, as an adjunct to the next large-scale development at New England. Before we can discuss this it is necessary to consider the period from October 1858.

Hardly had the new workshops been completed when Sturrock was moved to comment on the state of the New England engine shed roof. He said .....*the covering of the roof of the original running shed was constructed of corrugated iron. It is now completely perished and must be entirely renewed, at a cost according to Mr. Brydone of £440. I think that corrugated iron is not a suitable material for the covering of engine stables and as Peterborough is the only stable so covered on the railway I have no doubt that a similar expenditure will not be required.....*

Four years passed until another flurry of activity commenced on 20th May 1862, the Locomotive Engineer asking for an enlargement to New England erecting shop, and .....*certain machinery, including an engine lift (for the station shed) for the repair of engines.....* The proposed shop extension was referred to the Executive & Traffic Committee to see if they thought it was necessary. The result of the Committee's findings is not known - neither is the response to Sturrock's request, on the same day, for 50 additional cottages .....*for*

Endless additions and alterations at Peterborough lent a hotch potch air to the place. The station coal stage in particular, provided evidence of this 'growth by accretion'

K.Leech Collection

engine shed, was 40ft wide, 270ft long and dead-end in pattern, with access from the north. As such it largely filled the gap between the original shed and turntable and also covered the raking-out and blowing-off pit installed only a year before. So, strictly speaking, Sturrock was correct in his intimation that engine shed space had not been 'extended'.

First estimates for the development of New England Works were given on 3rd April 1857 at an estimated cost of £4,968/4/7d, yet only one month later the Locomotive Engineer seems to be justifying his case all over again, this time with the estimated price increased by exactly £825. What in fact happened in the 1857/8 development was that an additional building was put up, a three road spare engine/paint shop, added on to the north side of the works building and probably explaining both the hike in price and the unusually protracted construction time. The new erecting shop and ancillary buildings would also have covered the site of the 1852 turntable; this was replaced by a triangle laid out around the perimeter of the works, with its western side passing between the tender/paint shop annexe to the engine shed, and the erecting shop/spare engine shed. Little of all this is covered in any papers but all the details are evident on official plans

the workmen in the shops at New England..... Probably both proposals were turned down, for a few weeks later , on 19th July Sturrock made another two requests, the first concerning a new boiler shop for which he submitted plans, with estimates totalling £2,500. The second request related to the provision of 26 staff cottages, at an estimated cost of £120 each, for which it was immediately resolved that tenders be invited. Regarding the proposed boiler shop, expenditure was approved on 5th August, with tenders duly issued; contractor and final cost are unknown but the work was finished in 1863. Later in 1862 Sturrock turned his attention to the subject of gas supplies at New England. He complained generally about the fuel produced at the local gasworks and suggested the GN should generate its own. To illustrate, he declared that in 1860, the Traffic & Locomotive Departments paid £878 for gas of rather inferior quality. This was calculated on the consumption of 4.39 million cubic feet, at 4/- (20p) per 1,000 cubic feet. Sturrock estimated the cost of the GN providing its own gasworks at £612, less £160 for coke and tar as by-products - total cost: £452. When set against the amount paid in 1860 this showed a saving of £426. The provision of a company gasworks was approved and it duly appeared on a site about a furlong to the north of the engine shed.

Continuing with improvements, Sturrock next suggested the laying of a second water main, from Peterborough station to New England, also suggested was an additional pump for the Nene pumping station. Further details - costs etc. - will be found in the section on Peterborough station shed above. Two references come from the Minutes of 1863. On April 11th, the Locomotive Engineer asked for provision of a screwing machine and grindstone, at costs of £118 and £30 respectively. Purchase was sanctioned and it is thought these tools may have been ordered in connection with the boiler shop then in course of erection. Six months later, on 20th Octber, there was a request for a small extension to the school in the railway 'village' that was by then officially known as 'The Barracks'. The extension was intended for the use of the Mechanics Institute and the Board approved the work, which was completed on 9th May 1864, at an undisclosed price.

While the Mechanics Institute room was being built, Charles Sacre returned to Peterborough, to again take up the post of District Locomotive Superintendent, in succession to one James Johnson. It seems probable that Sacre had to 'eat humble pie' to regain his old position, because he had to serve a three month trial period, at the successful completion of which his appointment was confirmed, at an annual salary of £250 - the amount he was receiving when he left five years before.

Early in 1865 came the first of many improvements to be ordered over the next year. On 24th January approval was given for a 12ins screw lathe for the workshops at a cost of £185 and on 7th March comes the first mention of large-scale works at New England. Sturrock pointed out the need for more shed room at New England and Doncaster Stations, for the new engines to be delivered about the end of the year. Plans were submitted of the sheds he proposed to build, at an estimated cost of £17,607, including a Peterborough portion of £8,257. In addition to new engine shed accommodation, Sturrock proposed new turning and tender shops, and extensions to the erecting shop. The Locomotive Engineer also recommended provision of a further 25/35 cottages at Peterborough and the whole scheme was referred to the Stations Committees for the North and South Districts, to report their recommendations to the Board, with a detailed explanation of why he wanted the expansion. He said: .....*There is a lack of stabling room at New England for goods engines because the sheds are too small. The number of goods engines at New England is now 58, which will be increased to 68 by next winter and there is only standing room of 34. Of these about 20 are always away from home leaving 14 exposed to the weather on weekdays and on Sundays about 28. I contend therefore that these engines cannot be properly maintained and kept in proper order. Stabling room should be found for 12 engines and this can be done by moving the doors and extending the walls at each end of the shed by one engine length and adding the requisite number of principals to the roof. The jobbing and repairing shops in connection with the sheds are likewise too small and I consider it necessary to move the present smiths' shop into the turning and fitting shop so as to enlarge the latter, I would like an extra 50 cottages for staff employed at Peterborough.....* Sturrock did not repeat his March 7th requirement for a new tender shop. It was not excluded from the overall job, however, which was duly tendered to contractors, the successful bid coming from Messrs Rudd & Son, of Grantham.

The extra houses asked for *were* omitted from Messrs Rudd's schedule of works but on 11th April the Board did approve construction of 25 more staff cottages .....*in addition to the 25 recently ordered.....* (i.e. on 21st March). A fortnight later Sturrock said he needed two more planing machines at Peterborough .....*as the present ones are kept active day and night. The previous machines came from Messrs Buckton & Co......* As on a number of previous occasions the Locomotive Engineer's recommendation of a particular supplier did not carry any weight with the Board, which decided that tenders should be obtained from three selected makers. The outcome is not known, but when Sturrock presented a large shopping list of machine tools on 21st July 1865, his request received immediate sanction. He asked for the following:

1 Radial drilling machine - £196
1 Self-acting shaping machine - £140
1 15ins screw cutting lathe - £215
1 Bolt lathe - £60
1 Screwing machine - £119
1 Slide bar facing machine - £50
1 Lateral drilling machine - price not stated

At the same time, the Locomotive Engineer sought agreement for .....*erection of one engine weighing machine with necessary tables, at a cost of about £750 which was also agreed.....* Not content with that, Sturrock followed up by asking that the company's gasworks be exanded, as the supply would have to be increased to the new workshops; two more sets of retorts would be required. It was resolved that these be provided, using clay retorts .....*if these be more economical.....*

After that, Sturrock kept quiet for six months, during which time the various building works came close to completion and he was more easily able to assess any further reqirements for machine tools. Sure enough, on 9th January 1866, he asked for two more engine lifts for the shops at New England, one to be sited in front of the tender shop, the other before the running shed. As usual, he added a comment about a supplier of an earlier device, instancing in this case, Kirkstall Forge .....*who provided the previous lifts of that description, for a price of £200 each.....* The Locomotive Engineer thought that price would still apply; for once the Board did not require tenders to be called and permission for the lifts to be ordered was given on 3rd February. Purchases for the new and enlarged workshops at New England were completed on 10th March 1866, when a screwing machine and a Ryders Hammer were ordered at quoted prices of £137/10/0d and £140 respectively, to be installed in time for completion of all building works, later in the year. Apart from alterations to the erecting shop and other repair facilities, the major outcome of this project was that covered engine space at New England was increased by more than half. The three road tender/paint shop was taken over for use as a locomotive shed, its south end wall removed to make a through building; in addition the building, now nine roads, was extended again - not by one engine length but by 35ft so that overall it measured 305ft, a maximum extent which would pertain for the rest of its existence. Whether the north or south end was extended is not clear but probably it was the former. To compensate for loss of the tender/paint shed another three road building was added to the east side of the spare engine/paint shop on the north side of the works. Engines were still coaled from the stage at the north west corner of the engine shed, assisted now by half ton bucket cranes and with the coaling area between the stage and shed roofed over. The pair of engine hoists were placed at the south west corner of the works building, not quite as originally proposed. In that position they joined the hoist installed in the 1857/8 alterations; photographs from the late 19th century show all three hoists had their own buildings; whether these were provided at the outset is unknown. In the yard at the south east corner of the shed, the engine weighing machine was installed, complete with its own housing; on contemporary Ordnance Surveys it appears as an 'Engine Shed'! Finally the latest additions to 'The Barracks' brought the total number of GN dwellings to a maximum of 227. This period of development also witnessed departure of two servants of the Great Northern. On 9th May 1865 the obviously unsettled Charles Sacre again left the company, this time never to return; his successor as District Locomotive Superintendent was Mr. Hornby, who came from the same post in Boston District - he served the normal three months trial period successfully and had his appointment confirmed, at a salary of £300. Autumn 1866 also saw the retirement of Sturrock, who always maintained that Peterborough should have been the site for the Great Northern main works and came close to getting his own way. No doubt the latest enlargements at New England were a source of gratification to him and a nice point at which to end his career.

Such had been Sturrock's involvement with New England that the new Locomotive Engineer, Stirling, had little to do there for almost the entire thirty years of his office except for (inevitably) the persistent question of water. On 4th November 1868 the Locomotive Committee had its attention drawn by the General Manager to the supply at Peterborough; taken from the River Nene it was used for both locomotive and domestic purposes and while quite suitable for the former purpose, the same could not always be said of the latter. A new company, which had been formed to supply Peterborough with water, proposed satisfying all the GN locomotive needs; Stirling had declined the offer but what was not stated was whether employees had to continue with river water for their *single tap* per pair of houses. Almost certainly they did, for in 1875 there was an outbreak of typhoid in the GN cottages, Peterborough's medical officer recording thirty cases in one morning. The outbreak was quickly contained but the subject of water supplies would re-appear in future years.

1407 at the coal stage on 24th June 1922.

Terry Henderson Collection

New England, key to the vast coal moving operation that was the Great Northern. A long vanished labour, for decades it demanded rank upon rank of engines.

K. Leech Collection

New England from the south in Great Northern days. The building in the foreground was a weigh shed and beyond lie the various engine hoists. In the right background is the works.

R.Egglescliffe

Seven years elapse before New England again emerges from the Minutes, even then merely a reference to expansion of the already extensive sidings, for coal from the soon-to-be-opened Derbyshire & Staffordshire Extension lines. This was followed by another gap of five years, until 16th June 1880 when the Board approved expenditure of £141 for connecting inspection pit drainage at New England to Peterorough Corporation sewers.

In 1884 the subject of water supplies came to the fore again. Negotiations took place with Peterborough Corporation Waterworks which offered a draft agreement based upon charges of 4d per 1,000 gallons if consumption exceeded 100,000 gallons per day, and a further halfpenny if less, with a minimum of 50,000 gallons a day. Faced with increasingly unsatisfactory supplies from the River Nene, in terms of both quantity and quality, the GN Board referred the draft agreement to its legal department for scrutiny. In the meantime, drilling had started at New England and on 13th July 1885 it was reported that Messrs Hills & Co. had reached 275ft with no water being struck; authority was given to proceed to 400ft. By 1st October 1885 396ft had been attained through 'very hard rock and shells' but still no water; £600 had been spent so far and it was decided to go on to 450ft at 55/- (£2.75p) per foot. At that depth no water was present; exasperated the GN gave up and accepted the Corporation's offer, but some supplies continued to come from the river. In the following year the Way & Works Committee meeting of 6th May heard that the rent paid for company cottages in 'The Barracks' was three shillings (15p) per week. This was 'not popular' with the employees as speculators had built many other houses in the area with better facilities and at more attractive rates. The matter was passed to the Board, which agreed with the recommendation that the GN should provide wash-houses and install street lights and fix rents between 2/9d and 3/9d (14p and 19p). On 30th August 1893 a borehole by Peterborough station was brought into use, pumps sending water through the 8ins main to New England. The shed then shared the 100,000 gallons a day output with the station engine shed, thereby reducing reliance upon Corporation water supplies, a less than ideal situation, which was still over five years away.

On 2nd January 1895 authority was given for erection of a footbridge into the New England shed and works, spanning the goods lines to the east. This was deemed necessary after a number of accidents involving staff crossing the tracks. On 9th January the following year came first proposals for large-scale rearrangements at Peterborough station, a new locomotive shed for forty engines was mooted, to be sited at New England, even though it was acknowledged that there was very little spare space available. Nevertheless the matter was followed up and on 28th February 1896 the following estimated costs were presented:-

New engine line from New England North to Eastfield including signal works and permanent way:	£1,000
New engine shed:	£15,654
Enginemens' room and other outbuildings:	£500
New coal stage with tank over:	£5,006
Additional water cranes and mains:	£297
Pulling down and rebuilding the retort house:	£750
Permanent way and earthworks:	£6,508
	Total: £29,715

It is evident that at least part of the gasworks site was to be given up for the new shed and on 4th June the Board decided to meet 'on site' on the 22nd to view the matter first hand. The visit took place, after which the subject was to be studied more closely. By 27th July these further investigations had revealed that additional works and costs wuld be involved. On that day, the Way & Works Committee heard an engineer's reort, accompanied by a plan .....*regarding the new shed for 40 engines, the new line from North New England to Westwood Bridge, and for additional sidings in lieu of those displaced.....* Estimated cost, including the mess room; coaling stage and new retort house already mentioned, now came to £41,000. The matter was referred back to the Board and on 11th August the Directors asked the Engineer to examine the proposals yet further. This he did, deivering a report dated 20th November 1896, read out at the Board meeting of the 23rd.

It stated .....*if it (the proposed shed for 40 engines) is erected on the site chosen, sidings will have to be provided for empty wagons, as shown on plans 1 and 2 now produced and which can be laid on land already belonging to the Company. Plan 1 shows 11 sidings capable of holding 300 wagons and would involve the taking down of some old cottage property. Plan 2 shows how the sidings could be arranged without interfering with the cottages. The cost of the respective scheme is estimated as under Plan 1, £33,908; Plan 2, £39,138.....* These have not been located but it was resolved by the Board that .....*this matter be referred back to the General Manager for further consideration.....* The General Manager's response is missing from the Minutes but from a March 1904 reference (see below) it is obvious that around the end of 1896, provision of a new engine shed at New England was deferred.

1898 brought a couple of changes, the second being very important. There was a proposal for an engine hoist, to be put up at the south end of the works on a dead-end spur, reached from the eastern end of the triangle; this was authorised but placed, in its own building, at the south east corner of the works with access from a spur running from the south west side of the triangle. On completion of the job, one or more of the older engine lifts was taken out. Of great significance, Ivatt was able to report on 18th October 1898 that at last, Peterborough's water problems were solved, with the borehole at Warrington .....*overflowing at the rate of 12,000 gallons an hour.....* The Locomotive Engineer proposed urgent installation of an 8ins pipe to New England, with a pair of pumps and an engine house at the well-head, the total cost put at £2,000. Ivatt added; .....*there is no doubt £1,000 per annum will be saved as soon as pumping starts.....* Naturally, approval was given and once the Warrington well came into operation pumping of River Nene water ceased and much less reliance was placed upon the Peterborough Corporation supply; retained only for domestic purposes in 'The Barracks'. In 1899 a second borehole was put down at Werrington proving equally fruitful.

By 1900 increasing traffic had brought congestion problems at the coal stage. On 4th October the Locomotive Engineer reported to the Way & Works Committee meeting that .....*there have recently been great detentions of engines coaling at Peterborough and it was desired to have a supplementary coal stage, the erection of which has now been put in hand at a cost of £930, estimated. This decision was taken as there was no Directors' meeting at the time.....* The Committee resolved the construction be approved and the matter reported to the Board. The new stage was completed early in 1901, it was sited at the north end of the shed yard, adjacent to the main line. Opening of the Crimpsall shop at Doncaster in 1901/2 brought major repair jobs to an end at New England Works, which thereafter was concerned with running repairs only. Even so, further growth at Peterborough was soon forthcoming. Traffic continued to expand and on 24th March 1904, the Way & Works Committee heard that the new engine shed which had been held in abeyance, 'should now be proceeded with'. Tenders for a new shed and coal stage were invited, with the successful bid, at £6,638, coming from Messrs. Arnold & Sons. After tender, a sand furnace in connection with the stage was ordered at £915, and also added was a scheme to adapt some of the arches under the stage for the use of cleaners, a lamp room etc. at a further cost of £300-400. The job was completed by early 1905 with a massive double-sided ramped coal stage replacing the 1852 coaling shed and 1901 temporary coal stage. Absorbing most of the project's cost, the stage was completed with its own sand house, and was brick built. A pair of tiled gable roofs covered the two wagon roads on the coaling floor, which had a maximum daily capability - in theory - of about 1,000 tons; a figure never to be achieved, needless to say. It should be added that although replaced, the structures of both the original coke stage and sand furnace remained in situ. That a sizeable 'new' engine shed could therefore be created for only a small proportion of £6,638 is explained by the fact that the GN merely resorted to conversion of most of the six road spare engine/paint shop, which formed part of the workshops establishment. This particular building was 76ft wide with a length of 300ft over its western three road section. The eastern portion was subdivided into three parts, reading from the north - an 87ft spare engine/paint shed, 83ft carpenters' shop and a further 130ft 'spare' shop that connected directly into the erecting shop. Only the north section became an engine shed, with the little money available being spent on cosmetics mostly; inspection pits were not provided, so the new accommodation could have been used for stabling only, but this would have freed space in the main shed for engine preparation and inspection purposes. On completion of the extension, all passenger engines were moved from Peterborough station shed to New England; very soon the procedure was adopted of keeping the passenger stud in the three road former tender/paint shop section of the main building, with goods engines housed in the remaining six roads and the annexe. The company also immediately embarked upon a rolling programme of roof renewals at New England that covered the period from March 1905 to mid-1908, and again during 1910.

In the period of the First World War GN staff in the Peterborough Locomotive and C&W Departments totalled 1106, including 189 engine drivers and 183 firemen. Even so, there was a shortage of manpower and women were recruited for the work of engine cleaning. In the late summer of 1916 Gresley obtained approval for expenditure of £160, to provide separate mess room and toilet facilities for the lady members of staff; work was completed on 25th November that year. Nearly two years later, on 4th July 1918, he approached the Locomotive Committee with recommendations for two schemes at New England. First, at an estimated cost of £4,870 Gresley proposed

Locomotive Committee recommended to the Board that expenditure for two drops be approved. Work progressed throughout 1919 and 1920 until by June of the latter year two engine pits were in use and four were 'in hand'. The 21st of the same month saw a request for another £161 expenditure to provide an additional road through the repair shop. This involved the filling in of an engine pit but excluded the removal or refixing of any machinery. On 6th August yet more money was sought, this time £56 for a wheel road in the repair shop; once again any cost of alterations to machinery was not included. By October 1920 it was noted that two pit roads were in use in the paint shop and two large sliding doors had been affixed to the south wall of the repair shop. In the next month two more sliding doors had been inserted in the east wall and the new wheel road was 'being prepared'.

A final GNR alteration was put in motion by Gresley on 22nd January 1922 when he sought yet more pit accommodation, this time for ash disposal purposes. The request was occasioned by increased engine turn-rounds, which were themselves the result of post-war

Inside the rearranged New England shops, which declined upon the rise of Doncaster despite all Sturrock's efforts to the contrary.
Collection K. Leech.

installation of an electric traverser in the erecting shop, and an hydraulic locomotive wheel drop, the latter from Messrs Cowans Sheldon, ...*to a pattern as supplied to the Lancashire & Yorkshire Railway.....* His second scheme suggested increasing accommodation for running engines by extending the two lines of the eastern section of the former spare engine shed through the paint shop, coppersmith's and carpenters' shop, all this to cost an estimated £2,860. At first only the cheaper scheme was approved for the first proposal did not include costs of the wheel drop and traverser and a decision was deferred. By 25th July Messrs Ransomes & Rapier had quoted a price of £1,790 for the traverser, which was accepted but it was not until the following 3rd October that the Locomotive Engineer could report about the wheel drop. He said Cowans Sheldon were willing to supply the drop at a price of £1,200 to which had to be added a cost of £600 for the necessary pit and foundation. Gresley then remarked that he had since asked for a wheel drop for Kings Cross, and Cowans Sheldon had offered a price of £1,160 for each, if two were ordered. The

shortening of men's hours. An estimated cost of £900 was quoted by the Locomotive Engineer but he added that the new pits would lead to a saving in wages of £400 per year - overtime payments presumably. The Locomotive Committee recommended the scheme to the Board, which gave its approval. Two pits were provided outside the southern end of the nine road shed. One of 64ft was placed on No. 3 road and a second of 48ft on road No. 7. Roads were numbered 1-14 (by the LNER) reading from the west.

The LNER was slow to effect any improvement at New England but when changes did come they were on the grand scale! A scheme was put forward and approved late in 1930 for a 500 ton capacity mechanical coaling plant and a 250ft 'wet ash pit' which would entail the relaying of a greater part of the north locomotive yard and the provision of sidings for coal wagons. As an adjunct to the ash pit a rotary sand dryer was to be installed which had the capability to blow dried sand into elevated storage hoppers. In addition, shed (and yard) lighting would be converted to electric operation, a measure to enable demolition of the no-longer economic GN gasworks and thereby provide a site for the mechanical coaler and wet ash pit. Removal of the gasworks was completed by the spring of 1931 and from then the whole project took almost one and a half years to accomplish. Despite its displacement by mechanical plant, the New England ramped coal stage was retained as a standby and after 80 years water continued to be stored in the original tank. Later in 1937 foundations and sub-structure for a water softening plant were provided alongside, on the site of the original coke stage, the installation coming into use during the next year. The tall tower of the softener became a local landmark and its output solved, for the time being anyway, the problems of soluble salts inherent in the Werrington water source. In this modernised condition New England entered the war which quickly made its mark. In 1940 a bomb fell between the south locomotive yard and the Empties Yard, where an engine and a half was standing at a water crane. Tragically driver George Ruff was killed, fireman Joe Charlton badly injured and some material damage caused. Fortunately this seems to have been the only instance of the effects of war upon New England and its staff - except for the sheer hard work of course.

There were no other incidents it would seem but the war took its toll at New England - the shed and men were grossly overtaxed as the East Coast route groaned under the weight of war working. The crucial factor was labour rather than money and only essential work, which could be demonstrated as necessary for the war effort, could hope to obtain the necessary sanction. The shed roof was accordingly allowed to deteriorate and much of it was in poor state by the 1950s. It was largely rebuilt by British Railways in a two year period from 1953, in concrete and asbestos.

Amongst the last improvements to be made came in 1957. Six ash pits were rebuilt and new drainage installed - which pits were involved is not clear. After this New England continued to serve steam and an increasing number of diesels until January 1965 when it was closed to steam. It was intended that complete closure would be effected in June 1967 but this was deferred due to the workload and lack of experienced staff at the nearest main line diesel depot, Finsbury Park. Closure was only put off for fifteen months though and New England finally succumbed on 30th September 1968, to end 116 years of very intensive operational life. Demolition followed during 1969 and today the site is partly covered by a large Post Office parcels depot, opened in 1970, and an Electrification Fixed Equipment Maintenance Depot, opened on 14th July 1987. Construction was hindered by the still extant and masive concrete foundations of New England shed.

Peterborough was the base of a District Locomotive Superintendent (DLS) from the time such posts were created in 1858 until it came under Kings Cross (with a code of 34E) during a 1958 BR reorganisation. There were a number of locomotive outstations or sub-sheds, the longest-lived being Stamford, which opened on 1st November 1856 and closed on 2nd March 1957, although engines cntinued to use the shed yard until 11th October 1958. Another outstation, much more short-lived, was Ramsey, opened 1863/4 and closing about 1885 when New England started sending out an engine to work the branch on a daily basis. Late in the nineteenth century Boston Locomotive District was abolished and that depot, together with its sub-sheds of Horncastle (opened August 1855), Spilsby (1st May 1868) and Wainfleet (11th September 1871) all came into Peterborough District. Horncastle closed around 1918 and Spilsby followed early in World War Two but Wainfleet appears to have survived into the 1950s at least. Under BR though Boston and therefore Wainfleet, were made subordinate to the Lincoln DLS, leaving Peterbrough with Stamford once again. There had been other additions during LNER days however - the former Great Eastern Railway shed at Peterborough East, opened in the 1840s and closed on 30th April 1939 - and Grantham. The latter had been a District centre in its own right in GN times and came to Peterborough with its outstations until it too was made subordinate to Kings Cross in 1958.

As regards engine duties and allocations, the 1855 GN Rule Book shows New England's sole responsibility to have been workings to London and return - these were all goods trains of course, mostly coal. We know from earlier notes that in 1858, 55/60 engines were 'in steam daily' at Peterborough (including the station shed). Early in the spring of 1865 it was reported that 58 goods engines wereoperatingfrom New England, a number that had increased by about a dozen in the following December, with another 30 or so engines on order and due to be based there. It was this great increase in the allocation that prompted the 1866 expansion of the depot. In April 1867 Nottingham

duties had been added and in that month a deputation of enginemen met Stirling to ask if they were going to be expected to run two return trips a day to Nottingham. The Locomotive Engineer said no, except 'in an emergency', when if the 10 hour working day was exceeded, overtime would be paid. A dozen years later the WTT shows that New England was operating 72 main line goods workings a day - and their return empties of course - exactly twice the number run by the next busiest shed, Doncaster. By then the allocation was well in excess of a hundred, reaching over two hundred by the end of the century. Manchester workings were part of the New England duties by that time and on 1st May 1902 Ivatt informed the Way & Works Committee that loco crews running to Manchester had asked to come on duty for the return working after the expiration of 8 hours instead of the normal 9 hours. The Locomotive Engineer endorsed the mens' request which was approved by the Committee.

By 1905 New England had taken over all passenger workings from Peterborough station shed and the District allocation in that year was 252, of which 206 were at the main shed. Slightly smaller figures were evident in 1912, with New England hosting 195 out of the District's 241 engines but 1918 saw the allocation back to a figure of 207; during the same year weekly coal consumption averaged 2,600 tons - or over 135,000 tons per annum. At Grouping, only 180 engines were on the strength, while around the turn of the year 1930/1 the figure was some six engines more. Of that number a Sunday visit would find a good proportion 'at home' as on 16th November 1930, when these residents were noted:

A1 4-6-2
2557
A3 4-6-2
2747
C1 4-4-2
3282, 3290, 3293, 3294, 4400,4403, 4408, 4409, 4410, 4445, 4447
C2 4-4-2
3255, 3256
C12 4-4-2T
4507, 4509, 4512, 4516, 4521
D2 4-4-0
4334
D3 4-4-0
4342, 4343
J3 0-6-0
3302, 3315, 3337, 3368, 3384, 3717, 3731, 4037, 4081, 4092, 4109, 4120, 4155, 4163
J4 0-6-0
3392, 3394, 4044
J6 0-6-0
2706
J52 0-6-0ST
3980, 4052, 4209, 4211, 4218, 4219, 4220, 4221, 4224, 4225, 4265, 4267, 4269, 4270, 4277, 4278, 4279, 4280,4289, 4290
J56 0-6-0ST
3608A
K1 2-6-0
4638
K2 2-6-0
4654, 4681, 4682
K3 2-6-0
114, 116, 121,125, 134, 156, 170, 180, 208, 4006, 4007
01 2-8-0
3478, 3483, 3484, 3487, 3488, 3492, 3494, 3497, 3498, 3501
02 2-8-0
5392, 5405, 6284, 6308, 6314, 6496, 6509, 6557, 6587, 6593, 6604, 6619
P1 2-8-2
2393, 2394

In the repair shop:
C1 4-4-2
3279, 4429
C2 4-4-2
3987, 3989
C12 4-4-2T
4504
J1 0-6-0
3012, 3013

J6 0-6-0
3580, 3608, 3609
K2 2-6-0
4684
K3 2-6-0
92
O1 2-8-0
3470, 3474
O4 2-8-0
6495, 6554
Q1 0-8-0
3409

Allocations continued to vary slightly, with 189 in August 1933 and 201 just before nationalisation. After two and a half years of BR Eastern Region management there were 213 engines stationed at New England, with the following lines 'signed' by the footplatemen:

Kings Cross to York
Skegness
Joint
Mablethorpe loop
Loop
Colwick
Grimsby-New Holland (a very unpopular duty)
MGN to South Lynn and odd trips to Kings Lynn
Peterborough-Boston-Grantham-Peterborough

Wartime brought workings over the emergency curve at Sandy to Oxford and, in the middle 1950s, when engine numbers had fallen to 167, additional lines signed were:

Hunstanton
Ramsey North
Fletton loop
Sandy-Goldington Power Station, Bedford
Retford-Worksop
Retford-Sykes Junction
Essendine-Stamford (for Light Engine changes at weekends)
Newark-Lincoln-Grimsby
Hitchin-Letchworth

By April 1959 the allocation of New England had been quite drastically reduced to 111 and it was around that period, following closure of the M&GNR, that other lines were signed, those to Kings Lynn via March, and Wisbech to Magdalen Road. However these were a short-lived feature.

The shed's roster in 1961 is not known but the WTT for that year shows pilot and trip duties operated by New England as being:

9 pilots - Fletton (6 shunters, 3 transfers)
3 pilots - Station 'I' 'O' 'Q'
9 pilots - NWE yards (5 yard; 4 trips) (0-6-0 diesel)
1 passenger pilot (V2 normally)
Duty 'M' trips

Steam ended nearly four years later, with diesels reigning until final closure on 30th September 1968 although the fuelling point remained in use until 9th March 1969, when an alternative site at Spital was brought into use. During its final year the allocation was a mere 17 0-6-0 diesel shunters, a striking decline from the 150 locomotives of only twelve years before! Steam did reappear at the shed on two occasions after 1965 though; in 1967 an unlikely visitor was GWR 4-6-0 No. 7029 *Clun Castle* which called in on its way south to work a couple of specials from Kings Cross. The Castle's visit provided a good excuse for a 'trial run' and a New England crew showed the astonished pilot crew from Tyseley ex-GWR shed that their precious engine *could* be fired and driven GN fashion! Last steam locomotive to use the shed was preserved Standard class 5MT 4-6-0 No. 73050. It arrived only 18 days before the shed closed its doors for the last time, on the way to the Nene Valley Railway and resides there today.

New England locomotive history had been very long; for the first fifty two years, characterised by goods engines. Hawthorn 0-4-2s and perhaps even a few of the Bury-type 0-4-0 'Luggage' engines were the first residents along with some Sharp and Hawthorn singles. Sturrock's 0-6-0 designs formed the backbone of the complement including during 1865/70 the inspired but unsuccessful steam tender-equipped versions. Stirling 0-6-0s, 2-4-0s and 0-4-2s joined in the work of the shed with a solitary class E1 2-4-0 still present at the Grouping. Sturrock 0-4-2Ts were also seen at New England, later supplemented by various types of 0-4-4T. Of the latter, G2 Nos. 530A and 655 were still present in 1912 together with G5 No. 630 (all scrapped before Grouping) while G1 Nos. 939 and 943 lasted into early LNER days. Their main preoccupation had been the workings from Stamford until displaced by C2 (LNER C12) 4-4-2Ts. The latter also monopolised station pilot duties at Peterbrough; they numbered eight in 1935, seven around the end of the war and six still in 1950. Their demise came in 1958 with closure of the Stamford-Essendine line and for many years duties were shared with class N5 0-6-2Ts of which two were present from the early 1930s, increasing to eight in the late 1950s. Although popular the ex-GC engines never quite usurped the equally good C12s. Other tank engine classes included the ubiquitous Stirling and Ivatt 0-6-0 saddle tanks, with around twenty class J52 and J53 allocated for shunting and trip work. Their older J54, J55 and J56 sisters were also present in small numbers, with the last surviving J56 leaving the shed in 1932 and two of the final member of class J55 arriving during the early 1940s, to move away again in 1945. Gresley J50s were not a common sight until BR times and then only a handful were allocated - Nos. 68896 and 68976 in 1959 for example. The usual influx of ex-GER 0-6-0T designs followed the Grouping with J65, J66, J67 and J69s all seen for varying periods until the early 1950s. Slightly more exotic types were ex-NER J72, J76 and J77, the first for coal consumption trials in 1924 and the others for short visits in the late 1920s and early 1930s. There was also No 2529 of ex-H&BR class J75 coming to New England from Immingham and seeing out its days on odd duties until withdrawn in 1937. The only other tank engine of note was ex-GC Class L1 (later L3) No. 9064 which arrived in March 1947 for the specific purpose of working trains of coal to the power station at Little Barford. This solitary 2-6-4T stayed long enough to receive its BR number 69064, when it was transferred away. The other Class L1 2-6-4T - Thompson's modern machines - did come to New England, but only for storage after the 1960 electrification of the Liverpool Street services; N2 0-6-2Ts displaced by diesel sets from Kings Cross workings were also stored at New England for a time in the early 1960s. To close the section on tank engines, there are the Sentinels of Classes Y1 and Y3 to consider. Y1 No. 4802 arrived at Peterborough in 1926 to be assigned to the Engineers yard there. Later carrying the numbers 4992, 8133, 68133, 68133S and 'Departmental Locomotive No 6', the engine served in the one duty all her life until withdrawal in November 1955. A Y3 was allocated to Peterborough Engineer in replacement of No. 6, No. 68183 (ex-8183) which received Departmental No. 8 in October 1955 and served for just over three years, until withdrawal in January 1959

To return to goods engine types, we left their evolution with Stirling's designs, which were augmented from the later 1890s by Ivatt J5 (LNER J4) 0-6-0 types for example; they were still to be seen at the shed in the first half of the 1950s. From the end of 1902 Ivatt 0-8-0s of Class K started to appear; Nos 412-6 were the first to be allocated. By 1905 there were 25 'Long Toms' at New England, handling trains of coal and other produce to London. 1912 saw thirty three of the type at the shed and they formed the main freight power throughout World War One. After that war they were progressively replaced by O1 and O2 2-8-0s and from a peak of forty two in 1920, nearly all had gone eight years later, with the last example at New England leaving about 1930. Other Ivatt classes were J21 (LNER J1 & 2) and J22 (LNER J5). They were used on all manner of duties with the latter predominating on braked goods to London, while J21s also saw much use on local and summer extra passenger workings. J22 (J6) were also present in large numbers for many years - 16 at Grouping had grown to 29 by nationalisation, with 8 still present at the beginning of the 1960s. The modern J39s were not such prominent denizens of New England, with only six or so stationed there between the early '40s and the first days of BR; a few did return for a number of months in the mid-50s, however. Other 0-6-0 types came from the Grouped companies - a handful of ex-GE J15s in the middle of 1930 were of note and surprisingly some NER-designed J21s between 1936 and 1938 - they eventually found their way to Retford and Doncaster. Finally of note was the short stay of ex-GC 0-8-0s. Six Q4s came to New England in 1943 and were mainly used on M&GN lines until returned to their former haunts late in 1945.

No. 2394, one of the great 2-8-2s on the ash pits , 24th March 1935.

W.L.Good, cty W.T.Stubbs.

'Halt for one moment', an unusually genteel form of address, on 20th May 1938.

H.C.Casserley

Peterborough and its prosperity was mightily concerned with coal, though it lay far from any major field. It was to this stuff the denizens of 'The Barracks' looked for comfort in winter, with their miserable tap per pair of cottages. The company allowed its staff some preferential rates (see text) and any shortfall could usually be pinched. It is difficult now to imagine the absolute necessity to life that coal then was (and, of course, still very nearly is, despite much trumpeting to the contrary) and its constant movement powered and sustained a whole economy. In the foreground lies the eastern point of the shed triangle.

National Railway Museum.

O4 No. 6324 and an unidentified Q4 at the New England coal shed in 1933, with monstrous 500 ton coaler beyond. The old shed was an open, draughty place and the great height of its roof a disadvantage in conditions of driving rain and gusting wind.

H.N.James.

Atlantic No. 4454. The coaler remained in place long after the mechanical plant was put up. With its 'perambulator' coal tubs (a phenomenon largely restricted to the Great Northern and North Eastern, it seems) it continued at whiles to provide a gently decaying contrast and alternative.

The Deansgate Collection, Levenshulme.

The wet ash pits in March 1937. These pits, in various guises, were a feature unique to the LNER(though there were a number of foreign counterparts); ashes were extinguished in the concrete-clad water filled pit and subsequently excavated by grab crane. It was a vast subterranean, reeking mire; no accidents are recorded but the effects of a fall do not bear thinking about.

National Railway Museum.

Gresley Moguls were to be seen at New England from 1914 to 1963 (H4 - K3). The smaller types were present to the tune of thirty engines at the Grouping, used on fast goods and some passenger work. K3s dominated things though, with twenty allocated by the mid-1920s, growing to thirty four late in 1937 and thirty seven by nationalisation. Their numbers fell rapidly after that, to a little over twenty by 1950 and only five by 1959. During their time at New England the K3s were entrusted with all manner of prestige workings, for example, the Scotch goods from Westwood Yard to York, a train that required an average speed of 45 mph, with a load usually exceeding 600 tons. Equally strenuous were the 41 mph bookings on the Manchester service from Peterborough to Colwick and in the early 1930s the fast coal trains to London; they demanded working to Hornsey with 630 tons and returning with a 60 wagon train of empties in the 9 hour shift time. Slow pasenger work was also undertaken but the class declined in BR days and the last representative was No. 61835 which left in September 1963 after a year as stationary boiler.

Of the 2-8-0 classes, first arrivals of Gresley Class 01 were in 1913 and from then until 1936 about twenty were on the New England roster for heavy coal trains to London. Around fifteen trains a day were involved, the Peterborough men exchanging footplates at Hitchin with Hornsey crews. Three-cylinder 02s joined the 01s from 1921 and until the middle period of the Second World War around twenty five were allocated, growing to thirty five by the time of Victory in Europe, but all departed by the end of 1945. BR reintroduced the class to New England in 1950 with about four engines present for a short while. Grouping brought ex-GC 04s but they appear not to have been regarded in the same light as the GN 2-8-0s.

Although New England had about twenty from the mid-'20s for about ten years, they were used on less strenuous duties. A major feature was the arrival of Class 07 - the Riddles WD 2-8-0 - in February 1943. More came soon after and progressively replaced Gresley engines on Hornsey coal trains. Before the end of the war no less than thirty five of the 'Austerities' were at New England, assisted for a time in 1944 by ten of the 2-10-0 versions. After peace returned Austerities remained a fixture of the shed, the LNER making many purchases. So much so that by 1950 there were no fewer than 53 allocated, a position changed only by delivery in the mid -1950s of large numbers of BR 9F 2-10-0s. Even by 1959 with twenty five 9Fs allocated, there were still twenty WDs working from New England. While mentioning the 9Fs it is worth rememberng those extraordinary days when they were used on summertime extra passenger turns, and a number of instances of New England (and Grantham) crews reaching speeds of 90 mph down Stoke Bank.

Indelibly linked with New England are the two Gresley P1 2-8-2s. They came to the shed in 1925 and stayed there all the 20 years of their lives, in use on a regular turn, the 9.25 am New England to Ferme Park and 5.30 am return empties. As is well known, Nos. 2393 and 2394 were *too* good and became almost white elephants. Their full potential never realised, holding loops were of inadequate length for the longest trains they could haul. Of vastly greater flexibility were the 2-6-2s of class V2, No. 4774 of the legendary type first appearing in 1936. Numbers increased to twenty five by 1940, peaked at thirty four just before nationalisation and remained at around twenty five into the 1960s. First use was on the prestigious 'Green Arrow' goods train, the duties later extending to all manner of fast goods and assorted

The New England coaler in March 1934. The new plant required a pilot only for a few moments, when a new rake arrived, a contrast to the old stage which demanded more or less constant attention. Through the LNER period the task had been performed by class 56 tank No. 3608A and its principal problem, on the stage incline, was 'the stopping once up there, not the getting up.' This stalwart was withdrawn in 1932.

National Railway Museum.

Woodcock **at the south end of the shed in 1958, presumably prepared for a London working.**

V.Fincham

passenger work. A regular duty was passenger pilot at Peterborough station, the V2 stabled in the yard of the engine shed there - this practice lasted until the end of steam. In the '50s New England V2s had turns to such places as Newcastle and Grimsby (before the latter's route availability was downgraded) and in 1953 three of New England's examples were sent to the Southern Region to help cover the emergency withdrawal of 'Merchant Navy' Pacifics; the V2s acquitted themselves well on such trains as the 'Bournemouth Belle'.

Much smaller and earlier passenger engines at New England were the Stirling Singles and the various Ivatt classes of 4-4-0. The famous singles were in the twilight of their lives when they came to the shed and by July 1910 only Nos. 668, 776, 1001, 1003 and 1004 were left. Nevertheless they were kept on quite important turns until the advent of the First World War, during which they were withdrawn as as 'economy measure' never to be reinstated. One of their last regular workings was the nightly Peterborough - Kings Cross fast fish train, returning on the 5.20 am slow passenger. Ivatt 4-4-0 types had been at Peterborough from the late 1890s, based at first at the station shed. When it was reduced in status in 1904/5, they moved to New England - about eleven engines in all. Used on light passenger trains to such places as Spalding, Boston and even London, the 4-4-0s had reached seventeen in number by 1912, the figure dropping to eleven again at the Grouping. Numbers were maintaned at about half a dozen engines until the early period of the war, with the type fading out just after nationalisation. Also moved from the station shed were about four small-boilered Atlantics of Class C1 (LNER C2), joined about the same time by the first of their larger boilered sisters. The 'small' 4-4-2s were relatively few in number but the stud did stand at eleven for a time at the beginning of the 1920s. They were used on passenger services to Boston, Lincoln and Grimsby and took their turn on goods duties too. The 'large' Atlantics were much more in evidence with the original allocation as follows, a situation that pertained for many years:

288, 289, 290, 291, 1300, 1407, 1409, 1410, 1411, 1412, 1413, 1429, 1430, 1431, 1437, 1438, 1439, 1445, 1446 and 1447

Of these engines, the compound No. 1300 was always considered to be an odd man out even after conversion to a 'simple' engine in 1917, it

was never rostered for the most difficult duties and was withdrawn at the early date of 1924. The rest of the 4-4-2s were used on London and Doncaster main line turns until 1925, when increasing numbers of Pacifics caused them to be moved onto secondary workings. By 1936 though there were still twenty allocated to the shed:

3279, 3282, 3289, 3290, 3291, 4400, 4403, 4404, 4406, 4407, 4408, 4409, 4410, 4413, 4417, 4418, 4429 and 445.

Before advent of the V2s a regular duty for an Atlantic was the Peterborough passenger pilot. On 28th December 1938, No.4446 was so engaged when it was forced to relieve an ailing *Quicksilver* on the up 'Silver Jubilee', with a creditable performance through to Kings Cross. In that same year a quarter of the Ivatt C1s were based at New England but wartime wear and tear had its effect and by nationalisation only three were left. The last example at the shed was No. 2839 withdrawn in January 1950 after spending all forty four and a half years of her life at the shed. Major replacement for the 4-4-2s were Thompson B1 4-6-0s used on the East Lincs lines and stopping trains to Kings Cross, as well as some express goods turns. Ten B1s were working from New England during the 1950s with some more arriving by the early 1960s; a few were present when the shed closed to steam in January 1965. Class 4MT 2-6-0s of Ivatt LMS design first came to New England in 1950 with the then new No. 43058 subsequently joined by Nos. 43059-68/80-8, all fitted with tablet catchers for use over the M&GN route. When it closed in March 1959 they were quickly moved away - only six were on the roster in June 1959. How much longer they stayed is not certain - neither are the duties that the Moguls performed at that time.

Pacifics were not a feature at New England until the 1940s, except for A1 No. 2555 *Centenary* from January to October 1936. Three A1/3s came to the shed in 1940, joined by five more in 1942, some left early in 1943 until by the end of that year only three remained. A sudden influx began in March 1944 when another two arrived, then four in April, one more in May and a further two in June. The stud then stood at a dozen, declining to eight in August and September and to five from October to the end of the year. The large number of Pacifics working from the shed around the middle of 1944 was no doubt due to the preparation for, and immediate aftermath of, the D Day invasion, but

The Peterborough 'Light Tunnel' or 'Covered Inspection Pit' designed for use in the wartime blackout and unique to the LNER. As early as 1948/49 the new BR Motive Power Committee reported that it was in 'poor condition' and should be removed. Presumably its foundations had shifted.

J. Davidson

The rebuilt sheds in April 1959, from the north end. It was an unending task to rearrange engines for their subsequent duties; ex-GER 0-6-0Ts came from Peterborough East in 1939 and were assigned solely to 'engine setting', at both the north and south ends of the shed.

N.E.Preedy

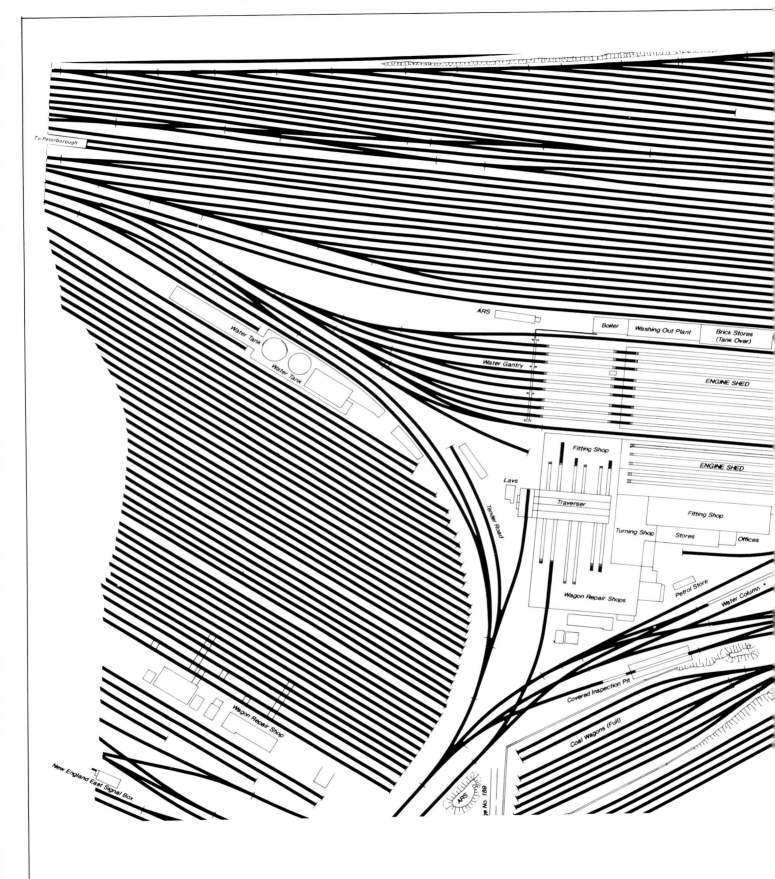

To Peterborough

Water Tank

Water Tank

ARS

Boiler | Washing Out Plant | Brick Stores (Tank Over)

Water Gantry

ENGINE SHED

Fitting Shop

ENGINE SHED

Lavs

Traverser

Fitting Shop

Turning Shop | Stores | Offices

Tender Road

Wagon Repair Shops

Petrol Store

Water Column

Covered Inspection Pit

Coal Wagons (Full)

Wagon Repair Shop

New England East Signal Box

ARS

e No. 189

NEW ENGLAND 1954

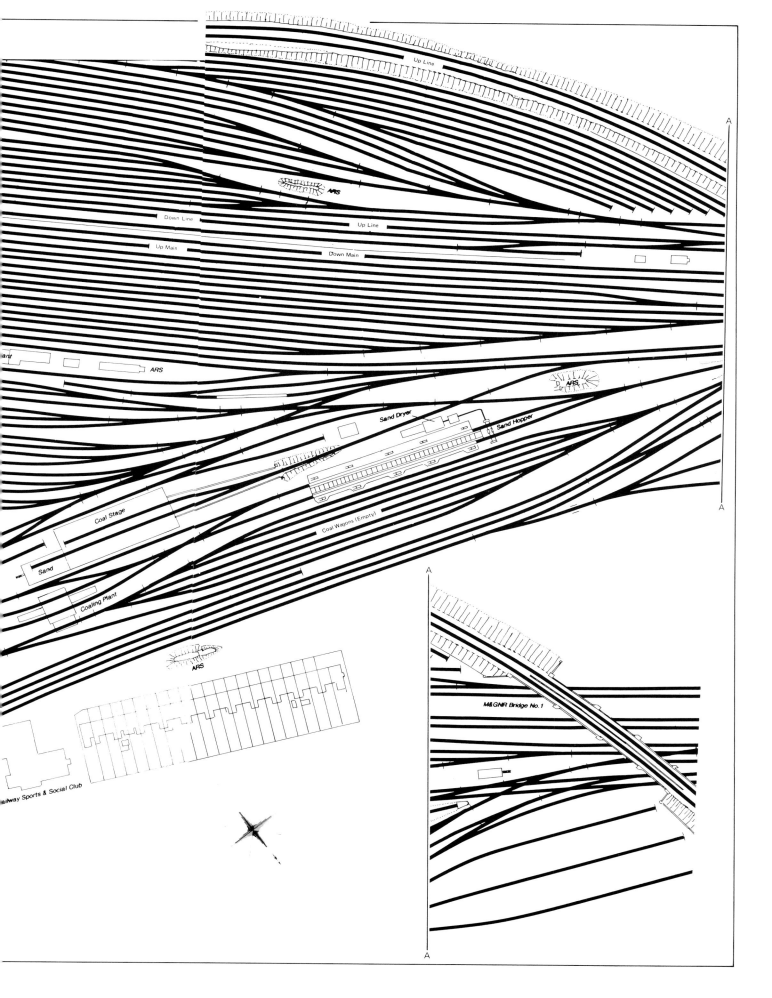

Up Line

Down Line   Up Line

Up Main   Down Main

ARS   ARS

Sand Dryer   Sand Hopper

Coal Stage   Coal Wagons (Empty)

Sand

Coaling Plant

ARS

Railway Sports & Social Club

M&GNR Bridge No.1

ARS

A

A

A

A

A

A

New England in 1958. Before arriving at the running shed most engines had already undergone four or five hours of servicing procedures, ash disposal and so on. On the wet ash pits alone there were four men continually employed, each dealing with eight locomotives per shift, with another five on a bonus rate of 9 old pence per engine. In other words a procession of 52 locomotives a shift.

V.Fincham

The shed on 17th July 1960. Originally examination was carried out at the shed itself, after servicing but in later practice engines were examined immediately upon arrival, before servicing commenced. This enabled replacements to be organised if serious defects were discovered.

Ken Fairey

1945 saw the numbers rise again to eight. A1/3s were reduced only in 1948 when A2s began to arrive. They were not present in the 1950s except for three members of the class right at the end of the decade; 60061, 60066 and 60067, from September to November 1959. During the '60s A3s came back again, with all eight on the allocation withdrawn or transferred away between April and June 1963. In October of that year six more came, 60054, 60062, 60063, 60065, 60106 and 60112 and they stayed until all were withdrawn in June and December 1964. The last three, which were incidentally the last of their kind on the GN section, were 60062 60106 and 60112 and they saw out their final days on the 9 am March-Doncaster parcels which they worked from Peterborough.

First of the various Thompson and Peppercorn A2 Pacifics at New England was the A2 No. 60533 *Happy Knight* in April 1948. It would appear that it was not a 'happy' engine for New England twice tried to lose it to Copley Hill, twice to Grantham and once to Doncaster, during the ensuing 11 years, but always she returned, the last time in September 1962 to be finally withdrawn in June 1963.

No peppercorn A1s were ever stationed at New England. This was not so with the A4s though. With the advance of dieselisation and closure of Kings Cross Top Shed no less than eleven of them came to Peterborough in an endeavour to find further useful work. They arrived in June 1963, comprised of:

60006 *Sir Ralph Wedgwood*
60007 *Sir Nigel Gresley*
60008 *Dwight D. Eisenhower*
60010 *Dominion of Canada*
60017 *Silver Fox*
60021 *Wild Swan*
60025 *Falcon*
60026 *Miles Beevor*
60029 *Woodcock*
60032 *Gannet*
60034 *Lord Faringdon*

Of the above, 60008 was withdrawn in the next month, most of the rest were stored and a few kept on workings mainly northwards until 60017/21/5/9/32 were themselves taken out of service in October and 60006/7/10/26/34 were transferred to Scotland.

New England in 1967, closed to steam.

Roy C Brown

Grantham,'the abode of dragons'.

NO. 222 GREAT NORTHERN. 7 FT. SINGLE.

GRANTHAM

Acts of Incorporation of the Great Northern and Ambergate, Boston, Nottingham and Eastern Junction Railways received their Assents in close succession, on 26th June 1846 and 16th July 1846, respectively. Before long, the Boards of the two companies were talking about joint working at Grantham and a minor GNR Act of 22nd July 1847 cleared the way for a Joint station in the town. Ambergate Company trains were the first to enter Grantham, on 15th July 1850, with completion of the first section, twenty two miles route, from Nottingham. In the event, it was the only portion of the Ambergate Railway to be built; it would be some years before the GN reached Grantham and the Ambergate company's initial terminus was situated at Canal Yard, a basin on the Nottingham-Grantham Canal owned by the company. A small engine shed was provided, single road and probably constructed in wood. Little else is known about it though it would hardly have been adequate, even for the meagre Ambergate locomotive stud, but coke and water supplies must have been laid on, probably a turntable too and possibly some form of rudimentary repair arrangements.

Great Northern services to Grantham did not commence until 1st August 1852, when the last section of its main line opened between Peterborough and Retford. In anticipation of joint station working, the Ambergate company had already constructed a connecting line, by-passing the Canal Yard terminus, to join the GN at Barrowby Road Junction, just north of the main line station. However, one month prior to commissioning of the Peterborough-Retford line, an Act empowering the GN to work the Ambergate Railway in its entirety had been rejected by Parliament, after much lobbying on behalf of the Midland Railway. Undaunted, one day after the GN reached Grantham, the Ambergate company exercised its rights under the Joint station Act and commenced running its trains over the connecting link, into the station. No longer needed, the Canal Yard terminus closed on the same day, but the adjacent goods yard and engine shed continued to function. In the reverse direction, the GN started its own Grantham-Nottingham service on 2nd August, but as

is well known, it initially failed on the first day, following the infamous 'arrest and imprisonment' of a GN locomotive, by the MR at Nottingham.

While that affair was being sorted out, Ambergate engines and stock maintained the Grantham-Nottingham timetable until, on 24th May 1853, the way was cleared for the GN to recommence its own operations over the line. The MR, presumably placated, did not oppose a second attempt at getting the GN to run the Ambergate Railway and on 1st July 1855 an Ambergate Company Act was duly passed, empowering just such an arrangement.

In preparation for this the GN Board had decided early in 1855 to provide locomotive and carriage sheds at Grantham *to house Ambergate Company rolling stock*. Around the same time, on 17th April, Sturrock asked that a travelling crane for breakdown purposes be stationed there but on that occasion the engineer's request was denied. Exactly when the engine and carriage sheds beside the Joint station opened is not clear, but certainly they were in use late in 1855; final cost of the buildings was £2,450. The two single-ended, brick built sheds had arched entrances and adjoined each other. Each had two roads, under a slated gable roof and measured 172 ft. by 30 ft. (carriage shed) and 35 ft. (engine shed). The engine shed was the portion furthest west and an 80 ft. by 20 ft. coke stage had to be positioned between the carriage section and the station. A basic water supply was laid in, fed from Grantham Waterworks, but no turntable was provided. With the new shed's opening, the original Ambergate building at the canal basin was closed but for some years seems to have been incorporated into the thriving goods yard; the date of its final demise has yet to be discovered.

Ambergate locomotives that came into GN custody were a mixed and motley bunch. 'Express' power was in the form of three 4 wheeled Cramptons, built by E.B. Wilson & Co.; they became GN numbers 218-220. Next in sequence came 221 and 222, which were 6 wheel Singles, by R & W. Hawthorn and E.B. Wilson respectively. Ambergate goods engines were represented by a 6 wheel four-coupled Wilson (GN 392), and three 6 wheelers, also by Wilson - Nos. 391/3/4. it is quite probable that the Cramptons were early candidates for withdrawal, but how long they, or the remaining Ambergate engines

Manchester Sheffield & Lincolnshire 4-4-0 at Grantham, when it was a changeover point for Manchester-London expresses.
Collection Dave Banks

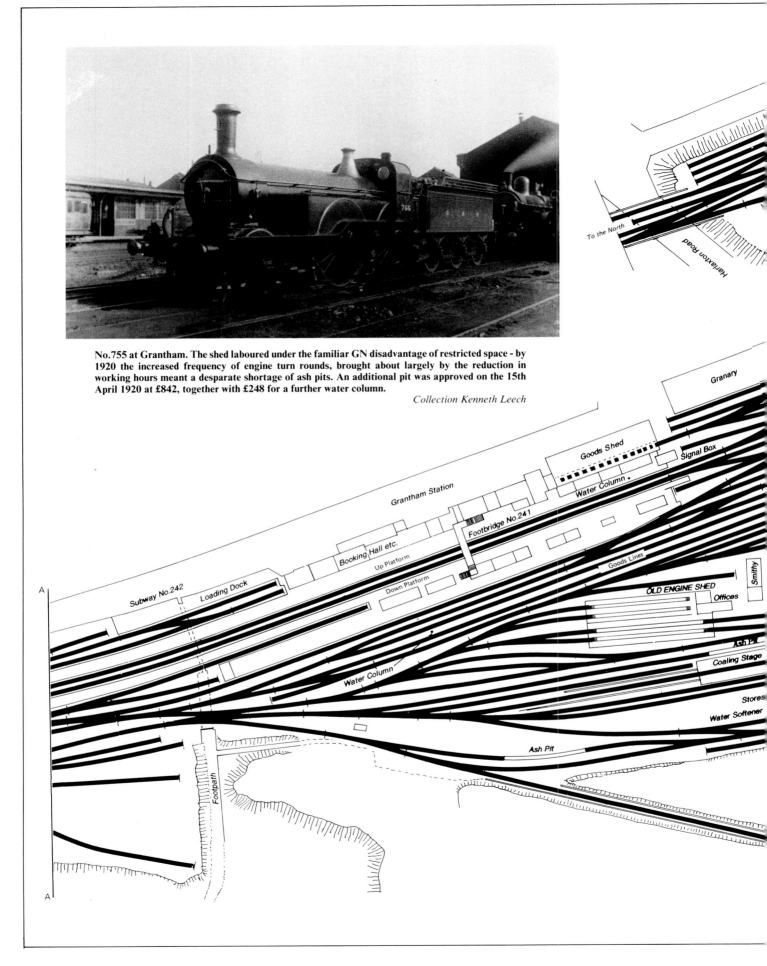

No.755 at Grantham. The shed laboured under the familiar GN disadvantage of restricted space - by 1920 the increased frequency of engine turn rounds, brought about largely by the reduction in working hours meant a desparate shortage of ash pits. An additional pit was approved on the 15th April 1920 at £842, together with £248 for a further water column.

Collection Kenneth Leech

To the North

Harlaxton Road

Granary

Goods Shed

Signal Box

Water Column

Grantham Station

Footbridge No.241

Booking Hall etc.

Up Platform

Goods Lines

Smithy

Down Platform

OLD ENGINE SHED

Offices

A

Subway No.242

Loading Dock

Ash Pit

Coaling Stage

Water Column

Stores

Water Softener

Ash Pit

Footpath

A

GRANTHAM 1956

To Peterborough

Bridge No.240

Crane 10T

Water Column

Signal Box

Level 200

Weigh Machine

Ramp

Toilets

Springfield Road

Fitters

Coal Stack

Coal Stack

NEW ENGINE SHED

Class Room

Scrap Bins

Shearlegs

Sand Drier

Ash Pit   Water Column

Coaling Plant

Storage Road

ARS

0-6-0 at Grantham in September 1938.

W.L.Good,cty W.T.Stubbs

survived, is not readily apparent. On 10th April 1858 Sturrock made a further request for a breakdown train for Grantham, ...*similar to that at Peterborough, which cost £160 in November 1853.....* For a second time, the GN Board obviously did not think of Grantham as a place of importance and refused to meet the locomotive engineer's requirement; it would be many years before the Board changed its mind (see below). 15th May 1860 saw the Ambergate Railway formally change its name to the Nottingham & Grantham Railway & Canal Company and on 1st August of the following year the GN commenced a leasing of the company, which would be continually extended until the Grouping, when the Nottingham & Grantham finally lost its nominal independence to the LNER.

The year 1862 saw Sturrock obtaining approval for installation of engine pits and water cranes at Peterborough station to enable engines to run through from Kings Cross to Grantham. This immediately brought about an increase in the strategic importance of Grantham engine shed and on 20th May 1862 the engineer sought sanction for a turntable there. It took until 24th June for the Board to say yes, when the estimated costs of £700 were approved. In due course a 40 ft. example was installed between the carriage shed and station, at the end of the coaling spur. Later in 1862, on 1st September, Sturrock followed up with a report saying that with engines now running through from Kings Cross, ...*extra accommodation is needed (at Grantham) which I do not have. The carriage shed is in a 'proper position' for the Locomotive Department and not now useful for Traffic Department purposes, being too small, but Mr. Leith refuses to part with it. Would the Board please intervene.....* On 9th September, the General Manager and Locomotive Engineer were asked to report further and by 27th October Mr. Leith had obviously been 'convinced' because Sturrock presented the Board with the following schedule of estimated costs:

Convert carriage shed to engine shed	£750
Provide new carriage shed and sidings	£750
Provide new water crane	£130
	£1630

Sturrock calculated a saving of £2,000 per year would be made by working engines through to Grantham via Peterborough, and the Board duly approved the above expenditure. By mid-1863 the work had been completed; the new carriage shed, of two roads, was erected by the north end of the down platform. A contemporary plan incorporating the alterations also depicts another carriage shed, scaling 118 ft. x 36 ft. at the rear of the engine shed and at right angles to it; origins of this building are not known.

Following the shed's increase in importance, the Locomotive Foreman and Inspector of Way each merited company accommodation and a Minute of 9th May 1864 records that two such cottages were under construction. This was soon followed, on 25th July 1865, by a petition from other company servants at Grantham, seeking the erection of workmen's cottages, a request finally granted on 16th October 1866. On that day, 17 cottages were approved, at a cost not to exceed £100 each, ...*to be built upon land about the station yard.....* they were for occupation by both Locomotive and Traffic Department staff. On 1st November 1865 £220 was sanctioned for the removal of an engine pit and water crane at the north end of the down platform, to enable it to be extended. The new carriage shed survived this alteration but was nevertheless to be relatively short-lived, being removed for further platform works, before June 1878.

Water problems plagued Grantham over the years. Soon after the GN arrived in the town, the Waterworks found itself unable to furnish a sufficient supply for the railway's needs and the GN put up a 37,000 gallon tank on its own tankhouse, at the top of the station approach road. On 12th March 1867, the General Manager reported that: .....*the water supply at Grantham, for engines and station purposes, having been insufficient during the past winter, the Waterworks Company has agreed to put in a new meter, but in order to increase the pressure, it is essential to raise the company's tank. That will cost £183, but at the same time it is desirable to increase the size of the tank, which will cost a further £120.....* The Board resolved that both jobs should be done and there the matter rested until 2nd December 1871 when the General Manager again reported: .....*the Agreement with the Grantham Waterworks Company will expire on 5th July 1872. The locomotive engineer states that he will not be able to arrange a sufficient and reliable supply from the Grantham and Nottingham Canal, so therefore, new terms will have to be arranged with the Grantham Waterworks Company. The current terms are £275 per annum for any amount not exceeding 100,000 gallons per day - or 1.8d per 1,000 gallons - and 3d per 1,000 for any quantity above 100,000 gallons per day. The Waterworks Company have intimated that on any new contract they will be asking 5d per 1,000 gallons, but the engineer thinks they will accept 4d, and enter into an agreement for 14 or 21 years, at that rate.....* It was resolved that the General Manager and Locomotive Engineer should try to make an arrangement with the Grantham Waterworks Company for 4d per 1,000 gallons.

The outcome of those negotiations is unclear but by 17th July 1873 Stirling had to report to the Way & Works Committee that *.....the 4 ins. main supplying the engine shed was insufficient.....* proposing its replacement by a pipe of 6 ins. diameter. To undertake such a job using GN employees was estimated to cost 9/10d per yard, whereas the Waterworks Company had quoted a figure of 3/7d per yard. Quite why the two costs should be so disparate is not explained, but needless to say, the Water Company got the job! The next development came in 1876 when for a third time the Loco Engineer asked for a breakdown train to be stationed at Grantham. It was a case of 'third time lucky' and in due course the train arrived, equipped with a standard 8 ton hand-powered crane, built at Doncaster 'Plant'. Thirteen years then passed before mention of Grantham shed next appears in a GN Minute book. On 25th May 1889, Stirling reported to the Locomotive Committee that: *.....the roof is very unsafe and when repairs are undertaken, can the shed be extended? 37 engines are stationed there, but there is room for 10 under cover, which means a lot of shunting to get engines in for washout and minor repairs. The extension proposed would cover a further 10 engines; the whole job, including roof repair is estimated at £2,600. If this shed were to be still further enlarged it would enable the company to run trains to York and Leeds with only one stop.....* The outcome was that the roof repairs were done, but the increase in accommodation was limited to the extension of the original two road engine shed portion by a mere ten feet or so, at the rear; this entailed removal of the carriage shed there. In addition, it was made into a through building, with both tracks extended for about 85 ft. to buffer stops. Arched exits were used but at the same time those at the front of the shed were replaced by a single square entrance, with a steel lintel above; the former carriage shed retained its arches. At the same time the turntable was moved from beside the shed to a less cramped location at the very top end of the yard, north of a pedestrian subway and the space made available by its removal put to use for a set of shear-legs. This relocation was to cause problems early in 1892; on 7th January that year the Engineer told the Locomotive Committee of a collision between two engines on the turntable road. Stirling suggested the company took possession of part of the recently acquired Union Workhouse so that the land could be used for an additional connection between the 'table and the north end of the shed yard. This would mean pulling down the Fever Hospital and widening the embankment, with consequent extension of the subway, involving 1,000 cubic yards of earthwork filling, the whole job costing an estimated £915. The Locomotive Committee recommended to the Board that the alterations be proceeded with, which was approved.

Just over three and a half years later, on 9th October 1895, Stirling was again after more land, this time for additional coal stacking. The site proposed lay along the northern edge of the shed and involved taking down a wall, removing and re-erecting the enginemens' room and a considerable amount of earthwork. Estimated costs were £454, these being quickly sanctioned. Whether Stirling's request was in anticipation of a planned expansion of Grantham shed is not known, as he died only a month later. His successor, Ivatt, certainly did have ideas about expansion and on 21st June 1896 announced that a new shed for forty engines was required at Grantham and should be located at the south end of the site, by Brick Kiln Lane bridge. The Board of Directors elected to visit Grantham to see for themselves, with the upshot that on 1st October 1896, tenders were invited for an engine shed for twenty locomotives, built in such a way as to permit easy expansion along its east side, for a further twenty. The job was to be dealt with in two parts; a separate contract for the foundations, because of the amount of heavy work involved, and another contract for the shed building, ramp coal stage and 'other works'. Successful tenderer for the foundations contract, which started straight away, was Messrs. Arnold, with a bid that has been impossible to ascertain precisely, but from available documents was in the region of £14,000.

Meanwhile, the shed building job went to Messrs. Dennett & Ingle, for a tendered price of £14,948/18/7d. Both these companies had worked for the GN before and moved with customary swiftness. So much so that by 2nd March 1897 though lamenting delays due to February's very wet weather, Ivatt was able to report thus on progress at Grantham: *.....the south and west walls are up to roof principals level and the pits are three quarters done. Extension of the subway has commenced and excavations for sidings are progressing.....* Completion came later in 1897, when the GN took possession of its new four road single-ended brick shed; in fact, the east wall was *not* built in brick but corrugated iron, in anticipation of future extension. measuring 300 ft. x 62 ft. the building had a standard northlight roof and stood some 210 yards to the rear, and slightly west of the first shed. This left it a considerable distance from the turntable and a second one of 52 ft. diameter was provided by the south west corner of the new building. On the same side, at the north corner, an engine hoist was installed, in place of the shear legs at the other building. The original coal platform was removed from its inconvenient position by the old shed too, replaced by the ramp coaler erected adjacent to the south west edge of the first shed; later, some of the arches beneath the coal stage were bricked-in, to form separate messrooms for footplatemen and cleaners. The ground set aside for a possible future building extension was used in the meantime for yet more coal stacking; enlargement never was effected, however. As at Kings Cross, the two sheds were soon being called 'Top' and 'Bottom' but in Grantham's case 'Top' referred to the southern most building. There are also several references to the appellations 'Old' and 'New' sheds at Grantham. Roads were numbered in the New Shed, with number 1 on the east side; at the Old Shed, they were named reading from the station side: Short Road, Long Road, Straight Road and Wallside; on one occasion, around 1936, someone tried to make the 'Long' even longer, driving a locomotive through the back wall!

It was not long before more adjustments were being made and on the very first day of the 20th century £180 was approved for extension of the siding beside the coal stack and an additional connection to the north turntable. Just 7 weeks later, on 19th February 1900, expenditure of a further £240 was sanctioned, this time to provide a hydraulic lift and pump for the engine hoist. More developments came in 1902, as part of a £9,957 scheme for new down goods lines. The north turntable was in the way of the new lines so it had to be moved and the GN took the opportunity to enlarge it to 55 ft. in the process. The engineer was able to report on 23rd December 1902 that foundations for the new turntable were being dug, following this up on 13th June 1903 with a request for £700 to provide additional sidings *.....necessary as the turntable has been moved south of the subway.....* plus an engine pit and water crane. After this Grantham keeps out of the Minute books for another 13 years until 25th November 1916 when as a wartime measure women engine cleaners had been employed and expenditure of £29 was authorised, to provide separate mess facilities and lavatories.

Over the years the District Locomotive Superintendent had responsibility for three outstations, at Sleaford, Leicester and Newark. Leicester had come first, opening in 1882, until it was transferred to Colwick around the period of the First World War. Next was Sleaford, again from opening, in about 1883, with two engines and four sets of men normally outstationed there. These arrangements continued until 30th September 1930, from which date Sleaford was transferred to Boston. Even so, a Grantham crew continued to travel to Sleaford each day, by train, to work the middle shift on Sleaford's pilot. Newark came under the Grantham DLS in June 1912, when it was transferred from Retford, together with responsibility for Muskham water troughs. Under LNER control, Grantham District was abolished and the shed and outstations were transferred to Peterborough District. Newark remained an outstation of Grantham until just before Nationalisation when it was transferred back to Retford again. While Sleaford and Newark were subordinate to Grantham, the main shed's Chief Clerk travelled by train on Friday mornings to Sleaford, and in the afternoon to Newark, with the men's wages; the method of paying Leicester Belgrave Road employees is not known.

The locomotive history of Grantham was illustrious, but began in a small way. For the first few years, it was primarily concerned with the maintenance of Ambergate Railway engines and services over the line to Nottingham until the 1860s, when it was established as a major engine changing point. Early Hawthorns and Sharps would soon have

Pacific on the Grantham 70ft turntable in June 1947. This had replaced a 55ft example, transferred to Bradford (for it was relatively new) in 1921.

Collection Kenneth Leech

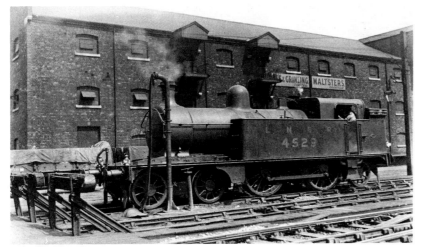

C2 in the engine siding at Grantham station in 1930.

R.S.Carpenter Collection

0-6-0 No.64172 on 4th June 1950. In LNER times (and it is not thought to have changed much by the early 1950s) the Grantham complement included some 120 sets of foot-platemen, under a District Locomotive Superintendent.

H.C.Casserley

Grantham in August 1938. The coaling plant was put up by Henry Lees, one of the major suppliers of such contraptions. Its installation speeded up the constant turnover of engines but ash disposal remained primitive. Even the relatively crude LNER wet ash pits were not considered suitable, possibly though lack of space.
National Railway Museum

been joined by Sturrock and Stirling 2-4-0s and 0-4-2s and from 1871 the latter's famous 8 ft. Singles were based there - No. 2 being the first to arrive. From 1887, variety was provided when the GNR/MSLR engine changeover point for Kings Cross-Manchester trains was moved from Retford. Parker's class 6D 2-4-0 (LNER E2) were common at first, replaced from about the early 1890s by Parker and Pollitt 4-4-0s. After the GN London-Manchester passenger trains were reduced to through carriage workings, a Great Central presence at Grantham was maintained, especially during 1914-1916, when the shed was used on a daily basis for workings to Nottingham, Sheffield and beyond; 4-6-0s of class B1 predominated.

By 1895, twenty-three GN singles of all types were stationed at Grantham, out of a total complement of about 50 engines. These included the following Stirling 8-footers: Nos. 2, 3, 5, 22, 60, 62, 93, 95, 221, 665, 771, 773, 777, 778, 1002, 1004, 1006. Their days, however, were numbered, with the introduction of Ivatt 4-4-0s and 4-4-2s imminent and by July 1910 only three (of the last nine) singles were working from Grantham - Nos. 95, 1006 and 1007; No. 1006 was to be the very last of her type, withdrawn on 14th February 1914. Ivatt 4-4-0s arrived, slowly at first, for there were still numerous 2-4-0s in service (seven Class E1 were at Grantham at the Grouping still, in use on locals to Derby, Nottingham and Stafford). By the early part of World War One, seven out of the fifteen first series of Ivatt's class D1 were on the Grantham allocation. They saw use mostly on the secondary routes to Boston, Leicester, Derby, Skegness and Mablethorpe, but did have some duties on the main line - in the York direction in particular, trains of up to twelve coaches and 415 tons were handled.

Summer 1924 saw ex-NER Raven Pacifics covering the 8 a.m. Newcastle-Kings Cross and 5.30 p.m. Kings Cross-Newcastle coming off and taking over at Grantham, where the first Gresley A1 had appeared the previous year. By the end of 1925 seven of the latter were allocated, reaching ten in the next year, when they took over the Top Link. The A1s worked Grantham-York-Kings Cross-Grantham or reverse and, when permitted to run to Leeds from 1930, took over the major London-Leeds workings. Such duties worked were the last leg

of the 'Night Scotsman', Grantham-Kings Cross, then hauling the 10.10 London-Leeds throughout, returning to their home shed on the 3 p.m. Leeds-London. By early 1935 thirteen out of the 79 A1/3s were allocated, a figure that fell to only four by Nationalisation, when the bulk of the important duties were being handled by a stud of ten Class A4 Pacifics, the first pair of which had arrived in 1938. A3s prevailed though, when the A4s went away again, in 1951. Before they left, Gresley's streamliners had been responsible for the 'Flying Scotsman', non-stop to Newcastle, and Grantham usually kept one A4 in special condition for the job - 60030 *Golden Fleece;* is recalled as a particular favourite for the turn.

For secondary duties, a solitary K2 2-6-0 was present for a few years in the early 1930s and a couple of V2s saw use in the later part of that decade, and again in the mid-late 1950s. Thompson B1s were seen from around 1946 but only about four came onto the allocation, a number which remained, on and off, until the 1960s. Another 4-6-0 type was the ex-GER B12 which saw use in the early BR period; they were used on trains to Skegness and Peterborough and also operated the Doncaster 'Parlies'. Other slow passenger work was covered by the various 0-6-0 types, of which Grantham had quite a few before Grouping - Stirling J4 and Ivatt J5 mostly (LNER J3 and J4), with Gresley's J22 (J6) also present. Before long, J6 were the major class, with eleven stationed there in 1933, at which time 8 J3s were allocated too.

Heavy goods engines were never much of a feature of Grantham until the Highdyke iron ore traffic was expanded, bringing ex-GC 2-8-0s to the shed in the late 1920s, holding sway until replaced in 1942 by an influx of twelve 01 2-8-0s. The 01s were present for only about two-and-a-half years before they gave way in turn to 02 2-8-0s of which seventeen were allocated by 1945. They were maintained at about that level until trickling away to Retford from the late 1950s. During 1946-1950 the 02s were assisted on the Highdyke traffic by some of the last remaining ex-GC Q4 0-8-0s of which a maximum of eight was stationed around Nationalisation.

Grantham's tank engine stud was also relatively small in number, with a handful of Stirling and Ivatt 0-6-0STs available for shunting. They were joined for varying periods after Grouping by ex-GE J66, J67 and J69 0-6-0Ts. One J68 No. 68638 even saw out its last year of service at Grantham, but J69s were employed on the last shunting duties. Passenger tanks were originally represented by Stirling 0-4-2Ts and 0-4-4Ts superseded by Ivatt C2 (LNER C12) 4-4-2Ts around the start of World War One. Here was another type noted for its 'staying' power and as a class it might even have beaten the 'Large Atlantics' tenure, with the very last C12 of all, No. 67397, withdrawn at the end of 1958.

The Grantham allocation stood at sixty by Nationalisation but a visit on the morning of Sunday 30th may 1948 found less than forty present, viz:

A3 4-6-2:
44, 83, 60107
A4 4-6-2:
8, 13, 14, 15, 18, 26, 32, 60007
B1 4-6-0:
1144, 1171, 1175
C12 4-4-2:
7382
D2 4-4-0:
2161, 2173, 62172
D3 4-4-0:
2000
J6 0-6-0:
4178, 4206, 4227
J52 0-6-0:
8816
Q4 0-8-0:
3229, 3234, 3240, E3243
V2 2-6-2:
806, 833, 858, 904, 60959
Total 32

This was not long before Grantham's allocation declined still further, to a figure of only 35 by August 1950. Presumably this derived from

Grantham northlight shed from the coal plant with attendant 'risk of falling coal'.

A.G.Ellis,cty Bruce Ellis

Grantham in July 1954.
Collection B.Matthews

the interruption to the turntable (see later); engines were transferred away and many do not seem to have returned, both passenger and goods. The number of locomotives stationed at Grantham slightly recovered to 41 by early April 1959, a figure that remained fairly constant until just before closure.

Modernisation of its most important engine sheds was a feature of LNER activities in the 1930s. Grantham was no exception and on 14th June 1935, a report to the Locomotive & Works Committee went like this: *.....64 engines, almost all passenger types, are located. The two sheds provide covered accommodation for 32. Locos are coaled from a single-sided elevated tip stage, with the quantity of coal consumed about 913 tons a week (47,500 tons per annum). New provision should include:*
1. A new 150' engine pit on an existing siding and a new siding with a 100ft long engine pit, beyond the coaling stage. The present pit alongside the stage is unsuitable because of the risk of falling coal.
2. A new Kelbus sand furnace, to be housed in a new building adjacent to the engine pits, as the present affair is old-fashioned and inconveniently positioned.
3. Electric lighting to be provided in the proximity of the coaling plant and engine pits. The present gas lighting is in general use in the yard and

will be continued.
4. A 200 ton mechanical coaling plant by Henry Lees & Co. Ltd., to cost £5,596/17/0d (installed by that company).
Other work as above carried out by LNER staff, to cost £9,524. Time of work to be 35 weeks, starting 19th March 1936. The scheme will enable 11 men to be dispensed with and effect a net saving of £1,410 per annum.....

The work was put in hand and completed more or less on schedule and would therefore have been just in time for a visit by two illustrious strangers on St.Valentine's Day 1937, when a pair of Great Western Castles arrived at Nottingham Victoria on specials, only to find that the turntables there were too small. So, what with it being a Sunday, with many crucial signalboxes switched out, there was not alternative but to send the Castles to Grantham's 70 ft. turntable. The visit was almost certainly the first by such a GWR type since the 1925 exchanges and the engines involved were none other than the 'Cheltenham Flyer' record holder for the Swindon-London run, No. 5006 *Tregenna Castle* and her sister No. 5045 *Bridgwater Castle* - both engines were from Old Oak Common.

Nothing extraordinary seems to have happened at Grantham during the war, when perhaps the extraordinary was almost an everyday event. It may be safely assumed that the shed's men and machines had to struggle against increasing demands upon their services, in a time of reducing manpower and considerably less than adequate maintenance. Like all of Britain's railway installations, Grantham shed emerged tired and run down from the war years and little could be done to remedy this in the company's last few years. In mid-1950 an unexpected setback occurred, which probably explains the sudden decline in the Grantham complement - the 70 ft. turntable went 'out of order', the exact cause of the trouble due to a collapse of the foundations under the pivot. The 'table went drastically out of balance, making turning almost impossible; the 52 ft. turntable by the 'Top' shed had unfortunately been taken out of use at some time before 1947, so for the period of the emergency, during the months of May and June, Pacifics were mostly transferred away and major engine changing suspended. Such locomotive turning that had to be done was carried out by utilising Barkston triangle, an eight mile round trip, with engines slotted into gaps in the busy main line

replacement, asbestos sheeting on a steel framework, was completed around 1955. The gabled roofs of the 'Bottom' shed had soldiered on through all this but by 1960 they finally reached such a state of dereliction that the shed had to be abandoned. With dieselisation in full swing, repair of the old building was out of the question and not long after falling into disuse it was demolished, after something like 105 years of service; the rear wall and adjoining offices, etc. were retained, the latter for use as a signing-on point.

After this it was only a question of time how long the remains of Grantham shed would survive. Diesels rendered the time-honoured practice of engine changing unnecessary, and when enough of them were in service and the early numerous failures had been overcome there really was no reason to keep Grantham shed open. Accordingly at the end of the 1963 summer timetable on 9th September the shed closed; in effect it shut on Saturday, 7th September, the last locomotives to be despatched (it is believed) being 4-6-2s Nos. 60108 *Gay Crusader* on a down passenger working and 60106 *Flying Fox* on a goods to Doncaster; it was very appropriate that two A3s brought to a close 108 years of history. Of the staff that remained, 18 drivers, 21

V2 No.60871 on 24th June 1958. The 2-6-2s are less well remembered than the various Pacifics which would be found at Grantham over very many years, from the Raven examples and A1s, A3s and A4s of the 1950s and early sixties.

R.C.Riley

services. The 70 ft. turntable was restored to use but only on a temporary basis for the clay soil made it difficult to reconstruct a sufficient new foundation. Accordingly, it was removed in 1951 for refurbishment and re-use, at Melton Constable of all places! That was not the end of its odyssey and after closure of the M & GNR in 1959 it was moved again, this time to Kings Cross where it saw out the days of steam until Top Shed's closure in 1963. The problem of turning engines at Grantham was resolved in 1951 by laying down a triangle on the instigation of the then District Locomotive Superintendent, John Blundell, on the open ground to the west of the two sheds - formerly occupied in part by the Union Workhouse. Even so, there was insufficient space to put down a triangle 'proper' and the two approach tracks actually crossed, at the nearest possible point to the triangle's 'base' track. This was achieved by use of a scissors crossing, an application that was certainly unique on the railways of Britain and probably overseas too.

British Railways next provided a new covering for the 'Top' shed; its northlight roof had decayed to a dangerous state and its wholesale

firemen and 21 cleaners were made redundant, but no fewer than 63 drivers, 53 firemen and 2 labourers were retained. They were housed in the block of buildings at the south end of the up platform, by Grantham Yard signal box. Some fitting staff also remained and had their own room and workshop at one end of the same building, exactly opposite where the 'Deltics' used to stop and render further conversation impossible!

After closure, the shed building and tracks remained in situ until 1964 and sheltered DMUs from the bitter cold of the 1963/64 winter. Clearance of the surviving structures commenced in March 1964, with the water softener the first to go. The work took time, however, and it was not until November that the coaling tower was demolished by explosives; even then the old coal stage still stood and may just still have been around in 1965. Around this time a diesel stabling point was established in the down goods yard but eventually that too became surplus to requirements. Today the southern end of the Grantham site is covered by a factory and a sand hopper complex, but the rest of the area is overgrown and derelict.

There are a number of 'lost' LNER branches in north London, some still lie in odd corners under trees and bushes, others wholly absorbed within the Underground network. The little shed at the end of the Edgware branch is almost wholly obscure and is known only from a simple plan - though it is in London now, the line was built through a damp open country of clay fields, orchards and farms and wondering yokels. Struck down at an early date, only the site (above, in 1914 and below, 1937) has been recorded.

The 1950s Society

EDGWARE

The fashionable North London suburb of Edgware was reached by the Great Northern on 22nd August 1867, by way of a branch from Finsbury Park, via other early suburbs at Highgate, Finchley and Mill Hill. The branch had been sponsored by the Edware Highgate & London Railway, incorporated on 3rd June 1862; it had originally arranged for the GNR to work all services but by an Act of 15th July 1867, the smaller company was wholly absorbed by the GN, immediately prior to opening of the line. In the takeover the GN also inherited the EH & L's powers for a proposed Edgware-Watford extension which, as it turned out, never came to fruition. With the Watford extension in mind, the layout of Edgware station was simple, having only the one platform. It was complemented by a single road engine shed, sited at the end of a long spur on the north side of the station. The dead-end building measured 65 ft. by 21 ft. and was built probably in wood on dwarf brick walls with a slated gable roof. A 40 ft turntable was situated immediately outside the entrance and a brick built coal platform, with 13,500 gallon water tank on top, stood about 100 ft. further along the spur. Arrangements were completed by a pit and water column adjacent to the stage, behind which ran a spur line, to accommodate a coal wagon. Despite the turntable, tank engines - Sharps and 0-4-2 Metros initially - worked the opening service of ten weekday return trains to Finsbury Park, with two on Sundays. This was typical of the service provided until 1st April 1872, from which date the Finchley-High Barnet branch was opened. At that time the Edgware-Finchley section was reduced in status to a 'sub-branch', having a shuttle service of fifteen weekday trains, with four at the weekend. The 1876 WTT shows one deviation from these workings, the first train of the morning, 7.53 a.m. to Moorgate Street. The engine worked in the previous night on the 11.05 from Kings Cross but all goods trains continued to be worked through during slack periods in the passenger timetable.

In his admirable history of the Great Northern Railway, John Wrottesley notes that by the middle of 1878, the cost of pumping water at Edgware was reputed to have become so prohibitive that the shed was officially closed from 1st July that year, and the staff were transferred to Kings Cross. This may have been a temporary arrangement for the 1881 WTT shows a Whistle Code (2 whistles) for *access to Edgware engine shed*. This may have been for coaling and/or watering purposes only of course, not stabling, but certainly the building was completely out of use only a few years later. During the winter of 1885 England suffered a freak blizzard, an apparently less than rare occurrence in that era. Such blizzards claimed many a building around the country, including a few engine sheds, Edgware

among them, and it was comprehensively demolished by the combined weight of wind and snow, never to be rebuilt. The water tank survived, however, together with the pit (and possibly the coal platform for a while), and continued in use, with an average of two-and-a-half million gallons of water taken annually, during the early 1900s. Water remained available until the end of steam working over the branch in BR days.

On 1st July 1897 improved services were offered over the branch the introduction of six through trains between Edgware and Kings Cross on weekdays. It appears the measure was not an unqualified success for by 1903 the Kings Cross trains had been reduced to two up and one down each weekday with one on Sunday. 0-4-4 Metro tanks had replaced the Sharps by then of course, with No. 510 an almost permanent resident on the branch. In 1904 the Metros were themselves replaced by Ivatt 4-4-2Ts which had a brief sojourn, before giving way in their turn to one of the first GN railmotors. The actual date was 19th February 1906, when a GN-built car took over. After six weeks service by the new machine Ivatt presented the following report to the Board, on 4th April 1906: .....*Between Finchley and Edgware, the railcar has largely taken the place of train services except on Saturdays and Sundays. Mileage over the 4 mile branch, for the month of March was 3,122 with 16,520 passengers being carried. Traffic receipts have shown an increase of only £9, with earnings per car amounting to 5d. per mile, while running costs were 7d.....* Ivatt concluded by saying the weather had been against all the GN's new railmotor services and he hoped for an improvement in performance to follow any improvement in the weather.

Despite the promise shown, the railmotors succumbed around the time of the First World War, to be replaced on the Edgware branch by 0-6-2Ts which henceforth remained the prime source of power. However, railmotors did reappear for a while at the end of the 'twenties, before finally fading in 1930; the last railcar on the Edgware branch was No. 51912 *Rising Sun*. At that time N2 0-6-2Ts re-established themselves, with Kings Cross engines handling passengers and Hornsey-based examples working the goods (mainly coal) services. The pattern remained thus until closure of the line in December 1961, when N2 No. 69523 was the last steam locomotive to visit the terminus, on a goods working, passenger trains having finished on 11th September 1939 - or rather, were suspended, as part of the works for bringing Northern Line tube trains to places like Edgware and Mill Hill East. The Second World War delayed the project but its eventual completion to a new Edgware terminus, only a short distance from the ex-GN station, ensured that LNER passenger trains were never reinstated.

After complete closure Edgware station and its environs were taken into private use, until surrounding property values made the site too attractive and it too disappeared under new building. The last traces of the engine shed disappeared during the redevelopment.

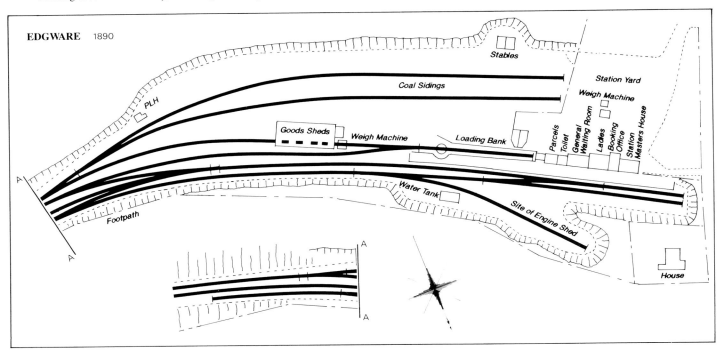

EDGWARE 1890

The little shed at St. Albans, which seems to have seen more use as an advertising device than an engine shed.

W.A. Camwell

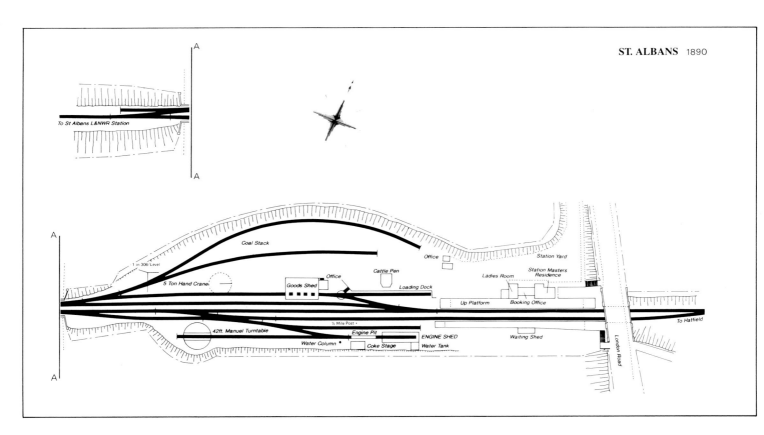

ST. ALBANS 1890

ST. ALBANS

The third and last branch line to be centred on Hatfield was that to the important Hertfordshire city of St.Albans, the *Verulamium* of Roman times. The branch line had been sponsored by the independent Hatfield & St.Albans Railway Company, which obtained the Royal assent to its Act on 30th June 1862. Subsequently, the H&SA arranged for the GN to subscribe £20,000 towards capital, and work all services from the date of opening, which took place on 16th October 1865. As was usual with most branch lines, an engine shed was provided at the terminus. It had been built by the contractor, one Mr. Rummens, who on 15th May 1863 had tendered to build the whole line and works, including the junction of Hatfield and St.Albans, the bridge over the GNR at Hatfield (replacing the level crossing near the junctions of the St.Albans branch, as required by the landowner, Lord Salisbury, as a condition of his sale of the land - the bridge cost £3,245), the station, sidings, goods shed and engine and carriage sheds at St.Albans, all for the sum of £60,000 cash, if paid two thirds cash, one third shares. Despite his offer being £3,000 higher than another tendered price, Rummens got the job.

As built, St.Albans comprised a one road, single ended building 55ft by 16ft in brick, with a slated gabled roof. An 1874 official plan shows the remaining facilities to have been a 40ft turntable, wooden coaling platform, a water crane and a 29ft ash pit outside the shed entrance. All this seemed fairly normal, but there exists quite a number of schools of thought that it was never actually used. Nonetheless, the 1876 WTT clearly indicates that an engine was stabling overnight, for the first train to Hatfield. What is more, the WTT seems to indicate that a pilot engine was employed from St.Albans to work trips to, and shunt Roe Green sidings. Whether this duty was fulfilled by the branch engine between passenger turns is not clear, but it is just possible that a second engine was stabled at St.Albans shed. By the next year, the WTT shows that the Roe Green Siding duty was undertaken by the Hatfield Pilot.

Initial services over the line, which would normally have been in the care of Sharps tanks, were quite ambitious, with the GN doubtless stealing some traffic from the LNWR, whose earlier St.Albans Abbey terminus was linked to the GN-worked branch. Whatever success the GN had was destined to be shortlived, as only three years after the Hatfield & St.Albans Railway opened, the Midland Railway commenced services over its London extension. With a station very conveniently situated to the town centre and a more direct and therefore faster route to London, the MR was soon capturing a major share of the traffic. Nevertheless the GN was 'saddled' with the H&St.AR and finally absorbed the company completely on 1st November 1883, by an Act which passed through Parliament the preceding 16th July; purchase price was £51,500. Before that it is evident the GN had decided to cease using St.Albans shed - undoubtedly through the Midlands success and its effect upon GN traffic - the WTT of 1881 makes no mention of locomotive facilities available at St.Albans. Seventeen years later, in 1898, another official plan shows that while the water crane and wooden coal stage were still in existence, the turntable and ash pit had gone and two lines of rail then terminated outside the shed, which was labelled 'stables'. It is quite probable the water crane was still in use at that time, but highly unlikely that locomotives could still take coal at St.Albans. Assuming the shed to have been used in the first years, then it seems to have been taken out of service sometime between 1876 and 1881, with 1876 almost certainly the year, given the switch of the Roe Green Siding shunting duty from St.Albans to Hatfield, between 1876 and 1877. The turntable probably had seen little use anyway, as Sturrock and Stirling 0-4-2 and 0-4-4 'Metro' tanks had succeeded the Sharps on passenger workings of which, by 1908, there were ten returns on weekdays and three on Sundays. After use as a stables, the shed became a store for many years; the entrance was bricked up in the process and latterly the building received a corrugated asbestos roof in lieu of the original tiles. In time, the coal platform and water crane were removed, leaving only the water tank, which adjoined the station building, to continue in use, supplying the traffic department. As such, the shed survived National-isation and eventual closure of the line to passengers, on 1st October 1951, with goods services ceasing on 5th October 1964. But, before the end, around 1956, spare siding space at St.Albans station had been put to an unusual use, as a railway hostel - employing surplus ex-MR and LNWR coaching stock. The shed also survived the subsequent purchase of the station by a company specialising in war surplus materials and thus, even very recently (September 1986), the little building could still be discerned, hidden among trees and shrubs, gradually mouldering away, surrounded by rusting armoured vehicles and other relics of man's warlike stupidity. The station too survived, in better condition, in use as offices, but the water tank, like the engine shed, was displaying extreme signs of its 120 years.

HERTFORD

The railways reached Hertford in October 1843, with the long-vanished 5 ft. gauge of the Northern & Eastern Railway, joined in the next year by the standard gauge Eastern Counties Railway and on 1st March 1858 came the Hertford and Welwyn Junction Railway. The Hertford & Welwyn ran from a connection with the GN at Welwyn Junction, north of Hatfield, to the Eastern Counties terminus. At first services over the Hertford & Welwyn line were worked jointly by the GNR and ECR, GN engines using the Eastern Counties engine shed and turntable.

After only 6 months, on 28th June 1858, the Hertford and Welwyn amalgamated with the Luton Dunstable and Welwyn Junction Railway, the new company christened, with some logic, the Hertford Luton and Dunstable Railway. Within three years, on 28th June 1861, it was absorbed by the Great Northern. The amalgamation of June 1858 had anticipated the completion of the Luton & Dunstable's line through to the GN main line, an event that finally occurred on 1st September 1860. Around this time the Eastern Counties pulled out of the joint working agreement for the Hatfield-Hertford line and Welwyn Junction station closed, with henceforth, trains from the branches running direct to Hatfield. With the ending of the Hertford line joint agreement, GN use of ECR engine facilities also ceased, and the GN rapidly put up a station of its own, at Cowfield, west of the ECR terminus and it can be assumed that a shed at the new station was opened simultaneously.

A consequence of the rapid change of events was the somewhat makeshift nature of that shed. Situated to the west of the station was a brick-built road overbridge, carried on five arches and to create its 'engine shed' the GN adopted the simple expedient of using the No. 2 archway, with a spur running through it to the west for some 25 feet covered by a 32 ft. extension building, probably in wood. Thus was created a 62 ft. x 17 ft 6 ins. building which also had the luxury of a 12 ft. ash pit immediately to the east of the bridge arch. No turntable was installed but though coke and water must have been available none of the plans inspected reveal the precise locations; in later years, however, a water standpipe was present at the west end of the station platform.

By 1861 the WTT shows the first goods train leaving Hertford for Welwyn Junction at 5.45 a.m. and the last goods service, from Hatfield, arriving at 8.40 p.m. The first and last passenger trains over the branch also started and terminated at Hertford, at 8.20 a.m. and 9.25 p.m. respectively. It is clear then that only a few months after cessation of the joint working, the GN was stabling two engines at Hertford overnight, outstationed from Hatfield. Initially these would have been Sharps tanks for passenger work and 0-4-2s and 0-6-0s for the goods. By 1876, however, the WTT shows only one engine staying at night, arriving at 9.38 p.m. and departing next day at 7.47 a.m.

Immediately adjacent to the extension part of the 'engine shed' was a cul-de-sac, which once formed a through road called 'Port Hill', with a matching cul-de-sac on the other side of the railway. The coming of the line had cut the road so the bridge was provided as a diversion, taking the name of Port Hill. On 4th July 1868 a resident of the cul-de-sac, one William Rolfe, made formal complaint to the GN about smoke emanating from the shed. The matter was referred to the Way & Works Committee, to consider its relocation to the other end of the goods yard with, in the meantime, ...*coke to be used instead of coal, to reduce smoke emission.....* It would appear the latter course of action was successful as Mr. Rolfe fades from the GN archive and no engine shed was, at that time, built further down the goods yard. An 1874 plan, however, shows a further proposal for a single road shed there, together with some new goods sidings. Creating room for the latter was almost certainly behind this second consideration to move the shed, but again nothing was done and an 1881 plan shows the

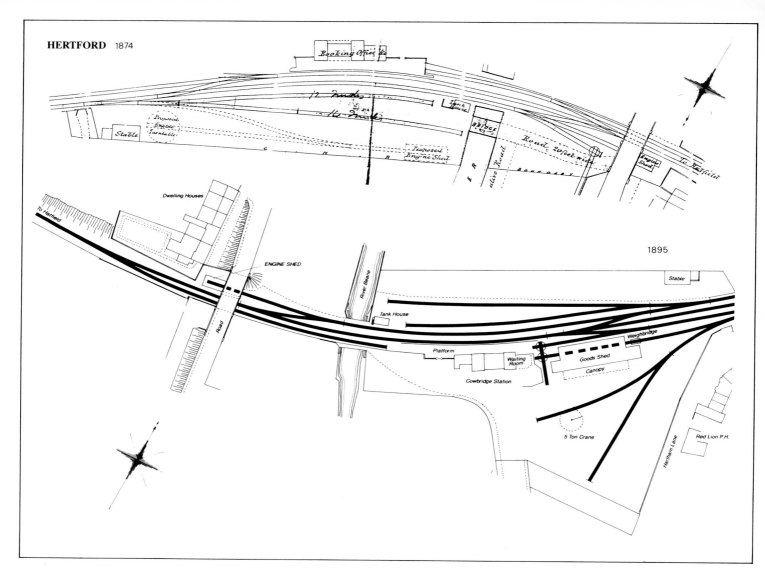

HERTFORD 1874

Booking Office &c

Stable

Proposed Engine Turntable

Proposed Engine Shed

Tank House

Bridge

Road, 20 feet wide

Engine Shed

To Hatfield

1895

Dwelling Houses

To Hatfield

ENGINE SHED

Road

River Beane

Tank House

Platform

Waiting Room

Cowbridge Station

Stable

Weighbridge

Goods Shed

Canopy

5 Ton Crane

Hartham Lane

Red Lion P.H.

'Luton Yard' and what remained of the engine shed in 1960.
Stephen Summerson Coll.

LUTON YARD

extended bridge arch to have still been in use. By then, services would have been handled by some of the Hatfield 0-4-2 and 0-4-4 tanks, with the latter surviving even the arrival of Ivatt's C2 4-4-2Ts in 1899. With the exception of the odd appearance by a 2-4-0, goods work largely remained an 0-6-0 job, until the advent of 0-6-2T types, which eventually became staple power for all workings. N1s arrived in 1907, N2s in 1921 and N7s *vice* N2 in 1924. Even ex-GC N5s appeared from 1934 to 1941. N2s returned, almost exclusively, by nationalisation and then N5s came back again too, to work most goods services until closure. Towards the end of steam L1 2-6-4Ts were said to have made forays over the branch, but this was probably on rare occasions only.

LUTON

The GN made a westerly incursion into Bedfordshire by way of a 20 mile branch from Hatfield, to the important towns of Luton and Dunstable. At the latter place, the line made a connection with an 1848 LNWR branch, from Leighton Buzzard. Originally promoted by the Luton Dunstable & Welwyn Junction Railway, incorporated on 16th July 1855, the first section, from Dunstable to Luton, was opened for goods traffic on 5th April 1858, with passenger services commencing on the following 3rd May. Only seven weeks later, the Luton & Dunstable amalgamated with the Hertford & Welwyn Junction Railway, to form the Hertford Luton & Dunstable Railway which was in turn absorbed by the GNR from 12th June 1861. Purchase by the GN was effected by varying the fixed dividend paid on the independent companies' original capital. When opened, there was no connection between the Luton & Dunstable and GN, who had agreed to work the line's traffic, so initial services were operated by the LNWR, from its station at Dunstable. An old Luton town plan of the time shows the somewhat rudimentary terminus provided for the opening with, at its western end, a single road engine shed, facing west. Probably of wooden construction, the single-ended building measured approximately 50 ft. x 15 ft. with a 40 ft. turntable sited off a spur, further to the west: coke and water are presumed to have been provided, but these do not appear on the plan. Whether the shed was erected by the Luton & Dunstable company or the LNWR is not certain, but anyway, its life was quite short. On 1st September 1860 the remaining twelve miles of line were opened, to Welwyn Junction and the GNR took up its working agreement. Within a month Sturrock was complaining that water arrangements at Luton were defective so it would seem that Luton's second shed - or at least a need for it- dates from that time. Certainly, it had been built by February 1862 because Sturrock again comments: *.....demand for water (at Luton) is now considerable and a pumping engine is required for the engine house built there for my department.....)* Sturrock then produced specifications for a suitable engine, from Messrs. Manning Wardle & Co., and on 4th December 1862 the Board sanctioned costs of £250 to purchase it. How long that pumping engine served is unknown but by the turn of the century, Luton Waterworks Company was supplying to the shed.

The primitive Luton station was rebuilt by the GN in 1863 and an official plan, produced two years later, shows the new layout, complete with second engine shed. This was located approximately on the site of the earlier turntable, facing east, and was a single road single-ended building, measuring 72 ft. x 21 ft. No turntable was provided but there was a coke stage with a 21 ft. pit alongside; a further pit, 46 ft. in length, was located inside the shed. Construction was in brick, with a 17,000 gallon water tank over the rear and a tiled pitched roof in front of it. At some time, yet to be discovered, a 20 ft. pitched roof extension was added on the western - ie. the rear - end of the shed.

Lack of a turntable had become a problem by 1883, so on 1st March that year, the Way & Works Committee approved expenditure of £500, for construction of the necessary foundations, at Dunstable *LNWR* station, with the 'table itself to be manufactured in the GN's own workshops. The 44 ft. 7 ins. 'table was duly installed and there matters rested until the last three years of the nineteenth century, when the Luton end of the section to Dunstable was doubled for about 1 mile. In addition, in 1897, the Way & Works Committee approved a £12,050 project at Luton, for construction 'of a new shed', warehouse and stabling accommodation. When finally completed, the job had cost in excess of £25,000 and included the complete resiting of the coal yard, onto ground that had to be specially acquired. The reference to a 'new shed' assuredly did not mean a new engine shed, and it was

probably soon after completion of the above mentioned works that Luton shed closed. Evidence of this is found on an 1898 Great Northern 2 chain plan of the branch, as amended in 1901. This shows the shed reduced in length, to 37 ft. by removal of the roofed section in front of the water tank, leaving the 17 ft. tank and 20 ft. extension at its west end. The shed had been made a 'through' building, with the line extending into an area of land at the rear which on 19th June 1902 became a workyard for one A. Giddings, Stonemason. It is faintly possible that the shed continued in service for a few more years, but by 1908 at least, it was serving as a store, specifically referred to as such in a contemporary article, on Hatfield and its branch lines, carried in the October and November issues of *The Railway Magazine*.

GN services over the branch were initially handled by Sharps tender and tank engines, then Metro 0-4-2T and 0-4-4Ts. In 1876 the WTT shows one of those engines stabling overnight at Luton, arriving on the 10.15 p.m. ex-Dunstable (which earlier formed the 9.16 p.m. ex-Hatfield). First working for the engine was the 8.10 a.m. passenger to Dunstable, then the 9.10 a.m. Dunstable-Hatfield. Although it is not certain, the same WTT indicates a second engine resting at Luton each night, for shunting the busy yard there. The Metros gave way to Ivatt C2 at the end of the last century - slowly at first, otherwise it would be interesting to speculate that the 4-4-2Ts capabilities may have been a prime reason behind closure of Luton shed, following a re-casting of Hatfield loco duties. But that is unlikely, with the Metros only really superseded when the first 0-6-2Ts arrived. Even so, when N1s appeared in 1907 they were found not to be ideal for the Luton branch, due to axle loadings. A similar problem plagued the N2s, when they came on the scene in 1921 and caused a number of derailments, particularly at Dunstable LNW. N7s initially superseded the N2s but the latter eventually returned in force, to take over a lion's share of the traffic - until September 1952 that is, when N2s were banned from the branch and N7s again took over all tank engine workings. The ban didn't wholly stick and N2s reappeared on goods work. Tender engines were also a common sight, on the branch goods, of which there was a considerable quantity - moving among other things, Luton's famous product of straw hats. That particular traffic had been immense in the years before the First World War, when straw had been a favourite millinery material - vanloads of hats were staple nightly traffic over both the GN and MR. In 1907, Vauxhall Motors opened its Luton works and before long, automobiles were being exported, via the branch to Hatfield and over the GER and NLR. In the other direction, the GER worked onto the Luton branch, via Hertford, bringing horses from Newmarket to Harpenden racecourse. Tender engines also took their share of passenger work, including the renowned Kings Cross-Dunstable through trains, of which in 1908, there were five up and four down, on weekdays. These saw heavy loadings and quite smartly timed schedules and Hatfield allocated certain engines to the duty. Ivatt D2 4-4-0s were regulars on the run, with Nos. 3041 and 3042 at Hatfield for many years, kept in 'crack' condition for these important commuter services. On Sundays, the Luton branch would see excursions to such places as Southend-on-Sea and engines like the 'star' D2s would be turned out for such trains.

In the latter part of the 1930s the D2s were replaced by Class J6 0-6-0s, a type which with J1s and J4s had earlier been used on Luton branch passenger work. During World War Two, Sentinel locomotives became a not uncommon feature at Luton, working at the Laporte chemical factory; Nos. 55, 61, 62, 63 and 65 and 86 were all noted on this duty. After the war N2, then N7 0-6-2Ts were the main source of power, as stated earlier, on a service that then consisted of seven down and eight up passenger trains each weekday, with an extra one down and two up on Saturdays. An additional working left Dunstable North (LNWR), at 7.53 p.m. to Luton, returning from there at 3.30 p.m. That train was actually a through working from Leighton Buzzard - usually push-pull, with Webb 2-4-2Ts and 0-6-2Ts giving way to LMS and BR Standard 2-6-2Ts. This was the sole survivor of an LNWR through service that once consisted of three return trains. Of the through workings between Dunstable, Luton and Kings Cross, only one survived - the 6.42 a.m. from Luton.

BR ceased passenger trains on 26th April 1965 and closure of Luton (Bute Street - as it had been known since 1st July 1950), to freight workings followed just over two years later. Before that had come truncation of the Hatfield-Luton line, with only the original section surviving today for mineral traffic, the portion of route from Luton to Dunstable. This is reached via a connection at Luton, from the former Midland line, opened on 3rd January 1966. Luton shed stayed through

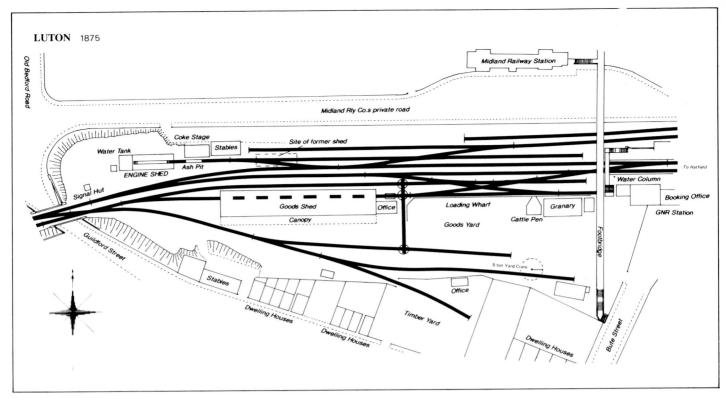

all of this, serving as a store and unusual form of gateway to Giddings stoneyard. The finale came in October 1970, when the shed was pulled down and its site, together with the stoneyard, was turned into a carpark.

SHEPRETH

A very short-lived engine shed was that provided at Shepreth, by the Royston & Hitchin Railway. Its Act of Incorporation was dated 16th July 1846 and subsequently an agreement was made for the GNR to work all services (it eventually absorbed the R & H on New Year's Day 1898). Built by Thomas Brassey, the Royston & Hitchin opened between those two towns on 21st October 1850. Passengers using the line were in the main, destined for Cambridge and completed their journeys from the Royston railhead by horse-drawn coach. A link with the Eastern Counties Railway and therefore Cambridge, was an obvious necessity, so the R & H soon commenced work on a 5 mile extension, to Shepreth, where it would make an end-on junction with the Eastern Counties, coming south. The Shepreth extension opened for traffic on 3rd August 1851 with the station again used as a change-over point for road coaches to Cambridge, pending completion of the ECR line. Among the arrangements at Shepreth was an engine shed, but little is known of its size, layout or precise location. All that is recorded is that the building was in wood with a 16 ft. turntable, which may additionally have served a carriage shed, erected at the same time and also of wooden construction.

Before completion of its route from Cambridge, the ECR had approached the R & H (GN) about leasing the Hitchin-Royston-Shepreth line and running trains from Hitchin to Cambridge, some of them conveying GN through carriages from London. The request met with a favourable response and an agreement was hammered out, to be effective from the date on which the Eastern Counties' Cambridge-Shepreth route opened - actually 1st April 1852. During negotiations for the lease, the ECR had pointed out that it did not require the engine and carriage sheds at Shepreth, a statement written into the leasing agreement at Clause 5. Four days before commencement of its operations under the lease, the ECR referred 'Clause 5' to the GN Ways & Works Committee, restating that Shepreth carriage shed was not wanted; as it was necessary, however, to provide a goods warehouse at Ashwell station, between Royston and Hitchin, Shepreth carriage shed (it was suggested) should be moved to Ashwell to fill the purpose. This was agreed and effected, but no mention can be

found regarding the fate of the Shepreth engine shed. Certainly, it does not show up on maps published a few years later, and when the GN repossessed the Company after 14 years of ECR leasing the company did not have any need to re-establish an engine shed. It is only possible to speculate upon its renewal and re-use elsewhere; see, for instance, the entry under Hitchin.

CAMBRIDGE

One of the world's premier seats of learning, the university city of Cambridge had earlier featured strongly in the evolution of companies that eventually became the Great Northern Railway. Once incorporated, the GN did not have Cambridge on its route map, the city having already been 'captured' by the Eastern Counties and Northern & Eastern Railways. Nevertheless, it did reach Cambridge, first entering the city on 1st April 1852, by way of through coaches over the ECR and ECR-leased Royston - Hitchin Railway. By 1856 the service consisted of three weekday and one Sunday return mixed trains - no separate goods were run at first.

Such through stock workings remained the status quo throughout the fourteen years of Eastern Counties leasing of the Royston company, ending on 31st March 1866. The Great Northern had already decided to run its own trains into Cambridge and arranged the necessary powers, to continue where the ECR leasing left off. The company was also determined to expand its operations in the city and to this end, came to an agreement with the GER for provision of GN staff and various offices at Cambridge station. However, the GER's general financial condition caused the GN expansion plans to become a somewhat protracted affair. It transpires that on 5th, 18th and 19th October 1866, meetings between the two companies took place, the upshot of which was a GER request for a loan from the GN, in the amount of £15,000. The GE wanted to borrow the money for a year, at 5% interest, maintaining that essential alterations at Cambridge station could thereby be expedited and more quickly allow the GN access. At the GN Board meeting of 30th October, the GE's situation was discussed and the request for a loan turned down. That decision must soon have been regretted, as by 27th November 1866, the GN Board were resolving to seek legal advice, because the GER had virtually halted work at Cambridge station. The next reference in the GN Minutes is from 23rd July 1867 and in those months the GE contractors, receiving no payments from their client, had walked off the site. This caused the GN Board at last to see sense and agree to advance £4,000 to the GER, which said it would repay the sum in 12 months and pay 5% interest in the meantime. The GE added that should it be forced to default on this arrangement, then it would empower the GN to recompense itself out of traffic receipts. By October 1867, the situation was obviously still in a shambles as the GN Board were then resolving to seek reimbursement for loss of earnings, due to non-completion of the Cambridge station works, and accept an offer, by another contractor, one Mr. Bell of Cambridge, to finish the job, for £800. All monies the GN felt it was owed would be taken from traffic receipts, after due advice had been given to the GER. Thus it was not until 1st January 1868 that GN staff were able to operate from their own offices at Cambridge.

Included in the GN/GE agreement was provision, by the GER, of locomotive shed facilities for use by the GN. In August 1865 the Great Eastern had offered .....*an engine house for not less than two engines.....* but initially, however, accommodation was achieved by allowing GN engines to share GE premises. Details of typical GN motive power outstationed at Cambridge in those early days were recorded in the diary of the GER's Cambridge District Locomotive Superintendent during 1866/67, George Macallan. The diary is today in the possession of Canon C.S. Bayes and the authors are grateful to him for the following information. Because the GN had to pay for water taken at Cambridge, Macallan kept records of consumption. He notes that about 5,000 gallons a day was being used by Sharps Single tanks Nos. 18 and 47, and 'Small Hawthorn' 2-2-2, Nos. 61 and 66.

Space considerations meant the presence of GN engines at the GER shed was a less than satisfactory arrangement, so it was not too long before the GER was required to erect a new engine shed for their guests. This was placed at the south eastern corner of the goods yard and, according to the GN's Way & Works Committee Minutes, was finally brought into use on 15th July 1869.

After its previous poor performance, the GE at least did the GN proud with their new shed. It was a handsome brick-built, dead-end structure of three roads, having a tiled gable roof. There were separate semi-arched entrances for each road and stores and offices at the rear, which provided a base for the 13,000 gallon water tank; a coal stage, covered by a pitched, tiled roof, stood adjacent to the spur leading to a 45 ft. turntable. Part of the London District, Cambridge was classed as

a sub-shed of Kings Cross and seems to have had a complement of four to six engines for most of its existence (four were reported in 1908, and again in July 1912). Fifty-six miles from London, and concerned with operations of a 'main line' nature, the allocation appears always to have been restricted to tender engines, although tank locos did visit of course. Sturrock and Stirling 0-4-2s and 2-4-0s featured among the complement in the 19th century, and even the latter engineer's legendary Singles, in the twilight of their lives. No. 1008 is remembered as a special favourite during its sojourn at Cambridge. Throughout the life of the shed the various classes of 0-6-0 also visited mostly on goods, but they could be observed handling the occasional passenger train. Ivatt 4-4-0 classes followed, then the first allocation of Atlantics - the small boiler version - and in 1908, these two types were involved with Kings Cross in the daily workings of eight up and down express passenger trains, five down and four up ordinary passengers and three down and four up ordinary goods. The allocation of Cambridge on 31st December 1922 was C1 Nos. 252, 253, 254 and 949 and B1 Nos. 56 and 62. The 4-4-0s would mostly be gone in a few years, to be replaced by the large boilered Class C1 4-4-2, which became the mainstay for some considerable time.

It was in this era of the 'Large Atlantics' that saw a Class V1 2-6-2T, temporarily allocated at Kings Cross, on trial (unsuccessfully, apparently), on Cambridge line trains, during the months of April to June 1931, a few months after the 'GN' shed was closed. GN Traffic staff had been withdrawn from the station as early as July 1912, but loco staff stayed until Grouping. Following formation of the LNER the GN shed maintained a 'stabling point' status, with administration from the GE depot, until 1930, when improvements at the latter enabled sufficient accommodation for engines working in off the former GN line. As it simply did not make economic sense for the LNER to keep two sheds in commission, all the company's loco work was accordingly centred on the ex-GE shed from January 1931. The above mentioned modifications there had robbed the C & W Engineer of repair space, so he was recompensed by adaptation of the former GN Shed into a wagon shop.

The depot served in its wagon shop role for over fifty years, to be closed by BR and lay empty for a while, before being demolished at the end of 1985, at an age of over 116 years.

The Great Northern shed yard. The building was put up with some ill grace by the Great Eastern, a company which despite an inferior financial position, maintained engine sheds of comparable, if not superior, qualities. An examination of the GE Running Department will reveal exactly how critical such a verdict really is! The two companies never seem to have got on at all, despite their joint involvement and the Minutes of both companies seem to indicate a lofty condescension on the part of the GN and a fear of being duped again in the GE camp.

Coll. Roger Simmonds

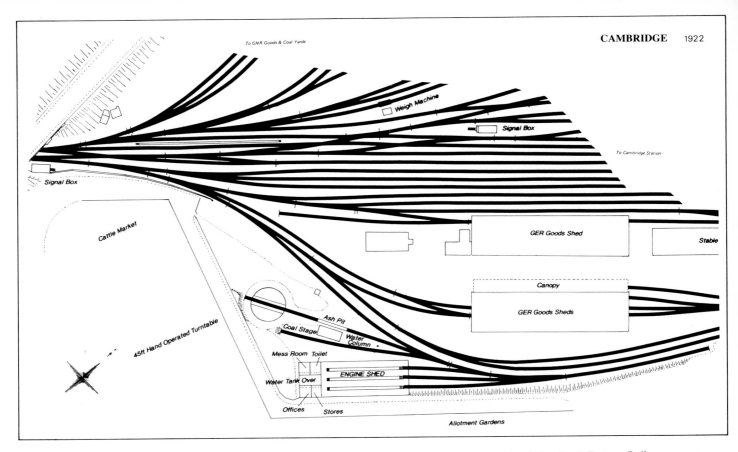

To GNR Goods & Coal Yards

Weigh Machine

Signal Box

To Cambridge Station

Signal Box

Cattle Market

GER Goods Shed

Stable

Canopy

GER Goods Sheds

45ft Hand Operated Turntable

Ash Pit

Coal Stage

Water Column

Mess Room Toilet

Water Tank Over

ENGINE SHED

Offices Stores

Allotment Gardens

RAMSEY

The GNR main line passed through Holme, just over five miles from the little market town of Ramsey, prompting private local interests to promote the Holme & Ramsey Railway Company, to link the two. The Act was obtained on 22nd July 1861 and almost a year later, on July 1st 1862, the Ramsey Railway signed a formal agreement with GN for the latter to work the line for a period of seven years. Given the easy terrain, construction was swiftly undertaken and thus it was early in 1863 that the line was declared ready for opening. However, when the GN engineers inspected the works, they found that construction had perhaps, been too swift! Lineside fencing was incomplete and, more importantly, some of the drainage ditches were too shallow for an area that could only be described as 'wet'. All defects were put right, but not without some to-and-fro, if one reads between the lines of the Ramsey Company's Minutes, and the line eventually opened for traffic on the second anniversary of the granting of its Act.

At first, services ran to a temporary terminus, for the local company had been trying to sponsor interest in an extension of its line - the Ramsey & Chatteris Railway which, if successful, would have determined the position and type of station to be provided at Ramsey. Very soon it was apparent that such an extension would not be viable, so construction of a permanent terminus was embarked upon, with opening probably around mid-1864. It is thought that the Ramsey engine shed appeared as an adjunct to the permanent station, but as the 45ft by 15ft building was constructed in corrugated iron, it is quite possible that it had stood by the temporary station, later to be taken down and re-erected. Precious little detail is available, although some sort of coke stage and water supply must have been provided, but it is fairly certain that a turntable was not installed.

Traffic was worked by locomotives out-based from Peterborough and changed over on Wednesday or Saturdays, when there was a through returned passenger train from Ramsey to Peterborough. Locomotives in early days would likely have been Sharps or Hawthorns - or possibly the 2-2-2T and 0-4-2T rebuilds of some of the first tender engines. Later would have come the Sturrock designed tender and tank engines, with all types undertaking passenger workings, plus a daily goods trip over the branch. The seven year agreement for GN

working came to an end, and the Great Eastern Railway moves prominently into the story, having maintained a shadowy presence for a number of years. The GER had also cast eyes upon Ramsey, supporting another independent concern, the Ramsey & Somersham Junction Railway, in its efforts to build a branch into the town from Somersham. In addition it proposed a link line, across the south eastern edge of Ramsey, to connect the two branches. So determined was the company that in 1865 it had tried to purchase the Holme & Ramsey, but the Bill had been rejected by Parliament, which nevertheless, passed the preamble for the Somersham line. With much persistence the Great Eastern tried again and in early 1870 was successful in purchasing the Holme & Ramsey Company outright. It was then faced with a problem, in that the Somersham Company could not get its own line into the town from Holme for five years. After this period had all but passed the Somersham line was still not started and the GE negotiated again with the GN and finalised a formal 21 year lease, signed on 1st July 1875, to continue the latter's operating powers. This lease was renewed in 1896 and 1917 for although the branch from Somersham did finally get to Ramsey, opening on 16th September 1889, the connecting line was never built. As a final note to this interesting story, the Somersham-Ramsey branch which, incidentally, had its own shed at the terminus, became a GER/GNR Joint undertaking on 1st January 1897 and afterwards, did very occasionally see a GN goods train.

Returning to the little corrugated iron shed at Ramsey North - as the station was later called - Great Northern engine workings from Peterborough were recast about 1885. This enabled a locomotive to be sent daily from New England, to work the Holme-Ramsey branch, returning in the evening. On outward and homeward journeys it hauled a goods train; it effectively rendered Ramsey engine shed surplus to requirements and it went out of use. However, probably because of contractual obligations incorporated in the GN's first 21 year lease, the GER, as owners of the shed, were not asked if the building could be demolished until 1897, shortly after commencement of the GNR's second 21 year leasing term. The GER consented to the GN undertaking the work and that the agreed scrap value of some £50 could be offset against the GN's capital expenditure. Whether Ramsey's coal and water supply was retained after the GN ceased using the shed is not known, but this is unlikely and certainly by the early twentieth century the only water available for the branch engine was at Holme.

MARCH

An Act of July 1863 empowered the GNR to build a line from Spalding to the Great Eastern bastion of March. The route was opened for traffic on 1st April 1867, nineteen days after the GN had invited tenders for provision of a turntable at March. This was duly installed but something must have been very defective because by mid-1868, the GER was complaining about it being 'out of order' (presumably it led to GN crews asking to turn their machines on the GER 'table)! A Great Northern Directors inspection of the Spalding - March line took place at the beginning of October 1868 and in a subsequent report to the Way & Works Committee, comment was made on the need for exchange sidings and a transit shed at March, and for an engine shed to accompany them. The builders of the line from Spalding were contacted and in his letter of reply, the builder, Jackson, quoted £526 for realigning his company's sidings for GN purposes, £480 for erecting the transit shed, and offering the use of 'an old engine house'. The building had been put up by Jackson Bros. to house their own engine, used in the construction of the Spalding line. Of two roads, in wood, with a slated gabled roof, it was of good size - 175 ft. by 38 ft. and Jackson's offer was accepted. A contemporary plan shows a coal platform and 44 ft. turntable sited just to the west of the shed, but whether the 'table had been put in by the contractor, or was the GN's own fault prone device is not known. It was reached, as was the shed, from March Norwood Junction signal box (Whistle Code 2 short and 3 whistles, respectively). Strangely no mention was made at the time of recompense for Jackson's 'old engine house', not until a Way & Works Committee meeting of 16th May 1875, when £100 was approved for purchase of the shed and a cottage - the latter presumably used by the shed foreman. Seemingly, the GN got a bargain thereby, but March shed was hardly used extensively. The 1876 WTT for example shows only one engine stabling there, for a passenger service to Spalding, with all goods work in the care of Great Eastern locomotives. The shed was therefore destined to have a short future. It continued to host 0-4-2s, 2-4-0s or 0-6-0s engaged on the sparse GNR workings until July 1882, when the March - Lincoln line opened throughout. At that time March shed was at last recognised as an excessive luxury, given the weight of traffic. It closed accordingly and no doubt was promptly removed. Thereafter, on the rare occasions that a GN engine required more than simple turning and watering, its crews would have sought access to the GER shed in the town, something that would soon present no problems, as the Spalding-March route became part of the GNR/GER Joint Line.

STAMFORD

The Stamford and Essendine Railway, incorporated by Act of Parliament on August 15th 1853, opened on 1st November 1856 with the GNR working all trains for 50% of the receipts. The first services consisted of four trains each way daily but as usual in those early days of high hopes, the scale of services was soon increased, to the point that could be described as 'lavish'. For example, the 1860 WTT shows nine return mixed trains running each weekday, and two on Sunday. Trains operated from Stamford, necessitating a locomotive, for which the S&E erected a brick engine shed, measuring 74ft by 20ft. The building had arched entrances and a roof that included a 10,000 gallon water tank above the front (eastern) end and a slated gabled roof behind. As such the shed provided cover for two tank engines but the single road passed through it to a buffer stop some distance in the rear, allowing extra stabling room. No turntable was installed and only the most basic of coke and water arrangements were available, the latter from the River Welland.

The Stamford and Essendine route abounded in sharp curves and had several weak underline bridges and services were worked from the first by small tank engines sent out from Peterborough. These would probably have been 'Little Sharps', and the rebuilds of the early Bury and Fairburn 'Luggage' engines. Such power held sway until New Years Day 1865 from which date Lord Exeter, instrumental in the promotion of the S&E line, and now in dispute with the Great Northern, took over working of the Stamford and Essendine. His first trains he ran composed of GN locos and stock, on hire, but this must obviously have been awkward, so ere long, his Lordship was hiring

rolling stock and motive power from the LNWR! In time, Lord Exeter drafted in his own private stud of locomotives, all 0-4-2Ts consisting of a Fairbairn design of 1855, a Manning Wardle of 1865 and an 1867 Hawthorn. Whether Lord Exeter's railway operations were maintained at their earlier GN levels is not known, but they must have been diversified to cope with expansion of the S&E. In fact, the 1867 Hawthorn 0-4-2T was almost certainly ordered because of expansion - the opening of a branch line from Stamford to Wansford, on 2nd August that year. The need to house a third engine gave rise to an extension of Stamford shed. Because of the obviously delicate financial circumstances under which Lord Exeter had to run his railway, economy was the watchword and this was starkly reflected in the nature of the building enlargement. Quite simply, it consisted of nought but a wooden structure, some 27ft long, appended to the rear of the brick shed; the roof was tiled, gable type, and followed the contour of the original. Still no turntable was installed, but a new coal platform was put up, outside the front entrance and a water standpipe appeared opposite; whether these were added with the wooden building, or were later improvements, is not clear.

After seven years the two protagonists settled their dispute and the GNR returned, to formally lease the S&ER with effect from 1st January 1872. Lord Exeter's three engines were taken into GN stock as Nos.501, 502 and 503 but were replaced in 1876/7 by four new 0-4-2Ts built specially by Doncaster for the S&E. These were Class F7 and they took the number 501-3 and 161 - the last specially built as a spare engine. The second No.503 acquired the interesting nickname of the *Welland Diver* early in its career, by virtue of the fact that it spent some time sitting on the bottom of the river! The locomotive was eventually rescued but its chimney remained in a watery grave and is almost certainly still there today. By 1910 Stamford's little tank engines were working the following services - more lavish even than those of 1860:

Daily

Stamford-Essendine: 11 return passenger, 4 return mixed and 2 return goods.
Stamford-Wansford: 3 return passenger, 8 return mixed and 2 return goods.

Daily when necessary

Stamford GN station to Stamford MR station: 3 return goods.
Stamford-Lime and Foundry sidings: 3 return goods.

In addition to the above there was the interesting daily through coach from Kings Cross to Stamford, which left London at 5.00pm. A 'permanent' lease of the S&E was empowered by a GN Act of 3rd July 1894, remaining in force until the Essendine company came into the LNER at the Grouping. In 1913 the civil works over the branch were improved, to enable larger engines to operate it and Nos.501-3 went to the scrapyard - No.161 had preceded them by six years. Services between Essendine, Stamford and Wansford were then in the care of Stirling 0-4-4WTs and class G5 No.630 especially, was a long-term resident at Stamford.

By mid-1919 the days of the 0-4-4Ts were clearly numbered and a £55 job was authorised for Stamford shed, entailing the taking down of the original brick arches, reforming them to a wider dimension, and fixing doors. It was a preliminary to the arrival of class C2 4-4-2Ts at Stamford, in place of the Stirling engines. The Atlantic tanks began an association that would last for more than 38 years, and would be amongst the class' last duties. Three were allocated in 1920 and the same number were there at the end of October, 1931, by which time all services over the Stamford-Wansford line head been withdrawn - the precise date of withdrawal was 1st July 1929.

Stamford-Essendine continued to keep usually two C12s occupied, even into BR times. It was after Nationalisation that the inevitable wind-down commenced, with the closure of Stamford East (GN) station to passenger traffic on 2nd March 1957 - trains being diverted to the ex-Midland Stamford Town station. It would seem that Stamford engine shed was 'officially' closed from the same date, but it continued to accommodate the single engine now required to run the branch - for example, 4-4-2T No.67376 was in residence on 21st April 1958. Six months later, on 11th October 1958, No.67398 was the branch engine, which completed its two week stint at Stamford on that

Atlantic tanks at Stamford in marginally more prosperous times.

Coll. J.E. Kite

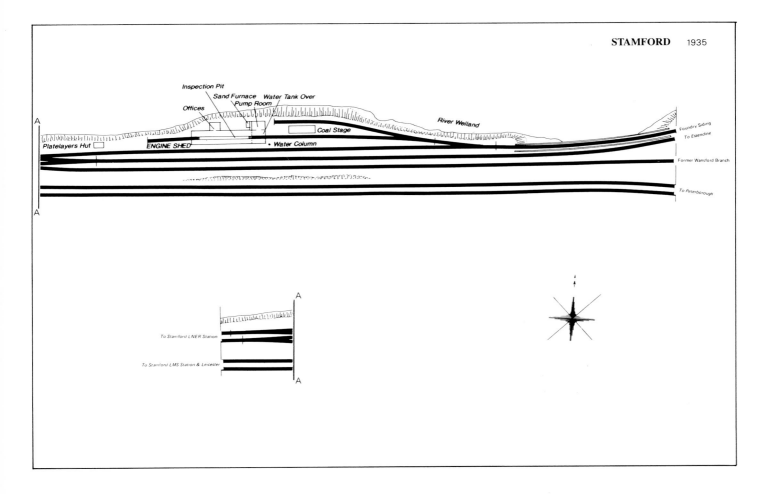

STAMFORD   1935

Inspection Pit
Sand Furnace   Water Tank Over
Offices   Pump Room
River Welland
Foundry Siding
To Essendine
Platelayers Hut
ENGINE SHED   Coal Stage
Water Column
Former Wansford Branch
To Peterborough

To Stamford LNER Station
To Stamford LMS Station & Leicester

day, and was to return to New England. Its replacement was ex-GC N5 0-6-2T No.69293 and it was that class that came to dominate services over the S&E, until final closure, on 15th June 1959. At that time, the engine shed was finally 'closed' to subsequently be demolished at a date yet undetermined. Today little trace remains of the GNR at Stamford but the former Midland Railway route from Peterborough of course still passes through the town.

LEICESTER

The city of Leicester had a population of around 100,000 even by mid-Victorian times and the potential traffic beckoned to the GN Board. The company obtained powers to build a railway into Leicester in an Act dated 28th July 1873, but it would be nine years before it achieved this aim, though an offshoot of what some considered to have been an ill-advised Joint Line venture with the LNWR, which Act received its Royal Assent on 30th July 1874. The eight mile branch from the GNR/LNWR Joint line at Maresfield Junction, to Leicester (Belgrave Road), opened to goods traffic on 15th May 1882, with passenger services commencing on 2nd October that same year. An optimistically grandiose terminus was provided, along with the usual goods shed and yard. The engine shed was perhaps more in keeping with the line's true worth, having only three roads and scaling 135ft by 40ft. Brick built, the dead-end shed featured the then fashionable northlight pattern roof. In fact, Belgrave Road was the first GN shed to have such a covering, launching a building style that would last for about fifteen years, until the company realised the maintenance liability it had bequeathed itself. Facilities at the shed were completed by a 45ft. turntable (later extended to 47ft.), and a coal stage, equipped by a basket crane and topped by a 56,000 gallon water tank. The only other addition which seems to have happened throughout the life of the shed was a set of shear-legs in the coal yard at the rear of the building. That was in the late 1890s and was followed by an 8 ton hand crane and tool van, for accident purposes - they do not seem to have been overtaxed.

A tortuous journey faced GN trains leaving Leicester, before they gained their own metals proper, in either the northward or southward direction. The former route was over the Joint line to Bottesford or Saxondale Junctions, on the Grantham-Nottingham line, while going

south, the Joint route was again used to Dryton Junction. From there GN services had to traverse some eighteen miles of the LNWR Northampton-Peterborough line, until the first minor junction with another GN line, at Wansford, followed by a further five miles of LNWR route, into Peterborough itself. The WTT of 1st October 1900 amply illustrates the secondary nature of the Leicester services, with passenger trains venturing merely along the branch to Loseby and back, or no further afield than Peterborough, virtually devoid of traffic of any sort.

With regard to which Locomotive District should have responsibility for Leicester, the GNR seemed to have some problem in deciding where it should lay! On opening, the shed was made subordinate to Grantham, which was in the North District, whereas Leicester itself was officially placed in Derby District! The anomalous situation took some time to be put right, when Leicester was reconciled with Colwick (Nottingham) at a date around the end of World War One - or possibly, not until the Grouping. Whatever the main shed though, Leicester initially sported a complement of about seven locomotive. At first these would have been the various Sturrock and Stirling 0-4-2, 2-4-0 and 0-6-0 classes, with the odd tank engine thrown in. With the gradual displacement of Stirling Singles from main line workings two of them arrived at Leicester, from Grantham, in January 1902. These were Nos.2 and 5 and they were joined, in 1905, by No.1006, also from Grantham. These thoroughbreds saw out their days on Belgrave Road passenger turns, especially to Peterborough, via Medbourne, a service which was withdrawn about 1916, never to be reinstated. At about the same time No.1006 moved to Leicester, Ivatt 4-4-0s were allocated for the first time, to start an association that would last for more than 40 years. His 0-6-0s were staple power too and in LNER days J1 Nos. 5007 and 5009 were particularly persistent residents. Ivatt J52 and Gresley J50 tanks were found on shunting duties and also taking their turn on the Loseby 'shuttles'.

To look after the engines, Belgrave Road had only a small staff. The shed foreman was invariably mechanically trained as he was more often than not without a skilled fitter. When a fitter was present he was usually temporarily outstationed from the main shed and undoubtedly would not have had the luxury of a mate. A few labourers for coaling and cleaning duties were probably available in the early days, but as time wore on the loco crews, themselves transitory in nature, would have had to 'do it yourself' more and more. Nevertheless, with the pride in the job that existed in those days, we may be sure that

No. 1339 at Leicester Belgrave Road. GN shed practice, in some unguessed at way, paralleled the LNWR, with early hipped roofs and subsequent (and largely unsatisfactory) essays in the northlight style. See, for instance, LMS Engine Sheds Vol.1, The LNWR, Hawkins & Reeve, Wild Swan, 1981.

Collection, W.A. Camwell

LEICESTER 1925

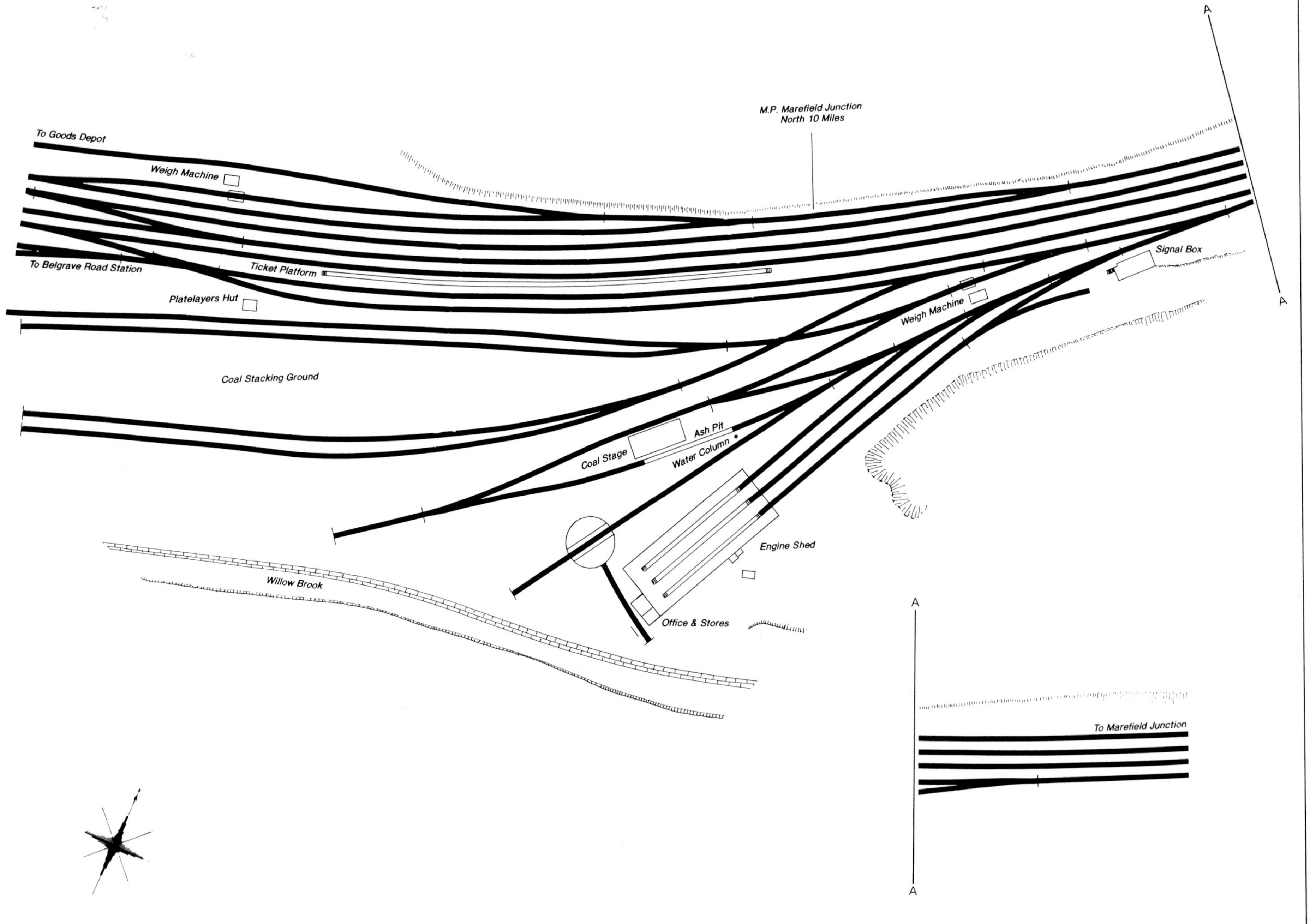

To Goods Depot

Weigh Machine

To Belgrave Road Station

Platelayers Hut

Coal Stacking Ground

Ticket Platform

Signal Box

Weigh Machine

M.P. Marefield Junction
North 10 Miles

Ash Pit
Water Column
Coal Stage

Engine Shed

Office & Stores

Willow Brook

To Marefield Junction

A — A

A — A

engine cleanliness generally lacked for little. Little change was experienced in LNER days, when Belgrave Road was supplied with locomotives from Colwick. The GN crews came from Colwick too of course, but this was amended in the last BR years; crews were supplied by the ex-GCR shed, but locos continued to be assigned from Colwick. All of which makes it difficult to be precise about the number of engines stationed at Belgrave Road at any one time - a figure which actually stood at three 4-4-0s and two 0-6-0s on the eve of Grouping. Based on the assumption that loco types would generally have kept to their pre-Grouping homes, it may be seen that the Belgrave Road allocation stayed at around five through the 1930s. But, just to confound that assumption, a former Colwick fitter, who spent some time at Belgrave Road, recalls a time in the '30s when the allocation was one J39 0-6-0 and three ex-GCR N5 0-6-2T! World War Two had its effect of course, to the extent that at one time in 1943, there were seven J2 0-6-0s at Belgrave Road. No doubt all manner of unusual types were to be seen there during those years: in October 1945 the complement was five J2 0-6-0s, Nos. 3071, 3074, 3075, 3076 and 3080. After the War matters quickly dropped back into the old routine but now B1 4-6-0s were regular performers on Nottingham - Leicester diagrams; even so some were regularly handled by Class J5 and J6 0-6-0s until 1955, evidenced by the allocation in October 1950: J6 64199, 64202, 64224, 64253, 64269, J11 64301 (Colwick's sole example at that time), J5 65497. In 1955, when Colwick received its first major influx of Thompson L1 2-6-4Ts they were well liked by the Colwick men and quickly became prime power on the Nottingham - Leicester turns.

Arrival of the L1s heralded the end for Belgrave Road shed. Not as a direct result it seems, but more because the building was ready to fall down! The northlight roof had largely succumbed around 1950 and with no remedial work being undertaken, the remaining structure became increasingly more tumbledown. Besides, such services as remained were being handled quite adequately by other depots so, in March 1955, Leicester Belgrave Road shed was closed, to be followed rapidly by demolition. The branch lingered for a few more years, keeping the water cranes and turntable in employment, but Belgrave Road's moment of glory - if it ever had one - was gone, and little now remains of one of the GN's less auspicious ventures.

HOLBEACH

This little shed was one of the most obscure, appearing and disappearing again by the end of 1866. It had been erected by the Norwich and Spalding Railway, whose Act was granted on 4th August 1853 and who subsequently arranged for the GN to work all its services. The line opened in sections, with the first eight miles, from Spalding to a temporary terminus at Holbeach, coming into use for goods only on 9th August 1858, passenger services commencing on 15th November in the same year. A small wooden shed was put up for the opening but details of its dimensions and ancillary facilities have not been unearthed.

The 1860 edition of the WTT shows five return mixed trains a day to Spalding, the first service leaving Holbeach at 7.55am and the last service terminating there: no Sunday trains were run. An engine would be required to stable overnight, sent out from Peterborough and doubtless changing over at Spalding when maintenance was needed or routine washouts became due. In those early years one can imagine the Holbeach duty entrusted to the likes of the Bury or Fairbairn goods engines, the first 0-6-0 or even the early Sharps and Hawthorn passenger types, and the tank engine rebuilds of those pioneer locos.

Extension of the N&S, to Sutton Bridge, was completed on 1st July 1862, and from Sutton Bridge to (Kings) Lynn, in November 1864. Holbeach shed was used by the locomotives working the extended services, including the interesting portion from Sutton Bridge to Lynn, which was operated by the contractor who built the line, using engines hired from the GN. This lasted until 1st August 1866, when the Bourn & Lynn Joint Committee took over services along the whole route. A GNR/MR partnership, the Bourne & Lynn was a precursor of the M&GNR proper, the line through Holbeach later forming a part of it.

This effectively brought to an end any need for a shed at Holbeach; it closed in December 1866 and was immediately removed, to make way for a new passing loop.

Belgrave Road hardly saw any intensive use but nevertheless deteriorated with almost unhealthy haste. By the 1950s there was little of it left.

W.A. Camwell

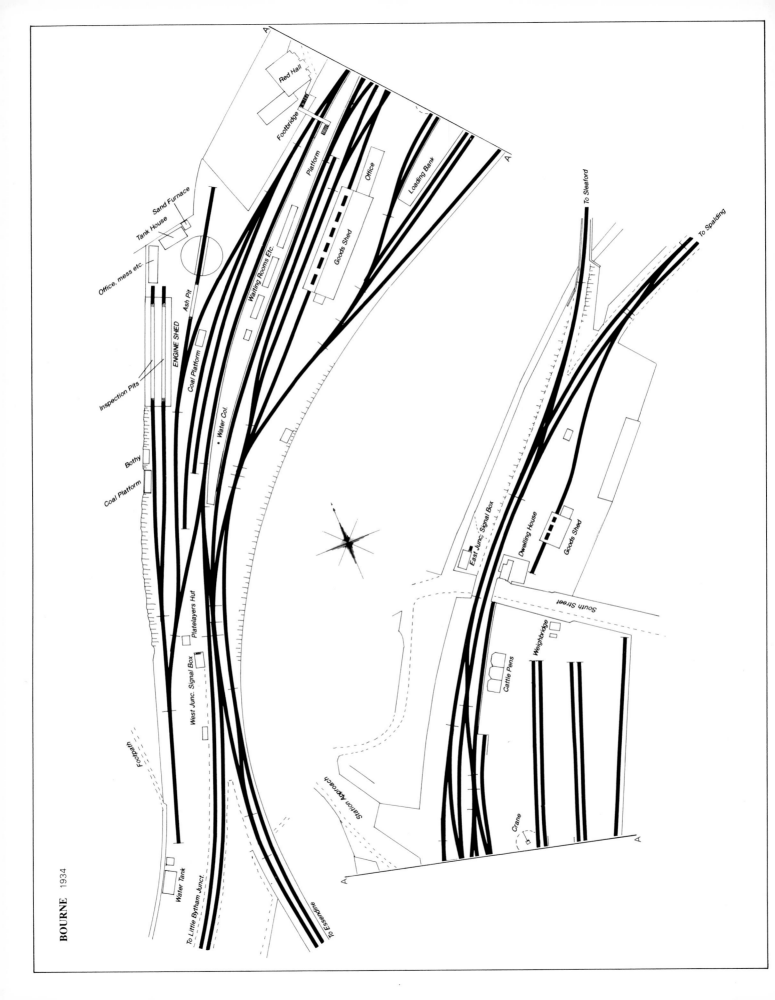

BOURNE 1934

BOURNE

The little south Lincolnshire town of Bourn (later and more widely known as Bourn e greeted the first of four railway routes on 16th May 1860, the Bourn & Essendine Railway, incorporated by Act of Parliament on 12th August 1857 and worked from the beginning by the GNR. The terminus was starting (7.10 a.m.) and finishing point for the Bourn-Essendine service, described in the 1860 Working Time Table as six weekday and one Sunday return trains; no turntable was provided and a tank engine, probably a Sharp 2-2-2, would presumably have been outstationed, from Peterborough. It was housed, according to a contemporary map, in a combined engine and carriage shed, a dead-end building of unusual layout, single road 42 ft. x 18 ft. engine shed at the front and a 50 ft. x 14 ft. carriage shed behind. A water tank, supplied from a well, stood outside the shed entrance on its own tankhouse but no fuelling arrangements are evident on the plan, though assuredly, a coke supply was laid on somewhere - on a platform under the tank, likely enough.

On 16th May 1864 the GN Act for absorption of the Bourn & Essendine was passed and on 29th June in the next year, the Act was granted for construction of another independent line the GN would come to work - the Sleaford and Bourne Railway. Before this could open, however, a second railway arrived at Bourne, on 1st August 1866, the Midland & Eastern Railway, a company supported jointly by the GN and Midland Railway, and running over the 9/1-2/ eastwards to Spalding. Although the way and works of the M & ER were maintained by the Great Northern, it seems sure that its services would have been worked by Spalding shed and kept separate from those on the Bourne - Essendine line. Bourne locomotive shed survived therefore to witness the opening on 2nd January 1872 of the third route, the Sleaford & Bourne; goods services commenced in October 1871, with passengers following on 2nd January 1872. The S & BR provided a Doncaster-built 45 ft. turntable and even though there was now a through GN route, between Essendine and Sleaford, the engine shed at Bourne continued in use, albeit in altered form. The carriage shed portion was removed and access to the engine shed made from the former dead-end. The track went through the shed and continued past the water tank for about 30 ft., to a buffer stop that closely encroached upon the down platform road. The building remained thus for the next twenty or so years, until the coming of yet a fourth line, the shortest, and yet probably the most notable.

The Bourne & Cottesmore Railway was sponsored jointly by the GN and MR and had Acts passed on 28th June 1888 and 24th June 1889. It ran westwards from Bourne, to make an end-on junction with the Midland line from Saxby, just east of the MR bridge over the GN main line at Bytham. In the event, the Bourne & Cottesmore enjoyed but a very short independent existence. Its (goods only) services did not commence until 5th June 1893, only 27 days before the Midland & Great Northern Joint Railway came into being, the new company taking over the B & CR's route.

Exactly one month before inception of the M & GNR, the Great Northern Board had opened tenders for construction of a new station at Bourne, complete with goods shed, stables, 'other works' and - a new engine shed. Tender prices ranged from £15,715 to £19,260, and the job went, naturally, to the lowest - from Arnold and Sons, a contractor often used by the GN. Quite when the new shed opened is uncertain, but passenger services commenced running over the Bourne & Cottesmore link on 1st May 1894, so it is logical to assume the new station would have been largely complete by then, and therefore the engine shed too. Quite how the building was arranged, whether one or two roads, has not so far been discovered. The only hints come in M & GNR Minutes of 1897-1898

..... 21st April 1897. The existing engine shed at Bourne, belonging to the GNR, but on land owned by the Joint Committee, should be transferred at an agreed price. The 'present two engine sheds' should be extended to accommodate six engines...... It is not really possible to clarify this reference, though it may be a simple error of wording - further references run thus: *4th May 1897: The Great Northern Engine Shed* note singular *at Bourne to be transferred to the Joint Committee. 6th July 1897: Estimated cost of extending the engine shed: £1,650. 2nd November 1897: Bourne engine shed extension contracted to be let to Messrs. J.W.Rowe, for £1,412/13/0d. 3rd May 1898: Bourne engine shed extension completed.*

The engine shed extended by Messrs. J.W. Rowe stood to the north of the very first building of 1860 which almost certainly had been closed and demolished in 1893/4. The new building was a two road brick-built structure, measuring 165 ft. x 35 ft., with both roads just passing through, to buffer stops immediately at the rear. It had a period northlight roof with tiles on the unglazed faces and the very unusual feature of square-section wooden supporting columns, instead

Bourne on 3rd October 1936. If the GN had remained in charge doubtless the place would have been a ruinous hovel by this time.
W.A. Camwell

Bourne, empty, in Joint days, or shortly after.

W.A. Camwell

of the normal tubular cast iron variety. Another notable feature of the shed was the two fireplaces provided along each side of the building. They stood 84 ft. apart, centred, and faced their counterparts on the other wall. The obvious purpose of the fireplaces was to keep the interior of the shed warm - a necessary precaution in such a notoriously bleak spot in wintertime. Another factor that may have bearing is that the shed faced north-south, although the site could more easily have accommodated it facing east-west. In the position erected therefore, Bourne's prevailing east wind would not have gained access to the building. The water supply continued to come from the well, but now was stored in a 19,000 gallon tank - probably of 1893/4 construction - sited in the yard, where also stood an uncovered coal platform. The 1872 Sleaford & Bourne 45 ft. turntable remained through all this and now lay between the shed and station; by 1920 it was being maintained by the MR, and in 1930 the LNER replaced it with a Ransomes & Rapier-built 60 ft. example.

With completion of the M & GN route it was not very long before it came to dominate traffic through Bourne. A natural progression from this was that the shed should be taken over by the M & GN, an event recorded as detailed above. No record of rental charges or purchase price has been found, but it is interesting to note that the M & GN paid the GN 5d. (2p) for each tender or tankful of water taken at Bourne. It was probably at the time of transfer that Bourne became outstation of Spalding, a situation which pertained until the end of the M & GN, when Bourne and Spalding became subordinate to Boston. As an aside, the M & GN also took over the GN station house, formerly an Elizabethan mansion known as 'The Red House' and supposedly where Guy Fawkes and Co. met, to arrange their dastardly deed!

While Bourne was still operated by the GN it housed the usual Sturrock and Stirling smaller engines - 0-4-2, 2-4-0 and 0-6-0s with 0-4-2 and 0-4-4 tanks replacing the Sharps and Hawthorn rebuilds. Midland Railway engines, which had been seen at Bourne since the Midland & Eastern's inception, had, with the opening of the Bytham link become an even more common sight, including three engines actually allocated to Bourne, transferred from Spalding. These were two 0-4-4Ts for Saxby passenger trains and an 0-6-0, for daily through goods service to London, via Saxby. Those duties ceased when M & GN engines took over, but haulage continued with MR-designed locomotives, in the shape of Johnson's 4-4-0s and 0-6-0s, both types forming the M & GN's initial standard stock. They were joined from 1900 by a dozen GN-pattern Ivatt 0-6-0s, which were used mainly on the western section and would therefore have been regular denizens of Bourne

shed. From then on the whole gamut of M & GN motive power would be seen at Bourne - through to the ubiquitous LMS Ivatt class 4 2-6-0.

Locos off the Great Northern itself still required access to the shed and were seen every day, working in from each end of the GN through route, on passengers and goods, and shunting at Bourne, before returning whence they came. Because of this, a second coal stage with separate enginemen's bothy were put up, probably in 1897, between the shed and running lines, thereby allowing GN engines to refuel without interfering with M & GN locomotive movements. This constant GN influence was maintained throughout and even at the end of LNER days for instance, Bourne's three pilot duties were performed thus: Number 1: Sleaford-based engine, arrived at 1.24 p.m. on a pick-up goods, which it shunted, then formed up and worked the 3.15 p.m. goods back to Sleaford. Number 2: Engine from Bourne shed, which had worked in on 2.35 p.m. ex-Spalding (Spalding No. 2 Pilot duty): shunted Bourne yard 4.35 p.m. - 6.20 p.m., then departed on 6.25 p.m. goods to Spalding. Number 3: Peterborough engine, arrived working 7.10 p.m. passenger ex-Essendine, shunted Bourne yard until 9.15 p.m., formed up and then worked 9.15 p.m. goods to Peterborough. (This engine - invariably J4 or J5 - had, in fact, worked the Essendine-Bourne passenger service all day, consisting of seven weekday return trips with a Bourne footplate crew working the middle shift).

No. 2 duty follows what naturally would have been M & GN practice, but Nos. 1 and 3 were obviously throwbacks to GNR days.

Such duties would have lasted until the demise began of all the lines out of Bourne. The first to go was the Essendine route - passenger and goods trains ending on 18th June 1951; closure of the Midland and Great Northern Joint followed on 1st March 1959, but only the Bourne-Saxby section was initially abandoned. Spalding-Bourne was retained, used as a long siding for goods trains that ran on to Billingborough, on the Sleaford route. The latter had lost its passenger service as early as 22nd September 1930, followed by complete closure of the Sleaford-Billingborough portion on 28th July 1956. However, Billingborough-Bourne continued to see a daily return goods train until even that remaining service was withdrawn, from 15th June 1964, followed by Spalding-Bourne, on 5th April 1965.

Long before this sad end, Bourne shed itself had closed - in 1953 - to linger, slowly decaying, until it was demolished in turn, eleven years later. The turntable had been taken out some years previously, for re-use at Peterborough East, from where it was in turn saved for posterity by the Nene Valley Railway.

SPALDING

For many years a large trading centre, by way of the River Welland, Spalding's business in corn, wood, coal and timber, plus the products of its breweries and bone, flour and saw mills, ensured it would be on the GN map from an early date. So it was, when on 17th October 1848, the first section of the 'Loop' line opened, from Peterborough, via Spalding, to Boston and Lincoln. The projected Ambergate, Nottingham, Boston & Eastern Junction Railway also had designs upon Spalding and that company's deposited plans include one for what would have been Spalding's first engine shed. It was intended to site it north of the station, but beyond the Wensover Road level crossing, on the west side of the line. The proposed building was 120 ft. x 60 ft. covering just two roads, which converged just before a 40 ft. turntable. From the turntable another spur gave access to the main line. Of course the Ambergate Company failed to get beyond Grantham, so the planned shed never materialised.

The GNR did install a 23 ft. turntable and watering points at Spalding, the latter acquiring a steam pump in an £80 job authorised on 15th April 1851. The Norwich & Spalding Railway opened on 9th August 1858, from Spalding to Holbeach, where a small engine shed was put up to house the engine working the line, but in December 1865, in anticipation of further developments at Spalding, the GN General Manager commented that *a larger supply of water would soon be required for locomotive purposes.* As Spalding Waterworks Company had already given notice of the termination of its existing agreement, from 6th January 1866, the General Manager had asked the Locomotive Engineer to see if an independent supply could be arranged. Sturrock had reported back, saying that given the nature of the ground he did not think another supply could be arranged for an outlay of less than £4,000. The Board rapidly resolved that an offer should be made to Spalding Waterworks to supply any amount of water, at 6d. per 1,000 gallons. As no further mention of the matter has been found it is assumed the waterworks company went for the idea.

The 1866 developments at Spalding concerned the opening of the Midland & Eastern Railway, to Bourne, a company whose Act was passed on 29th July 1862 supported by the GNR and MR, who would work all services jointly. The Midland & Eastern route was brought into use on 1st August 1866 and part of the works at Spalding included a two road brick-built locomotive shed, having arched entrances at each end and a slated gable roof. 50 ft. by 30 ft., it was put up by the Midland Railway, but along with the rest of the M & E's 'way and works', the GNR was responsible for the building's maintenance. M & E rental charges were shared by the GN and MR, at £24 per annum each, but fuelling arrangements were divided, GN engines getting theirs from an open platform which the company maintained, while the Midland coaled from wagons. Around the mid-1880s there was talk of a divided coal stage and the GN engineer was asked to draw up a plan but nothing came of this. Later, the platform would have a manually operated bucket crane installed, but not until BR times was a (partial) cover provided.

On 1st July 1883 the Midland & Eastern was incorporated into the confusingly named Eastern & Midlands Railway, an act that presaged formation of the Midland & Great Northern Joint Railway exactly ten years later. The E & MR was another Great Northern/Midland joint concern and individual areas of responsibility remained unchanged from M & ER days. So, parochial rates on Spalding shed were paid by the GN, who also settled water and gas charges, and had the task of maintaining the turntable. The latter survived opening of the Spalding to Lincoln GN/GE sponsored line in 1881 but on 2nd June 1887, the GN loco engineer at last conceded that at 23 feet, Spalding turntable was less than useful. Stirling asked for £1,000 to site a new 'table by the station (not the shed, which lay a few hundred yards south), and by June 1888, a 44 ft. 7 ins. turntable was in place. (Years later it would have its capacity enlarged by one foot, by use of extension rails).

From 1st January 1892 the Joint Committee put up the rent for Spalding shed to £84. Stirling and Johnson (MR) agreed that the rental cost, and £56/10/0d per year, for maintenance, gas, etc. should be shared and 1/6d be charged for each boiler washout - indicating the use of 3,000 gallons thereby. The GN had to face these new charges for one year and eight months beyond the formation of the Midland & Great Northern Railway, on 1st July 1893. The costs were ended by an agreement of mid-January 1895, in that the company's locomotives were immediately to be withdrawn from Joint Line duties, and from Spalding shed entirely, from 2nd February 1895. With the Great Northern's departure, M & GN engines were to assume full responsibility for work on the line. It was the GN's passing from this particular scene that one of those instances of staunch employee loyalty to the company came into focus, receiving mention in the GN

Spalding on 20th March 1938.

H.C.Casserley.

Spalding, of exquisite neatness, on 23rd October 1936, with engines Nos. 36, 74, 76, 77 and 90.

W.A Camwell

Spalding in 1948. The tiny place managed a cosmopolitan atmosphere, with a variety of visiting engines even in BR days. They usually heralded from South Lynn, March, Boston, Grantham and so on but B12s from Yarmouth Beach and B16s from York could be found together in 1957.

Photomatic

Way & Works Minutes, those of the Joint Committee - and probably the MR too! It seems that immediately before the M & GN takeover, the GN used to stable 4 engines at Spalding - two outside and two occupying all available space inside the shed. At the same time the MR kept two engines there (but for long would have preferred four!), these also being parked outside of course. The number of M & GN locos stabled (in the open) is unknown, but with the prospect of a complete removal of GN locomotives the M & GN claimed use of inside stabling and quickly took it up. However, with only two days to go before the GN departed Spalding, on 30th January 1895, a GNR driver, shunting engines, pointedly stabled his own company's machines inside the shed, forcing those of the M & GN to remain firmly outside! This personal comment on what the driver obviously thought was a backward step for his employers brought a sharply worded letter from Mr. Marriott of the M & GN, to Mr. Grindling, at Kings Cross. What Grindling said in his reply is unrecorded but it can be assumed that GN driver had a good laugh only two months later, when on 1st April 1895, the M & GN commented that gale damage to Spalding engine shed would cost £2,000 to put right!

From 1866 Spalding was an outstation of Peterborough, which supplied Sturrock and Stirling 0-4-2, 2-4-0 and 0-6-0 types. Shunting would have largely been in the care of tank engine rebuilds of early types, soon superseded by Stirling's early saddle tank designs. From June 1893 three MR locomotives were allocated to Spalding - two 0-4-4Ts and an 0-6-0, for work to Saxby, via Bourne. The 0-6-0 was soon moved to Bourne shed, while the two tanks remained at Spalding until full M & GN working commenced, when the 0-4-4T also went to Bourne. Even so, GNR (LNER) types did visit regularly, as may be seen from the following list of engines found on shed on 20th May 1934; M & GN 4-4-0 Nos. 21 and 27, 42 and 49; 0-6-0s Nos. 84 and 88 and LNER J6 No. 3593. On Tuesdays - Spalding market day - a GN Atlantic, of large or small boiler versions, would work a train from Peterborough and because the Spalding 'table was too small, the engine would make use of the M & GN triangle Spalding No. 1 - Welland Bank Junction-Cuckoo Junction and back to Spalding shed.

The M & GNJR ceased to be a separate entity on 1st October 1936 and LNER engines reappeared in numbers, sub-shedded again from New England, under the charge of a foreman fitter from Doncaster. Although workings over the former M & GN remained Spalding's main preoccupation, the depot did have a few turns elsewhere. On all services, Ivatt 4-4-0s were common, including the pioneer No. 3400, by then LNER Class D3. Regular visitors to Spalding for servicing were ex-GC B2 4-6-0s, working London trains from Immingham, handing over to Ivatt Atlantics or K3s to continue southwards.

By the summer of 1946, the WTT listed the following duties, weekdays only:

Dep. shed 4.55 a.m. Arr. Down Yard 5.00 a.m. No. 2 Pilot, shunting and transfers to sugar beet factory, then works 2.35 p.m. goods to Bourne. Arr. 4.35 p.m. Shunt until 6.20 p.m.; Dep. 6.25 p.m. goods to Spalding Arr. 8.30 p.m.

Dep. shed 5.45 a.m. Arr. Up Yard 5.50 a.m. Dep. 6.10 a.m. goods to South Lynn. (As required runs to Holbeach only).

Dep. shed 5.55 a.m. Arr. Up Yard 6.00 a.m. Dep. 7.10 a.m. goods to South Lynn.

Dep. shed 9.20 a.m. Arr. Down Yard 9.25 a.m. Dep. 9.35 a.m. goods to Lincoln.

Dep. shed 11.45 a.m. Arr. Up Yard 11.50 a.m. No. 1 Pilot, shunting Up and Down Yards, 4.00 a.m. Mon. to 6.00 a.m. Sun

Dep. shed 11.45 a.m. Arr. Up Yard 11.50 a.m. Dep. 11.45 a.m. SO Fruit to Sutton Bridge. 12.00 noon SX Fruit to Sutton Bridge

Dep. shed 1.00 p.m. Arr. Up Yard 1.05 p.m. Dep. 1.15 p.m. goods to Sutton Bridge.

Dep. shed 1.45 p.m. Arr. Down Yard 1.50 p.m. No.3 Pilot, shunting Beet Factory and Down Yard, 2.00 p.m.to 8.00 p.m. or earlier if finished.

Dep. shed 2.05 p.m. Arr. Up Yard 2.10 p.m. Dep. 2.14 p.m. goods to Holbeach.

Dep. shed 2.25 p.m. Down Yard 2.30 p.m. No.2 Pilot, shunting Down Yard, then works 3.10 p.m. SX goods to Donington Road; 4.35 p.m. goods to Gosberton; 6.15 p.m. goods to Spalding; shunt; 11.30 p.m.

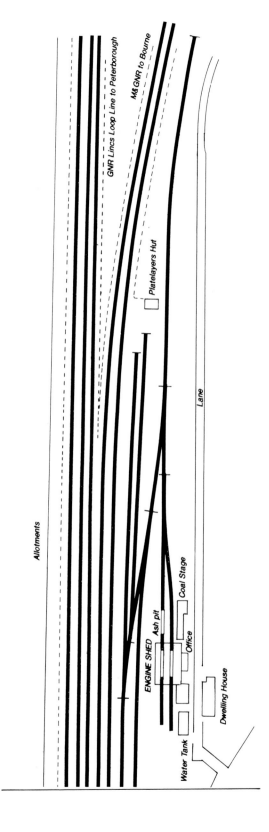

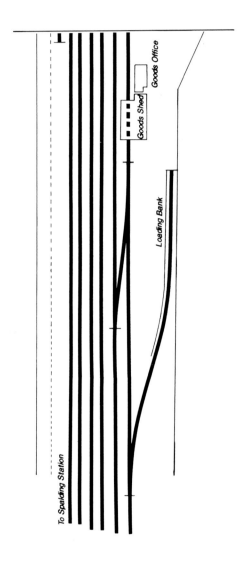

Allotments

GNR Lincs Loop Line to Peterborough

M&GNR to Bourne

Platelayers Hut

Lane

ENGINE SHED

Ash pit

Coal Stage

Office

Water Tank

Dwelling House

To Spalding Station

Goods Shed

Goods Office

Loading Bank

goods to Whitemoor; light engine to Spalding.

Dep. shed 2.30 p.m. Arr. Up Yard 2.35 p.m. Dep. 5.05 p.m. SX goods to New England.6.40 p.m. SO goods to New England.

Dep. shed 3.30 p.m. Arr Down Yard 3.55. p.m. Dep. 4.05 p.m. goods to Doncaster.

Dep. shed 4.30 p.m. Arr. LMS Yard 4.32 p.m. Dep. 6.10 p.m. goods to Saxby.

For a typical allocation necessary to work the above, we turn appropriately to a visit made on Sunday 12th May 1946, when the following were stabled at the shed : 0-6-0 J3 No.081, J4 No.082, J6 Nos. 3526, 3535, 3542, 3558, 3567, 3597, 3603, 3634, J17 No.8171, 2-8-0 O3 No.3465 (from Frodingham). Note the absence of tank engines - a long standing phenomenon, which came to an end in 1948, with allocation of a Stirling 0-6-0ST, succeeded by an LMS standard 3F 0-6-0T, then an ex-GER J66 0-6-0T. In 1938 there had been a trial of a C12 on local passengers to Bourne, but after only one day the engine went back to New England shed.

A bizarre resident of Spalding, from July 1940 to July 1943, was armoured locomotive WD 'M'. In reality this was ex-GER Class F5 2-4-2T No.7748 and it was equipped with an LMS-supplied armoured tender, to increase its radius of action. Needless to say it saw none and was restored to its normal condition on being 'demobbed'.

On 29th December 1957 Spalding was made subordinate to Boston shed which, on the same day - a Sunday - had fifteen engines recorded as outstationed at Spalding, 4MT 2-6-0s Nos.43059, 43061, 43062, 43064, 43065, 43080, 43083, 43085 and diesel No.11160. The change of 'parent' shed was the last change of significance at Spalding, which continued to function until Monday 7th March 1960. From that date the shed was closed, leaving diesels D2023, D2024, D3490 and 11179 to stable in the yards. In fact the last steam engine left on Saturday March 5th, 43095 giving valedictory salute on its whistle as it went to work an evening goods to Whitemoor. Earlier in the day the departure of 43147 had been strangely appropriate, as the modern engine still carried a M&GNR tablet catcher on its tender.

After closure, the turntable was taken out during the following April and subsequently the shed was demolished - a fate that in time befell four of the six railway routes into the town. The original Spalding - Boston section of the 'Loop'; the M&GN, including the 1893 avoiding line; the GN/GE Joint route to March - all these are gone. Today, Spalding is famous for its bulb fields and annual flower festival, which in part explains why it remains, precariously placed at the centre of a secondary route - the 'Loop' from Werrington Junction and on, via the former GN/GE Joint Railway to Sleaford.

Ivatt 2-6-0s were increasingly common in the 1950s and Nos. 43060 and 43085 were at the shed on 4th October 1953. No less than a dozen further locomotives were also present: 64172, 64191, 64207, 64210, 64217, 64224, 64231, 64258, 64278, 64279, 68846 and 68880. A sobering reminder of the traffic levels now long vanished.

B.K.B. Green

Spalding shed in the autumn of 1953.

Photomatic

Spalding, 16th march 1958.

B. Hilton

WATER

The steam locomotive consumes vast quantities of water through-out its work. When one adds to the locomotives the myriad steam-powered pumps and workshop machines, foundries, hydraulically-powered goods depots, boiler washout apparatus and, in later years, electricity generating plants, employed by all railways, then the finding and distribution of water can be seen to have been a matter of prime importance.

Like all other companies, the GNR spent huge sums on the provision of adequate water, discovering very early on that not to do so could cause expensive problems! Such an instance was noted by the Lincolnshire Committee, in December 1848, after only a few months of the company's operations. At Boston, Lincoln and other places, water cranes were so placed as to require engines to leave their trains to replenish supplies. Furthermore, at Boston, Mr. Peto, of Peto & Betts, was employing several men in the task of pumping water and charging the company three shillings and sixpence (17p) a day, making a profit of one shilling (5p) in the process!

The tremendous amount of water used, even in the early days, was well illustrated on 23rd November 1865, in a traffic census at Hitchin (taken because of severe congestion south of there), revealing the following information about water consumption at just one of the company's minor centres:

In the Down direction, 78 trains took water - 17 GN passenger and 37 goods; 8 MR passenger and 10 goods; 6 GER passenger and goods.

In the Up direction, 79 trains took water - 17 GN passenger and 36 goods; 8 MR passenger and 12 goods; 6 GER passenger and goods.

Plus two locomotives taking water at the MR shed.

Therefore, if a not over-generous 1,250 gallons was taken, on

Hornsey water softener with attendant sludge tender and accompanying mire, 1936.

The Thompson Society

average, by each of the 157 trains and 2 MR locos, this would mean the day's consumption to have been nearly 200,000 gallons, not counting any that must have been taken by locos standing at the GN shed. This works out to something in the region of 73,000,000 gallons a year! Further figures, for Sunday 19th, to Saturday 25th November 1865, show 822 locomotives taking water.

Moving on to the turn of the century, the following are details of annual water consumption and costs, for the shed at Ardsley:

1898: 29,674,000 gallons 8d. 1,000 gallons: £ 992-2-8d.
1899: 37,204,000 gallons 8d. 1,000 gallons: £1244- 2-8d.
1900: 40,498,000 gallons 8d. 1,000 gallons: £1353-18-8d.
1901: 39,640,000 gallons 8d. 1,000 gallons: £1324- 6-8d.

(The above price calculations include what is assumed to have been a small 'annual charge' of three or four pounds: the suppliers were East and West Ardsley Urban District Councils and Morley Corporation. (To the above must be added some 16 million gallons a year, taken from the GN's own borehole, on site).

To expand on the above costs, figures of estimated water consumption for the whole of the GN's West Riding District, for the year 1895, make interesting reading. At that time the company were paying widely varying charges for its water. These ranged from the half penny per 1,000 gallons, from Brierley Local Board and Pudsey U.D.C., through the sixpence and sixpence halfpenny for Leeds and Bradford Corporations' supplies, respectively, to the exorbitant 11d per 1,000 gallons of Halifax Corporation's water. When applied to the total estimated water consumption for the year, of 164,586,000 gallons, these varied costs gave a total bill of £5,624-3-8d; a considerable sum in those days - and this for just one of the GNR Districts! As a pointer to costs in other Districts, we move forward a few years, to 1899. On 27th July that year, Ivatt reported that annual water costs in the Locomotive Districts were:

LONDON District, at an average 6d - 1,000 gallons: £12,000
NOTTS District, at an average 6d - 1,000 gallons: £ 504
BRFRD District, at an average 6d - 1,000 gallons: £ 2,000
LEEDS District, at an average 6d - 1,000 gallons: £ 1,412

From the above and preceding table it would seem that in Leeds District, Ardsley was responsible for about 88% of total water expenditure: this was almost certainly not the case and the dis-crepancy, together with the very low figure for Nottingham, is inexplicable.

As the system developed, it can be appreciated that the company would have been wise to forecast its water requirements as accurately as possible, and arrange for suitable supplies to be on hand. In this way a pattern emerged, whereby in urban areas water came from the local waterworks company, or council, while in country districts the usual sources were rivers, streams, wells etc. Sometimes, when the costs were justified, water from a particularly good source would be piped over quite long distances. Such an example was Bawtry, where from 1902, River Idle water was piped to Scrooby troughs, some two miles south, while in 1906/7, a pipeline was run to Doncaster shed, about eight miles north. The latter was a major exercise with the contract for the fifteen inch main let on 6th August 1906, to Stanton Iron Company and Docura & Sons, at an authorised cost of no less than £20,000!

In later years, when traffic and thereby the demand for water had increased, the GN resorted more and more to boring for supplies on its own property, hoping to create wells of the artesian type, or where necessary, of the pumped type. These endeavours met with mixed success. Boring really started in earnest in 1899, after Ivatt had presented the figures given in the last table. Large experimental bores were started at the following places:

LONDON District: New Southgate £ 650
BRDFRD district: Bradford Loco £ 500
LEEDS district: Leeds (Copley Hill) £1,000
NOTTS district: (Location unknown) £ 650

In addition, a catchpit and main were to be installed at Soothhill Tunnel (between Batley and Woodkirk), at a cost of £500, to tap the water resources of that very wet subway. Total outlay in this flurry of drilling was at least £3,300.

WATER SOFTENING

Despite the many exhortations of the GNR analysts, installation of water softening plants was never undertaken by the company. However, in 1902, after much canvassing by the 'Desrumaux Automatic Water Softener Co. Ltd.', the GN did accept a small version of that firm's patent equipment, for a period of trial. It was installed at Ardsley, and the terms of the trial were that the plant should work for two years, at a cost to the GN of £100: for comparison purposes, the GN would have the option of installing a high capacity (220,000 gallons/day) D.A.W.S. plant, at a cost of £2,500; the trial softening apparatus was duly installed, but unfortunately, the outcome is so far unknown. Presumably the company was not too impressed, despite its contemporaries (like the Great Central and Hull & Barnsley Railways') adoption of softening in a big way and it was left to the LNER to foot what must have been a very sizeable bill for the large scale provision of softening apparatus. The LNER soon noticed that boiler repair costs were very much lower in the Scottish area, with its inherently softer water and Gresley brought in T.H. Turner, a metallurgist and chemist to work with a group specifically to deal with the matter of water-softening. Turner was very influential and had much to do with the programme of softener installations that began in the early 1930s, plants appearing at numerous places along the former GN (and GE) main lines, and other places. All major GN sheds outside the West Riding Division were equipped with softeners, as were the water troughs, and the tall circular structures, with attendant paraphernalia and old locomotive tenders, in use as sludge carriers, became a normal part of the railway scene. Not before time, when one re-reads some of those 1905 analysts' reports!

An adjunct of water treatment, the automatic blow-down valve, while adopted by the LMS, was rejected by Gresley. Although such valves did prolong intervals between washouts, and reduced priming, Gresley's objection was that it wasted heat (he was a great devotee of hot water washout plants). Despite the LNER's expenditure though, water treatment could only be effective if *all* feed waters were softened, and this was never achieved by the company.

WATER TROUGHS

Although water troughs were in common use on a number of railways, well before the end of the nineteenth century, it was mid-1899 before the GN considered their employment. Ivatt presented a report nominating two sites, at Werrington and just north of the River Trent at Newark; to allow through running between London and Leeds. Each set would consist of troughs in the up and down mainlines, supply tank and feed pipes and cost £5,000 - £6,000. The set at Newark would entail extra cost for a new tank, pumping engine and pipes, to the tune of about £2,500. In addition an occupation road, crossing the lines at the proposed site of the troughs, would have to be closed, at a further cost of £100 - £150. The total cost of the exercise would be about £14,000, plus £15 - £20 each engine, for fitting pick-up apparatus. Ivatt strongly recommended early action on this matter. The GN Board concurred, and in late 1900, the first set opened, at Werrington. The actual date of the first pick-up was 18th November 1900, when locomotives Nos. 1366 and 1369 made an experimental run in each direction. The Newark set - actually at Muskham - opened a short while later. A further set followed, a little way north of Scrooby, in 1902, obtaining its water from the River Idle, at Bawtry. It was this third set, in fact, that finally allowed non-stop running from London to north of Doncaster. Some confusion had reigned in the railway press at the time, when the January 1902 issue of 'Locomotives & Railways' reported, in the section devoted to the GN, that:
.....additional water troughs are being laid down between Hatfield and Welwyn..... This report, although in error at the time, did point to the fact that there was need for yet a fourth set, in the 76 miles separating Kings Cross and Peterborough. It did finally appear at Langley, a few miles south of Stevenage, where trial borings had been made in 1908. The new troughs were brought into use in October 1918, six years after first authorised, and shortly after completion of the Hertford Loop line, to Langley Junction. The Langley set was identical to the earlier installations, in being sited in up and down fast lines only, with the troughs themselves 600 yards in length, and measuring 18 ins. wide by 6 ins. deep. Water depth was, however, no greater than four-and-a-half inches, which was considered best to avoid excessive wastage and

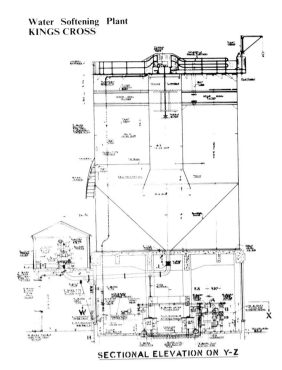

Water Softening Plant
KINGS CROSS

SECTIONAL ELEVATION ON Y-Z

avoid flooding the track. Each trough held about 6,000 gallons, from a 14,000 gallon tank beside the line, under the control of automatic level valves. The water for Langley came initially from a borehole 100 yards deep with boiler/pump house, to a 100,000 gallon storage tank, from where gravity took it to the lineside tank. Cost of the installation had been some £15,537, quite an increase over that for the initial two sets, sixteen years before!

Before water softening was initiated, the site at Muskham, receiving its water direct from the River Trent, presented the GN with two unusual phenomena. The first was the growth of algae in the troughs, while the second was the almost permanent colonies of minnows and sticklebacks! Fish are not normally known for their intelligence so the enginemens' stories of the fish swimming to the far end of the troughs, when they heard a train coming, can safely be assumed to have been fanciful! It is not known if Scrooby troughs shared the same features with their River Idle water, but softening removed the algae and fish eventually of course. However, the widespread introduction of the process was a slow business and eyewitnesses have told of fish in locomotive tanks into the 1950s. Perhaps the famous escapade of the Reverend W. Awdry's Thomas the Tank Engine and the fish had its founding in fact!

As the table of water supply points shows, the 1906 estimates of annual water consumption at troughs averaged about 50 million gallons, for each of the three sets then in use. This equates to some 68 trains a day, picking up at each location, if the average pick-up is taken as 2,000 gallons (4,000 gallons would become the norm with the arrival of the Pacifics). This was proof enough of the trough's value, which makes it all the more surprising that the GN tarried so long before resorting to their use.

WATER STORAGE

Having found a supply of water, it then must be taken to a storage vessel of some type, from where gravity could be utilised for its final delivery. On the GN such storage devices were, in a few rare instances, of wooden construction, but wrought iron tanks were usually employed costing, in the first orders placed (on 22nd June 1848) as follows:

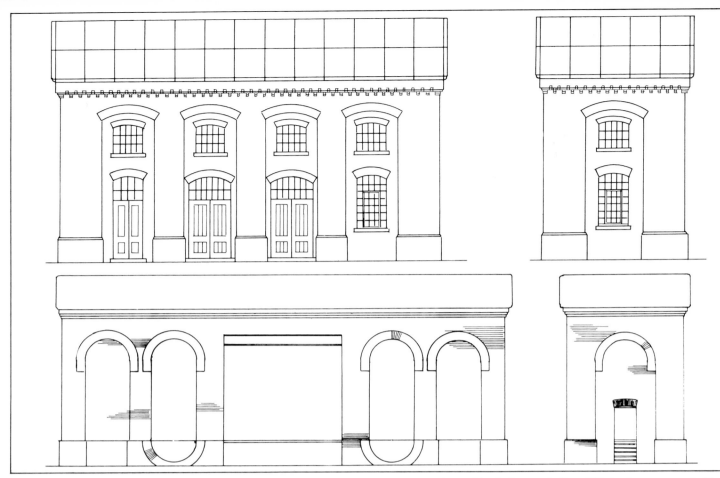

*Photo:***29,000 gallon lineside water tank and crane at Spittlegate, Grantham.** *Elevations :top* **Lincoln** *. bottom* **Leeds Wortley 1857.**

From Messrs. Lloyds Forster & Co. of Wednesbury, to supply 20 water tank kits containing all necessary plates and girders, within 9 miles of: Peterborough - £8 per ton; Spalding - £8/5/0d; Boston - £8; Tattersall - £8; Lincoln £7/17/6d.; Doncaster - £8. In addition to supplying as specified above, Lloyds Forster were to deliver to each site and 'fix'.

Tanks employed by the GN varied enormously in capacity from 1,500 to 200,000 gallons. Typical dimensions were, in 1893: Peterborough (Crescent), 36,377 gallons (41 ft. by 21 ft. by 6 ft. 6 ins. - later enlarged). At New England, the big 128,000 gallon tank scaled 97 ft. 6 ins. by 25 ft. 2 ins. by 8 ft. 6 ins. Enlargements were invariably effected by raising the sides, through the addition of a further row of plates, usually 4 ft. in height. Such an extension, at Doncaster Station, in 1860, cost £108, while 2 years later, in a widespread exercise, tank capacities were increased at Hitchin, Peterborough, Grantham, Newark and Retford, at costs varying from £100 - £600.

The tanks could be seen all over the system; on station platforms, by the lineside, in goods yards and especially, at the engine sheds. They were commonly sited above coaling stages but elsewhere would usually be placed atop stone or brick buildings, necessarily of substantial construction and often of imposing edifice. Where sited in such a way, the space beneath the tank was used for various purposes, for pumping machinery, storage, staff mess accommodation and, in a few instances, as office space - which must have made for noisy ceilings!

Strongly built though the tanks were, mishaps did occur, such as at Huntingdon on 4th March 1866, when the General Manager reported *that the 30,000 gallon tank over the stationary engine had burst.* In consequence some 120 tons of water had caused damage to the road where it fell, washing away the contents of a coal wagon standing near. Two weeks later the loco engineer was able to report that the failure had partly been caused by defects in the plates and partly by errors in the placing of transverse ties, when the tank was enlarged.

Where demand for water was not expected to be high - for example, at minor goods yards and the smaller stations, a combined water tank and crane was normally employed. These 'parachute' tanks, as they were sometimes called at unit costs of £75 (1887), £125 (1896) and £225 (1905), held no more than 3,000 gallons and were meant only for topping-up purposes.

The Ardsley 'coal hole'. Practice again was borrowed from other companies.

National Railway Museum

WATER CRANES

Water cranes were to be found in varying styles, usually dependent upon their location. In yards, where tracks were closely spaced, a central column and flexible hose(s) would normally have been adequate. Platform-mounted cranes demanded swivelling cantilevered arms, a type that was also found in yards where space permitted. Eventually to be numbered in their many hundreds, GN water cranes had a small beginning, with just twenty ordered by J. Cubitt on 22nd June 1848, as follows:

From Messrs. Beecroft of Kirkstall Forge Leeds, within 9 miles of: Peterborough - £42/6/0d. each; Spalding - £42/4/0d.; Boston - £41/10/0d.; Tattersall - £41/12/0d.; Lincoln - £41/0/0d.; Doncaster - £41/0/0d.

On 5th November 1850 Cubitt wanted to order eight more cranes, but pointed out that as the present ones were too low and too near running lines, accidents had been caused. He was told to investigate further before ordering more water cranes and it was not long before the GN were manufacturing their own. Thenceforward, the company's annual estimate books were never without at least one job involving the provision or relocation of a crane, a process which continued through the LNER period to culminate in high-capacity overhead watering gantries at Kings Cross and New England, provided by British Railways.

FROST PRECAUTIONS

One of the major problems faced in storing water, in the British climate, is the yearly threat of freezing. As is well known, the normal way of protecting railway watering apparatus was by provision of small furnaces, or 'Devils' as they were sometimes known, etc. which usually had long flues, to carry the heat up to outlet pipes, etc. The GN working timetable included a section entitled 'Coal for use at stations' which detailed its permitted use, while all the time exhorting the company's servants to exercise stringent economy. However, the WTT did recognize the importance of not letting water supplies freeze, so it gave the following instruction, couched in the usual lofty prose of the time - in this case, 1912: .....*During frosty weather and when there is apprehension that the water in the cranes may be frozen, coal may be supplied from the station stock for the fires at the water cranes, at the undermentioned places:*

Aslockton/Edgware/Hucknall/Royston
Batley/Essendine/Ingrow/Shipley
Caythorpe/Hertford/New Barnet/Sutton in Ashfld
City Road/High Barnet/North Bridge/Willoughby
Clayton/Holme//Ramsey/Wood Green
Daybrook

One may only speculate at the anti-freezing arrangements that were permitted at any place not on the WTT list!

GN WATER SUPPLY POINTS

The main points of supply were listed by the Locomotive Department in a register, with an overall numerical order, subdivided by Locomotive District. Annual estimates were made for consumption, divided where appropriate, amongst suppliers. For a glimpse of the estimated water consumption in the first decade of the twentieth century, when services were approaching their zenith, it is interesting to compare two years, 1901 and 1906, to observe the variations in forecast water requirements. As added interest, analyst's reports are given about the suitability of the various water supplies, for use in locomotive boilers. Such reports had been prepared on an ad hoc basis since the 1880s but when the company finally realised the importance of such work at the beginning of the twentieth century it set up its own analytical laboratory; thenceforth, water quality was monitored at all points of supply and recommendations made for the remedying of defects. The analyst's reports date mostly from 1905: they provide for a fascinating appraisal of the often daunting problems faced daily in the running department and an excellent indication of the very complexity of a Victorian/Edwardian railway. It can be found as an appendix in *Great Northern Engine Sheds Part Two*.

The Ardsley coaling plant. The general neglect of pre-Grouping days ensured that plenty were required on the GN section of the LNER.

National Railway Museum

COAL, ASH & SAND

It may rightly be said that in mid-nineteenth century Britain, coal was the lifeblood of the Nation. Certainly it was the *raison d'etre* of many a railway company's existence, including the GNR and to an ever increasing extent as the century wore on. Of course, along with water, coal was also the lifeblood of the steam locomotive, so the purchase, distribution and economic use of the fuel, were paramount features of the Locomotive Department's activities.

In the earlier years of Britain's railways coke was the fuel deemed best for locomotives and it was not until the latter part of the century that coal finally replaced it. On the GNR, Archibald Sturrock was at the helm during the all-coke period, though he pursued trials with coal and his reign saw the start of the transition to it. Ever the careful Scot, Sturrock decided very early on in his GN career that general coke costs should be reduced. On 11th May 1850, he commented, in a report to the Board, that he thought the amount of coke used was 'too high'. He continued by declaring consumption *could probably be reduced* by offering some form of reward to enginemen, based on the percentage of coke conserved above a certain average. This average would be determined by himself, according to work done from the various stations, and be modelled on the amount of coke used on the Great Western Railway. This was a compliment to his erstwhile employers, who were always in the forefront in striving for fuel economy.

Thus were created the celebrated 'Coke Premiums', which must have been a success, for they were perpetuated for more than a quarter of a century. However, they may have led to a situation that arose in 1854, when a Mr. Middlemas reported to the Board that *coal was being pilfered from wagons in coal trains*. The drivers were blamed, using the coal in their own fireboxes, but Mr. Middlemas suggested the loss could be written off as 'bad debt'.

Sturrock's next idea for coke economy was put to the Board on 11th August 1850, when he noted that the major permanent engine sheds were nearing completion. He advocated the provision of coke furnaces to his own design which, if approved, would cost £50-£60 each and *.....effect great economies by allowing the use of refuse coke for locomotive firelighting purposes.....* His idea was adopted.

Still with the economic bit between his teeth, Sturrock next suggested to the Board, on 14th March 1851, that instead of running special trains for the transport of coke, it should be brought to the various sheds by ordinary goods trains *.....as is the practice on other railways.....* He went on to instance the GWR (again), MR and Y & NMR. It is not known if the Board agreed to Sturrock's suggestion, but it may be assumed so. Naturally, in later years, consumption became so great that fuel had to be transported in whole trainloads - something that became one of the most common sights on Britain's railway system. *Much of interest regarding fuel in the early years can be found in the GNR 'Comparative Costs Statements' and many figures from the 1850s and 1860s are detailed in the appendices to Part Two of Great Northern Engine Sheds.*

COAL STACKING

Not all coal delivered to the GN was used straight away. Like most other railways, the company employed coal stacks at many of its sheds, to buy in the summer when coal was cheap, and as a form of insurance against an interruption of supply. Thus it was, on 28th February 1899, the Board learned that coal stacks at various depots were being repaired and the coal 'on the ground' currently amounted to 44,000 tons. Stacking was to continue at Kings Cross, Doncaster and Lincoln, while 2,000 tons would also be put down at Retford, before the end of March. When stacking was completed, there would be 50,000 tons laid which, with the exception of Lincoln, Boston and a few other 'small places' would all be Best Yorkshire, and would include 1,000 tons of Welsh coal at Kings Cross.

Just over five years later, on 27th July 1904, the General Manager reported that the company had 51,200 tons of coal on the ground (so things had not changed much from 1899), and he asked for sanction from the Board to lay down a further 1,500 tons in the immediate future. The Board approved this additional stockpiling.

With so much invested money just 'lying around' as it were, suggestions were made that perhaps coal stacks ought to be protected from the vagaries of the British climate. So, in April 1894, estimates were obtained for provision of a cover for the coal stack at Doncaster

Carr, one of the largest, containing 3854 tons of coal. Use of 10 ft. x 10 ft. corrugated iron sheets was envisaged, to be erected in bays of six, 3 sheets by 2, mounted on supports. The total cost was estimated at £1,178, so it should come as no surprise that the idea was dropped, never to be resurrected! Stacks, certainly in later years, could lie almost forgotten and the coal could deteriorate quite disastrously.

LOCOMOTIVE FUELLING

In the beginning, simple coke platforms - or stages - were provided at frequent intervals along the main lines, not necessarily at the sheds. This was due to the limited fuel capacity of the early engines, of course, as well as the greater bulk of coke compared to an equivalent weight of coal. As time progressed and locomotive outputs increased, the lineside stages gradually disappeared but even as late as 1880 places like Newark, roughly halfway between Peterborough and Doncaster, still sported coke stages beside both up and down main lines.

Locomotives normally received their fuel at engine sheds, where men shovelled it direct from wagons, or stockpiles on stages in all weathers. After a while the men's lot started to improve - if such is an appropriate word; roofs appeared over a number of stages and in some places hand baskets appeared. A form of mechanisation gradually came about, with hand-operated crane and tub systems, of about half a ton capacity, only those at Kings Cross later gaining the benefit of steam power. Further improvements followed with the introduction of an elevated coaling stage/wagon ramp, at Ardsley, in 1892/3. During the latter part of 1890 most of the large sheds, with the notable exception of Kings Cross, benefitted from this sort of arrangement but it still demanded the manhandling of coal from wagon to locomotive. In fact, hand coaling remained in use to the end of steam at the smaller sheds - only at the bigger depots was man finally relieved of this onerous burden, by the introduction of fully mechanised coaling plants.

These mechanical coalers were introduced not by the Great Northern but by the LNER, in a programme that started in the mid-1920s, and carried on until the advent of World War Two, although one or two did appear after that time as part of postponed pre-war schemes. They ranged from simple skip-hoists, loading half a ton at a time, to massive 500 ton capacity coal towers, at places like Kings Cross, New England and Doncaster. That at Doncaster appeared first and because of its shape, was soon christened 'The Cenotaph'. Powered by electricity, it operated by lifting an entire wagon to the top of the tower, and tipping the contents into the bifurcate bunker. From there, up to four engines could simultaneously be loaded, at two tons a minute each. Automatic slakers were employed at all necessary points, to keep down flying coal dust - a vital feature when sheds were sited in built-up areas.

Smaller mechanical plants for the secondary sheds were also

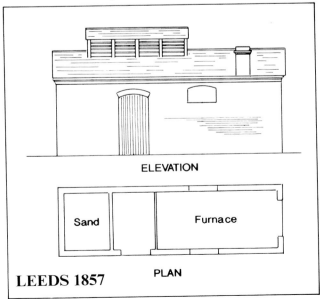

ELEVATION

| Sand | Furnace |

LEEDS 1857   **PLAN**

introduced by the LNER. These were usually of 200 tons capacity (Bradford was 175 tons and Ardsley 300 tons), and while the first examples operated in a manner identical to the 500 ton plants, the method of charging was finally changed, to where wagons tippled into subterranean bunkers, with skips hoisting the coal from bunker, to top of the tower.

LOCOMOTIVE COAL WAGONS

Originally, of course, all engines burned coke, which was consumed in much greater quantities than the later coal, so the fleet of wagons dedicated to transporting it was quite large, even in the earliest days, and numbers increased rapidly, for example, in 1851 the GNR had 200 coke wagons, increasing to 500 only four years later. The same number was in use in 1871, by which time coal was in general use and by 1874 the GN had been able to reduce its loco coal wagon fleet to just 208.

The standard loco coal wagon was a 4-plank open type although 5, 6 and 7-plank mineral wagons were also used. About the end of the nineteenth century the company introduced larger wagons, of 15 and 20 tons capacity and even some 30 ton bogie types, which were vacuum braked and designed to run in full trainloads, for 'better benefit'. The 15 tonners were delivered in two styles: 18 feet long, with a single drop door on each side, and 19 feet, with a single drop door per side, plus two 'cupboard' doors. The latter design found favour with the LNER, being manufactured in some numbers by that company for wide-spread use over its system.

ASH DISPOSAL

Coal burning locomotives produce large quantities of ash and clinker. A task as onerous as hand coaling, and one that usually accompanied it, when locos arrived 'on shed', was that of ash disposal. Here, men faced hot, dirty and sometimes dangerous jobs, cleaning char from smokeboxes and boiler tubes, and removing clinker from firebox grates. All of the waste material was deposited in ashpits, or simply dumped beside the track, but wherever it went, it later had to be manhandled again into wagons, for eventual disposal. Not all this refuse was dumped, however; large amounts were used for landfill, ballasting lightly laid track, creating pathways and, in winter, as a covering for iced-up areas. That not required for such purposes was disposed of. For many years, one of the main dumps for Great Northern ash was at Conington Tip, between Holme and Abbot's Ripton. (In fact, Conington Tip still serves today, for disposal of railway refuse, and will continue to do so, after the East Coast main line is electrified).

Such gruelling work, involving thousands of tons of ash a year was never completely mechanised. The LNER introduced 'Wet Ash Pits' at the bigger sheds, but even these required man power for the initial task of getting the stuff from locomotive to pit. Small grab cranes, conveyors, rocking grates and self-cleaning smokeboxes were other aids, but basically, despite all the investment, ash disposal remained one of the steam locomotive's most unattractive features.

SAND

Sand was an indispensible aid, from the earliest days, to maintain adhesion between locomotive driving wheels and the rails. It was delivered to the rail by gravity, either by hand, or from containers on the engine (steam-blowing came late in the history of steam development) and had, by necessity, to be dry and free-flowing. Thus most sheds had their own sand drying facilities - a bin, room, or separate building, with a furnace, from which the footplatemen could draw supplies to top up the locomotives' sand boxes.

No apparent changes were made to this system during GNR times, but the LNER did introduce a fairly radical development, usually as an adjunct to 'Wet Ash Pits'. This comprised a rotating drum sand dryer, sited adjacent to the pits, and capable of drying up to two tons of wet sand per hour. From the drum, sand was blown by compressed air into two elevated hoppers, one at either end of the pits, each capable of holding ten tons of dry sand. Outlet pipes were taken from the hoppers, down to within one foot of rail level. From there, under the control of stop valves, locomen could fill buckets, for tipping into the engines' containers! This was an apparent anachronism, re-establishing itself, but on reflection, the notion of power-blow sand directed onto locomotive bearing surfaces was probably sufficient to deter the LNER from completing the labour-saving features of their device.

It would seem the GNR obtained its supplies of sand from at least one major source, Nuthall Sand Siding, situated near Basford in Nottinghamshire. Trains ran from Colwick to Nuthall, when required, so it is probable that Colwick was the clearing house for sand, distributing it all over the system on an 'as required' basis. In LNER days, and into the BR Eastern Region era, sand for the GN Section came from a sand siding - name unknown - situated on the down side of the main line, about a mile north of Retford. That deposit was exploited until the 1950s, when Scunthorpe steelworks began providing abrasive fines. This material, a by - product of steel- making, had a distinct advantage over sand in that it did not require drying and came ready bagged for use. There were almost certainly other sources of sand besides Nuthall and Retford of course, but none so far, have been identified.

ACKNOWLEDGEMENTS

Producing a book which records a history as complex as that of the engine sheds of the Great Northern Rly requires imput not just from the authors but from many people; operational and retired railwaymen, society stalwarts, civil servants, librarians and a host of private individuals willings to give advice, time and the loan of collected material. All of these people have made the years of *graft* something of a pleasure and we would like to record our thanks to them all. If we have failed to acknowledge anyone it wasn't intentional, we'll get you next time!

Certain people have bent over backwards to help us reach our goal, in particular the 'Twins'-Chris Hawkins and George Reeve and their ladies Wendy and Beverley respectively-who have always made us welcome at the Enfield and Pinner 'hotels' where hang-overs became the norm.

Others who have put up with our incessant letters, phone calls, visits, read proofs and supplied all manner of information, include Alex Appleton, J.S.Brownlie, Adam Cartwright, Sid Checkley, John Cockcroft, Chris Duffell, Bob Ellwell, Ron Fareham (thanks for Leeds Ron), Brian Fowler, Greg Fox, Leslie Franks, Terry Henderson, Brian Hilton, Eddie Johnson, Kenneth Leech, Brian Longbone, Dave Love, Philip Mason, Eric Neve, David Parker, Nick Pigott, John Rhodes, Allan Richardson, Steven Summerson, John Sykes, Richard Strange, Dick Tarpey, Peter Tatlow, Ray Townsin, Peter Townsend, Peter Waszak, G.Woodward and John Wrottesley. BR offices and the staff therein at Doncaster, Kings Cross, Manchester and York have all been willing 'shed some light' on the subject.

Railway societies always seem willing to help authors and we would like to mention in particular the GNR Society, Grantham Rly Soc, Gresley Soc and the LNER Study Group.

Staff at the National Rly Museum and the Public Records Office, Kew saw us so often that first name terms were usually in hand.

The following generously supplied photographs from their own camera's or collections: H.C.Casserley, W.A.Camwell, Roger Carpenter, A.V.Fincham, Alec George, A.R.Goult, Brian Green, Harold James, John Kite, Keith Ladbury, Alf Ludlam, John Meredith, Bob Miller, Syd Outram, Les Perrin, Neville Stead, B.M.Wykes. Cheers gentlemen.

As always with these listings, families are mentioned last but nevertheless are most important of all. Many thanks to Christine and Jane for enduring the last five years.